BlackBerry Enterprise Server 5 Implementation Guide

Simplify the implementation of BlackBerry Enterprise Server for Microsoft Exchange in your corporate environment

Mitesh Desai

[PACKT] PUBLISHING

BIRMINGHAM - MUMBAI

BlackBerry Enterprise Server 5 Implementation Guide

Copyright © 2011 Packt Publishing

All rights reserved. No part of this book may be reproduced, stored in a retrieval system, or transmitted in any form or by any means, without the prior written permission of the publisher, except in the case of brief quotations embedded in critical articles or reviews.

Every effort has been made in the preparation of this book to ensure the accuracy of the information presented. However, the information contained in this book is sold without warranty, either express or implied. Neither the author, nor Packt Publishing, and its dealers and distributors will be held liable for any damages caused or alleged to be caused directly or indirectly by this book.

Packt Publishing has endeavored to provide trademark information about all of the companies and products mentioned in this book by the appropriate use of capitals. However, Packt Publishing cannot guarantee the accuracy of this information.

First published: February 2011

Production Reference: 1160211

Published by Packt Publishing Ltd.
32 Lincoln Road
Olton
Birmingham, B27 6PA, UK.

ISBN 978-1-849690-48-5

www.packtpub.com

Cover Image by Sujay Gawand (sujay0000@gmail.com)

Credits

Author
Mitesh Desai

Reviewer
Vivek Thangaswamy

Acquisition Editor
David Barnes

Development Editor
Swapna Verlekar

Technical Editor
Aditi Suvarna

Copy Editor
Laxmi Subramanian

Indexer
Monica Ajmera Mehta

Editorial Team Leader
Aditya Belpathak

Project Team Leader
Ashwin Shetty

Project Coordinator
Joel Goveya

Proofreader
Steve Maguire

Graphics
Geetanjali Sawant

Production Coordinator
Shantanu Zagade

Cover Work
Shantanu Zagade

About the Author

Mitesh Desai is an IT consultant from London, UK. He has worked on several BlackBerry projects for numerous clients in many different network infrastructures. He also operates an IT consultant company—`www.it-problems.co.uk`.

He enjoys a busy lifestyle supporting many prestigious companies in the heart of Central London, but finds time to enjoy sports and music.

He is also available on `www.it-problems.co.uk` to help budding BlackBerry technicians.

About the Reviewer

Vivek Thangaswamy has been working as a solution developer in Software Technologies for more than six years now. He has worked for many top-notch clients across the globe. He started programming in a DOS world, then moved to C, C++, VC++, J2EE, SAP B1, LegaSuite GUI, WinJa, JSP, ColdFusion, VB 6, and eventually to .NET in both VB.NET and C# worlds and also in ASP.NET/MS SQL Server and more into Windows Mobile platforms. He also worked in Microsoft's latest trendsetter in Enterprise Collaboration Microsoft Office SharePoint Server accompanied with VSTO and .NET 3.0 frameworks. He started working in SharePoint from the version 2003 to the up-to-date versions. Now, he is more into Mobile platform Research and Development. Different domains and industries knowledge and experience eCommerce, ERP, CRM, Transportation, Enterprise Content Management, Web 2.0, and Portal. He is an expert in SAP B1 and SugarCRM consulting, focusing on Java ME, Windows Mobile, JavaFX Mobile, and Android. So basically, what Vivek does is answers more out in the newsgroups over and over, plus adding to its blogging about Microsoft Technologies, wraps it in a very readable and interesting format and more in technical writing. For his good technical knowledge, passion about the Microsoft Technologies, community involvement, and contribution, he has also been awarded the Microsoft Most Valuable Professional award for ASP.NET (once) and SharePoint (twice). He is the lead technology consulting advisor for Arimaan Global Consulting (www.arimaan.com).

Vivek completed his Bachelor's Degree in Information Technology (B.Tech) from one of the oldest and finest universities in the world, University of Madras and MBA (Master of Business Administration) in Finance from one of the largest Open University in the world IGNOU.

Writing is a passion for Vivek, he has written many technical articles and whitepapers based on different technologies and domains. He has also authored a technical book on *Microsoft technology VSTO 3.0 for Office 2007 Programming* — Packt Publishing. He was also a reviewer for Microsoft *Office Live Small Business: Beginner's Guide* — Packt Publishing and *Refactoring with Visual Studio 2010* — Packt Publishing.

www.PacktPub.com

Support files, eBooks, discount offers and more

You might want to visit `www.PacktPub.com` for support files and downloads related to your book.

Did you know that Packt offers eBook versions of every book published, with PDF and ePub files available? You can upgrade to the eBook version at `www.PacktPub.com` and as a print book customer, you are entitled to a discount on the eBook copy. Get in touch with us at `service@packtpub.com` for more details.

At `www.PacktPub.com`, you can also read a collection of free technical articles, sign up for a range of free newsletters and receive exclusive discounts and offers on Packt books and eBooks.

PACKTLIB

http://PacktLib.PacktPub.com

Do you need instant solutions to your IT questions? PacktLib is Packt's online digital book library. Here, you can access, read and search across Packt's entire library of books.

Why Subscribe?
- Fully searchable across every book published by Packt
- Copy and paste, print and bookmark content
- On demand and accessible via web browser

Free Access for Packt account holders

If you have an account with Packt at `www.PacktPub.com`, you can use this to access PacktLib today and view nine entirely free books. Simply use your login credentials for immediate access.

Instant Updates on New Packt Books

Get notified! Find out when new books are published by following *@PacktEnterprise* on Twitter, or the *Packt Enterprise* Facebook page.

Table of Contents

Preface	**1**
Chapter 1: Introduction to BES 5	**7**
New features of BES 5.0	8
BES version 5.0 architecture	10
Databases	13
MAPI and CDO files	14
BES network requirements	14
BESAdmin account	14
Lab 1—installing BlackBerry Enterprise Server 5.0	16
Creating the service account—besadmin	16
Assigning a mailbox to the besadmin user	17
Assigning Microsoft Exchange permissions to the service account	18
Assigning Microsoft Windows permissions to the service account	20
Configuring Microsoft Exchange permissions for the service account	22
Enabling the database server	23
Creating the BlackBerry configuration database	23
Setting permissions for the service account manually	25
Setting permissions for the service account automatically	28
Final checklist prior to installation	29
Installing BES version 5	29
Applying the Maintenance pack	45
Summary	46
Chapter 2: Understanding and Administrating BES 5	**47**
Delivering messages	47
Sending a message to a BlackBerry device	48
Sending a message from a BlackBerry device	49
Setting security options	50
Understanding encryption	51
Setting the BES encryption method	53

Table of Contents

Protecting content	54
Sending PIN-to-PIN messages	54
Logging into the BlackBerry Administration Service	**57**
Lab 2	**61**
Logging into the console	61
Settings for the BlackBerry Administration Service	**62**
Creating administrators and administrative roles	63
Creating a role	64
Creating a group	66
Creating an administrative user	67
Activating the Enterprise policy	**70**
Setting a corporate peer-to-peer key	72
Regenerating the transport keys—main encryption keys	74
Summary	**74**
Chapter 3: Activating Devices and Users	**75**
Creating users on the BES 5.0	**75**
Creating a user-based group	**77**
Preparing to distribute a BlackBerry device	**80**
Activating users	**83**
Understanding enterprise activation	**84**
Activating a device using BlackBerry Administration Service	84
Activating devices over the wireless network—OTA	85
Activating devices over the LAN	86
Activating devices using BlackBerry Web Desktop Manager	87
Activating the device over the corporate Wi-Fi	87
Messaging environment	**89**
Synchronizing organizational data	92
Lab 3	**97**
Importing users to the BlackBerry Enterprise Server	97
Adding a user when the user is not present in the company directory lookup	99
Setting a disclaimer at the server level for all users	100
Setting activation passwords	102
Sending a PIN message	103
Applying a Level One message filter to a user	103
Summary	**105**
Chapter 4: IT Policies	**107**
IT policies	**107**
Creating a new IT policy	108
Assigning an IT policy	109

To a user	110
To a group	110
Rules for conflicting IT policies	111
Setting IT policy priorities	112
Verifying a user's IT policy	112
Change how an IT policy is sent to a BlackBerry device	115
Lab 4	**116**
Creating the Sales Team IT policy	117
Applying the IT policy to the sales group	120
IT policy settings	121
Resending the IT policy automatically to devices	122
Deactivating devices that do not have an IT policy	122
Troubleshooting IT policies	123
Summary	**123**
Chapter 5: Software Configuration and Java Applications	**125**
Overview of the process	**125**
Developing Java applications for BlackBerries	126
Creating a shared folder on the network	126
Application repository	131
Application control policies	132
Standard required	132
Standard optional	133
Standard disallowed	133
Software configurations	**135**
Creating a software configuration	136
Adding a BlackBerry Java application to the software configuration	137
Assigning the software configuration to a user	139
Job deployment	140
Default settings of a job schedule	140
Changing job settings of how applications are sent to devices	141
Installing Java applications on BlackBerry devices using the wired approach	141
Reconciliation rules for BlackBerry Java applications	142
Scenario one	142
Scenario two	143
Scenario three	143
Scenario four	143
Scenario five	144
Scenario six	144
Scenario seven	144
Scenario eight	144
Lab 5	**145**
Changing a standard application policy	145
Creating a custom application control policy	145
Assigning the software configuration to a group	146

Table of Contents

Deploying device software to BlackBerry devices 147
    Using Desktop Manager 147
    Using Web Desktop Manager 147
Updating the BlackBerry device software over the wireless network 147
Deploying device software using Web Desktop Manager—an example 148
Installing the BlackBerry device software 148
Creating the shared folder 150
Allowing the BlackBerry Administration Service to display
the device software configuration settings 151
Adding the shared folder to the BlackBerry Administration Service 152
Creating the BlackBerry device software configuration 153
Creating a software configuration for the BlackBerry device software 155
Assigning the software configuration to a user 157
Assigning the software configuration to a group 157
Summary **158**

Chapter 6: MDS Applications 159

Understanding and setting up our MDS environment **159**
Running MDS services **160**
Installing MDS runtime platform **161**
    Creating a software configuration to deploy the MDS runtime
    platform to devices 161
Logging in to the MDS console **167**
    Adding an MDS application (Expense Tracker) to the MDS repository 168
    Sending the Expense Tracker MDS application to BlackBerry devices 169
    Configuring IT policies with respect to MDS applications 170
Summary **170**

Chapter 7: High Availability 171

Understanding high availability **171**
    Understanding how it works 172
    Configuring high availability 172
    Examining the default threshold values and setting failovers 173
    Forcing a manual failover 174
    Introducing HA for databases 174
Using the BlackBerry monitoring website **175**
Setting up SNMP on the BES Server **176**
Summary **179**

Table of Contents

Chapter 8: Upgrades — 181
Upgrading from supported versions — 181
Upgrading considerations — 181
Replacing the BlackBerry manager — 182
Upgrading the database — 182
Upgrading options — 182
Upgrading procedure — 183
- Backing up the BlackBerry configuration database on an SQL server — 183
- Backing up the BlackBerry configuration database on lightweight MSDE — 185

Using the 'in place' procedure — 186
Upgrading your BES environment using the End Transporter tool — 187
Migrating users to the new BES server — 187
Recording the database paths — 187
Using the Transporter tool to move BES users — 188
- Understanding transport errors — 195

Summary — 196
Index — 197

[v]

Preface

BlackBerry Enterprise Server is a platform that extends corporate messaging and collaboration services to BlackBerry devices. It supports management and administration of devices, and also supports deployment of third-party applications on the BlackBerry device platform. The basics of installing BlackBerry Enterprise Server are familiar for most administrators, but the server is infinitely configurable and contains extended administration features.

This book focuses on BlackBerry Enterprise Server for Microsoft Exchange, providing detailed information on planning and implementing a BlackBerry Enterprise Server deployment. It will show you how to use the BES to manage the flow of e-mail data, ensuring that it is directed to its ultimate destination—the BlackBerry Smartphone. It covers all the new features of the BES version 5.0 and also looks at areas that have been enhanced from the previous versions. If you are new to BlackBerry Enterprise Server, then this is the perfect guide to help with your planning and deployment.

The BlackBerry Enterprise Server supports a variety of messaging platforms, including Microsoft Exchange, IBM Lotus Domino, and Novell GroupWise. As you begin reading this book, you will first learn about the two prominent features introduced with BES 5: BlackBerry Administration Service Console and Server Routing Protocol. As we proceed further, we will learn about 200 more configurable IT policies provided by BES 5 as opposed to the earlier versions. We will look at Mobile Data Service and third party applications that can be deployed to BlackBerry devices. We will also look at a monitoring portal included in the installation process of BES 5, which provides health scores to check the BES performance and a much more stable and robust SNMP. Written by mobile and wireless technology experts, this book provides a detailed approach to installing, configuring, and managing your BlackBerry Enterprise Server.

What this book covers

Chapter 1, Introduction to BES 5, provides an overview of the BlackBerry Enterprise Server version 5.0 environment and the features and services that are available within that environment. It also compares and discusses the components involved win the BES version 5.0 and the previous versions.

Chapter 2, Understanding and Administrating BES 5, covers administrative user roles, how messages are delivered, and other key elements of the BES. This chapter concludes with Lab 2, which gives a practical insight on how to use the BlackBerry Administration Service console and key elements we need to configure before activating users on our BES.

Chapter 3, Activating Devices and Users, looks at creating users and activating devices, as we now have a broad understanding of how BlackBerry Enterprise Server works.

Chapter 4, IT Policies, explores the capabilities provided by the BlackBerry Enterprise Server to configure and enforce a variety of policies for device settings. With the aid of the lab, we will be able to successfully create IT policies and assign them to our users and devices.

Chapter 5, Software Configuration and Java Applications, examines the controls available to administrators to enforce specific policies on to a BlackBerry device. We will be able to send device software and Java-based applications over the air or via a wired approach.

Chapter 6, MDS Applications, looks at the MDS applications that can be deployed to the BlackBerry Smartphone. It shows how to custom develop applications to run on the BlackBerries or use third-party applications to push on to the devices.

Chapter 7, High Availability, discusses the new features of high availability that is ready to use straight out of the BlackBerry Enterprise Server 5.0 installation. It also looks at the monitoring console that is built into the BES, which enables us to keep a close eye on the performance of our BES.

Chapter 8, Upgrades, introduces several options available to us to upgrade prior versions of BlackBerry Enterprise Servers.

What you need for this book

The following is the hardware recommendation for up to 500 users:

- Two processors, 2.0 GHz Intel Xeon
- 2 GB of memory
- 2 drives, RAID 1

The following are the system/software requirements:

- Microsoft Exchange Server 2003 SP2
- Microsoft Exchange Server 2007 with MAPI client and CDO 1.2.1
- Microsoft Internet Explorer 6.0 or higher

Any of the following operating systems:

- Windows Server® 2003 SP2 (32 bit or 64 bit)
- Windows Server 2003 R2 SP2 (32 bit or 64 bit)
- Windows Server 2008 SP2 (32 bit or 64 bit)

Who this book is for

This book is written for IT professionals and network administrators who need to implement a BlackBerry Enterprise Server. The text assumes basic familiarity with Microsoft Windows Server administration, but provides detailed instructions for administrators with varying levels of experience.

Conventions

In this book, you will find a number of styles of text that distinguish between different kinds of information. Here are some examples of these styles, and an explanation of their meaning.

Code words in text are shown as follows: "To execute the file use the `createdb.exe` command followed by the full path of the `BesMgmt.cfg` file."

A block of code is set as follows:

```
<system.net>
<defaultProxy>
<proxy usesystemdefault = "false" />
</defaultProxy>
</system.net>
```

Any command-line input or output is written as follows:

```
add-exchangeadministrator "BESAdmin" -role ViewOnlyAdmin
```

New terms and **important words** are shown in bold. Words that you see on the screen, in menus or dialog boxes for example, appear in the text like this: "Once all the services have started successfully, click on **Next**."

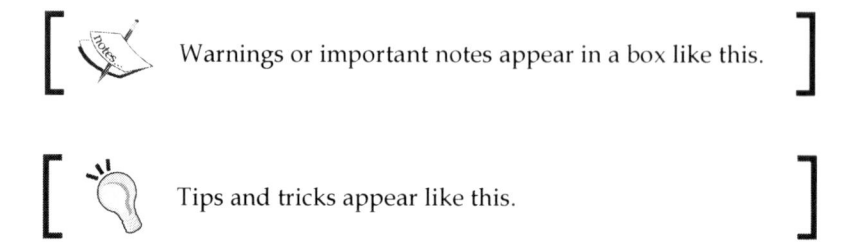

> Warnings or important notes appear in a box like this.

> Tips and tricks appear like this.

Reader feedback

Feedback from our readers is always welcome. Let us know what you think about this book—what you liked or may have disliked. Reader feedback is important for us to develop titles that you really get the most out of.

To send us general feedback, simply send an e-mail to feedback@packtpub.com, and mention the book title via the subject of your message.

If there is a book that you need and would like to see us publish, please send us a note in the **SUGGEST A TITLE** form on www.packtpub.com or e-mail suggest@packtpub.com.

If there is a topic that you have expertise in and you are interested in either writing or contributing to a book, see our author guide on www.packtpub.com/authors.

Customer support

Now that you are the proud owner of a Packt book, we have a number of things to help you to get the most from your purchase.

> **Downloading the example code for this book**
> You can download the example code files for all Packt books you have purchased from your account at http://www.PacktPub.com. If you purchased this book elsewhere, you can visit http://www.PacktPub.com/support and register to have the files e-mailed directly to you.

Errata

Although we have taken every care to ensure the accuracy of our content, mistakes do happen. If you find a mistake in one of our books—maybe a mistake in the text or the code—we would be grateful if you would report this to us. By doing so, you can save other readers from frustration and help us improve subsequent versions of this book. If you find any errata, please report them by visiting http://www.packtpub.com/support, selecting your book, clicking on the **errata submission form** link, and entering the details of your errata. Once your errata are verified, your submission will be accepted and the errata will be uploaded on our website, or added to any list of existing errata, under the Errata section of that title. Any existing errata can be viewed by selecting your title from http://www.packtpub.com/support.

Piracy

Piracy of copyright material on the Internet is an ongoing problem across all media. At Packt, we take the protection of our copyright and licenses very seriously. If you come across any illegal copies of our works, in any form, on the Internet, please provide us with the location address or website name immediately so that we can pursue a remedy.

Please contact us at copyright@packtpub.com with a link to the suspected pirated material.

We appreciate your help in protecting our authors, and our ability to bring you valuable content.

Questions

You can contact us at questions@packtpub.com if you are having a problem with any aspect of the book, and we will do our best to address it.

Introduction to BES 5

The demand for information to be highly available for corporate decision makers is ever so more crucial, as technology develops. No longer are we prepared to wait until we return to the office to get back to important e-mails. Due to the fast pace that business has taken in the 20th century, we are all accustomed to rapid response. The situation has been fuelled by Smartphone devices being introduced into the market to meet such demands. One mobile communication device that has stood out in the competitive market is the BlackBerry Smartphone.

The BlackBerry Smartphone was introduced in 1999 by **RIM, Research In Motion**, a Canadian-based company, to support push e-mail by delivering information over the wireless networks of mobile phone service companies, along with its own wireless infrastructure. The BlackBerry Smartphone uses push technology, so e-mails are effortlessly routed to the user's device without the need for synchronizing the BlackBerry Smartphone. As push technology is utilized as opposed to pull technology—which was the traditional architecture of a Smartphone—e-mails are delivered to the device in near real time, without the user having to poll the server to see if new mail has arrived. This architecture means that when an e-mail arrives in your inbox, a copy is immediately pushed on the BlackBerry Smartphone, which has increased their presence widely in all types of organizations.

For inexperienced IT administrators, the prospect of managing these high-end devices loaded with sensitive corporate information can be a nightmare. As the demand for BlackBerry devices grows within the corporate environment, the need for individuals who can expertly configure and administer the servers that support these devices will continue to expand. The **BlackBerry Enterprise Server (BES)**, provides the capability to deliver data to BlackBerry devices, set and enforce security and management policies for the BlackBerry devices, and so on. In short, BES is a vital tool to make sure that you have flexible, granular control over the BlackBerry devices that you deploy across your organization.

Introduction to BES 5

The installation, configuration, and management of a BES can be far from easy. With the help of this book, you should be able to simplify the implementation of a BES in your corporate environment. This chapter looks at the new features of the BES version 5.0.

We look at areas that have been enhanced from the previous versions—BES 4.x.x and lower. We then finish the chapter with the *Lab 1 – installing BlackBerry Enterprise Server 5.0* section.

New features of BES 5.0

BES version 5.0 has many changes, but there are two prominent changes that will captivate administrators who ever worked on any previous versions of BES. The first is the new web-based interface that has replaced the cumbersome BlackBerry Manager console. The new management tool—**BlackBerry Administration Service** console (also referred to as the **BAS**) allows administrators to use Microsoft Internet Explorer along with Active X plugins to control and administer the BES.

The second prominent change is the high availability built-in feature of BES 5.0; this allows us to plan for a disaster recovery straight out of the box. Unlike previous versions of the BES, where we had to look at third-party applications to help us create disaster recovery scenarios, BES 5.0 allows us to do this out of the box. The high availability component takes care of SRP lockouts, therefore no additional license is needed for the standby server. **Server Routing Protocol** (**SRP**) is a unique identifier that is used to communicate and authenticate your BES server with RIM BlackBerry relay circuit. In the previous versions, if the same SRP was used on two different BES servers in the same domain then the SRP would automatically lockout and one of the BES servers would be disconnected from the RIM relay circuit. This made planning for a disaster recovery more expensive as you would need to have purchased an additional SRP (which in essence is an additional copy of the BES software) in order to implement a successful disaster recovery plan.

Improvements have been made to the existing IT policies. BES 5.0 now provides an additional 200 more configurable IT policies as opposed to the earlier versions of BES, which we will look at in *Chapter 4, IT Policies*, followed by a lab examining IT policies in more detail.

As the need grows for not just e-mail messages being able to be viewed and delivered on BlackBerries but also to have a full Instant Messaging environment available on a BlackBerry device, this can be provided by **Microsoft Live Communication Server** (**LCS**), which will enable us to deploy a robust Instant Messaging solution.

With BES version 5.0, a monitoring portal (provided via a website similar to the BAS) is included in the installation process. In the previous versions, the monitoring tools had to be downloaded and installed separately. The monitoring software provides health scores to check the BES performance and a much more stable and robust **Simple Network Management Protocol** (**SNMP**) architecture is employed in BES version 5 (further information on SNMP can be found at `http://en.wikipedia.org/wiki/SNMP`).

General administrative failures relating to managing users and groups have also been addressed in BES 5.0, such as the ability to have users in more than one group, the ability to nest groups (place a group inside another group) and for the BES to then work out the correct effect IT policies, software configuration policies and security rights that should be applied to users when they find themselves in multiple groups. In the previous versions of BES this was not possible. We will examine this in more detail in *Chapter 4, IT Policies*.

> Similar to the Microsoft Technology of when users are in different security groups and the effective permissions are worked out except in the case of BES, the *least* restrictive role applies, and the highest ranked IT policy will be applied. Also note, these groups are created logically on the BES and have no correspondence to groups that exist in Active Directory.

The delivering of apps to BlackBerry Smartphones via the BES has also vastly improved. Now we can create and house a robust application repository, which allows us to create application lists to ease the management of apps as seen later in *Chapter 5, Software Configuration and Java Applications*.

There has been much improvement for the end user as well, with the launch of BlackBerry Device Software, version 5.0 software. Users can now see flags for follow up, and can manage and synchronize e-mail folders to make message filing simpler.

Introduction to BES 5

Another obstacle in the previous versions of the BES was the ability to only synch the main Outlook contact folder, which resides in the user's mailbox. In BES version 5.0, we have the capability to synch multiple address books within Outlook. The improvement is extended by allowing us to also synch distribution lists and contacts that reside in public and shared folders. There is also a new feature that allows the BlackBerry devices to access data directly from your organization's corporate LAN. This means that any shared folder, which has important information in it—that resides on the corporate LAN—can now be accessed securely, directly from the BlackBerry device.

We can now also push BlackBerry firmware updates for the devices by using **OTASL (Over the Air Software Loading)**, as seen in Lab 5.

Other advances in Microsoft Exchange have made the prerequisite setup more manageable due to the ability of the Microsoft Exchange to use a command-line shell. We can now apply and change the permissions more swiftly for user accounts.

BES version 5.0 architecture

BES, BlackBerry Enterprise Server, is the backend software that runs multiple BlackBerry devices in your organization, linking each one to your corporate e-mail server. The BES manages the flow of e-mail data ensuring that it is directed to its ultimate destination—the BlackBerry Smartphone. The BES also provides its own set of features and capabilities. The device management capabilities stand out the most in a BES. These allow us to have full control over BlackBerry Smartphones that are deployed within our organizations.

The core functionality of the BES has not changed; it still acts as a conduit between the messaging server and the Smartphone devices. Its ultimate goal still remains the same; it controls the data flow (be it e-mail, calendar, tasks, or third-party application data) between the servers on the corporate LAN and the wireless networks that the handhelds are joined to.

What has improved vastly in BES version 5.0 is the rich capabilities it now offers to administrators to manage the Smartphone devices. Those of you who are used to the previous version (version 4.x.x or earlier) of the BES, the first thing you will notice as an administrator is the new dashboard style administrator tool, which allows us to administer users more efficiently, offers hyperlinks and right-click functionality, so tasks can be achieved quickly and in a proper manner.

It is not just monitoring of the devices that has improved in BES version 5.0, but also the ability to set health scores on the BES and its components to ensure the system is running to its optimum. If it detects any change in the health of the system, alarm messages can be raised and disaster recovery plans can be brought into action automatically. Health scores are discussed in *Chapter 8, Upgrades*, in more detail.

From a backend perspective, the database has changed from the previous versions. The new database is more in-depth, schema tables are better written, and indexing has improved vastly. Previously, the database for the BES was just a hidden attribute, an important attribute but one that was never really managed by BES functions. In BES 5.0, we can now—without the need of third party applications—take control of the database, by running defragmentation, indexing, and checking database sizes, all from the BES 5.0 monitoring service.

Everyday management tasks such as the capability to provision devices, deactivate and wipe data from lost or stolen devices, and to enforce security policies have also improved with added functionality in the new BES management system, BAS.

> It is important to note that the BES still remains a distributed service. The BES is not a single service and it is made up of a dozen or so component services that combine to provide the functionality of the BES.
>
> These components can be installed on a single server or they can be spread out on multiple servers to offer greater scalability.

The components that make up the BES service are vastly similar to the previous versions of the BES. The following is an overview of these components:

Component Name	Component Function	New To BES 5.0
BlackBerry Administration Service	New feature that lets you manage the BlackBerry domain via a web interface—the new dashboard style management of the BlackBerry configuration database, which allows you to perform the core functions related to administering the BES.	YES
BlackBerry Monitoring Service	Used to troubleshoot and monitor the BES in your organization, it polls and collects SNMP data and then applies it to threshold values configured and alerts network admins when unhealthy scores are produced.	YES
BlackBerry Web Desktop Manager	A web-based application that provides similar features to Desktop Manager, so users can manage devices, backup, restore data, and update device software.	YES

Component Name	Component Function	New To BES 5.0
BlackBerry Attachment Service	Converts e-mail attachments into a format that can be viewed on BlackBerry devices.	NO
BlackBerry Collaboration Service	Encrypts the communications between instant messaging servers and the instant messenger client on BlackBerry devices.	NO
BlackBerry Configuration Database	A relational database that stores the configuration information for the BES components, using MS SQL.	NO
BlackBerry Controller	Monitors BES components and restarts any stopped services.	NO
BlackBerry Dispatcher	Handles compression and encryption for the BlackBerry data.	NO
BlackBerry Alerts	Used to send out any alert information from the monitoring component.	NO
BlackBerry Configuration Panel	A GUI view of the BlackBerry Configuration database, this utility allows us to make changes to the configuration database after the installation process.	NO
BlackBerry Mail Store Service	Connects to the messaging server to retrieve user contact data that the BlackBerry Administration Service requires. It synchs and updates the contact list to the BlackBerry Configuration database ensuring that the messaging server's contact lists and the contact lists on the BlackBerry configuration database are the same.	NO
BlackBerry Messaging Agent	Makes sure that the data between the BlackBerry configuration database and the user's mailbox is the same. It serves as the connection between the messaging server and other BES components.	NO
BlackBerry Synchronization Service	Synchs organization data, such as calendars, tasks, and so on, between the e-mail server and the BlackBerry devices.	NO
BlackBerry MDS Connection Services	Controls the access of online content and applications from the organization's intranet, or information published on the internet.	NO
BlackBerry MDS Integration Service	Enables BlackBerry MDS Runtime applications to interact with Enterprise backend systems via web services or using a direct database connection.	NO
BlackBerry Policy Service	Manages the IT policies, and IT administrative commands such as resending or provisioning service books for the BlackBerry devices.	NO
BlackBerry Router	Connects to the wireless network and routes data to and from BlackBerry devices.	NO

Databases

There are three main databases within BES:

- The BES database (the BlackBerry configuration database)
- Monitoring database
- MDS integration database

These databases can be held on a Microsoft SQL Server Desktop Engine or a Microsoft SQL Server 2005 standard, express, or enterprise edition. Selection of which database system to use will have an impact on future growth and scalability of your BES environment. MSDE is a lightweight version of Microsoft SQL server that can be installed during the BES installation process. The ease of implementation of the MSDE makes it a popular choice especially with smaller BES environments. The database size for MSDE is limited to 2 GB, which will limit the number of users you can have in your BES environment. The base configuration database is approximately 100 MB and each additional user requires 20 MB restricting BES implementations with MSDE to less than 100 users. You are not locked in if you opt to use MSDE as your initial BlackBerry configuration database, as you can upgrade the database to Microsoft SQL Server.

These databases can be created during the BES installation process as long as the correct permissions are assigned to the Microsoft SQL Server, prior to running the installation (see the *Lab 1 – installing BlackBerry Enterprise Server 5.0* section.)

The configuration database can be installed outside of the main BES installation by running the `CreateDB` executable on the `Besmgmt.cfg` file, ideal when running upgrades or when you don't have access rights to the SQL server due to network policies.

Using Microsoft SQL Server to house the BlackBerry configuration database provides greater flexibility and scalability, especially in the area of disaster recovery. There is no support for database mirroring when using MSDE.

For the monitoring service, we need to ensure that the SNMP service is running on all the servers that will be housing BES components. We need to configure SNMP service and the monitoring service itself. Once it has been installed, it will be shown in *Chapter 7, High Availability and Monitoring the BES*.

MAPI and CDO files

These files are required for the BES to be able to initiate a Remote Procedure Call to the Microsoft Exchange Server to read and locate the **GAL** (**Global Address List**, this is populated in Microsoft Exchange Server and is used to search for e-mail recipients in the organization) and other Exchange Server information, especially the device user's mailboxes, calendars, and so on.

These files need to be of a particular version (6.5.8022) and also they are no longer installed during the original installation of Microsoft Exchange Server 2007, as Microsoft Exchange Server 2007 does not use **Exchange System Management** (**ESM**)tools.

We need to make sure they are downloaded and installed from the Microsoft website prior to Lab 1. By running the executable in the download on the BES (the chosen server that will house the BES software) the MAPI and CDO files will be installed in the correct locations.

The BES uses the subarchitect of the MAPI to provide more stable communication software.

BES network requirements

The network requirements for a typical BES implementation are relatively simple. The BES should be installed in a high-speed, switched network environment. The number of hops between the messaging server and the BES should be minimized to ensure optimal performance. The other basic security requirement is that the BES should be able to initiate an outbound TCP connection to the BlackBerry infrastructure on TCP port 3101. This is one of the security features that has made the implementation of BES successful-you only need to open a single port on the firewall for an outbound connection for the solution to work. This minimizes any exploits via a firewall as you are only opening the single port for outbound connections.

BESAdmin account

As mentioned, the BES acts as a data traffic controller, so we need to make sure that it and the relevant components can authenticate into the Windows domain and messaging service available on your corporate network.

We do this by creating a service account for administrative tasks that the BlackBerry Enterprise Server needs to carry out and communicate with the Microsoft Exchange Server. The account has an Exchange mailbox associated with it. Generally, the accepted username for the service account is **BESAdmin**.

The BESAdmin account will need to have view permissions to the Exchange Server, so it can read data from the messaging server. The Microsoft Exchange Server holds e-mail information in the Information Store. The BESAdmin account needs to access this information so it will require relevant view and allow permissions on the Exchange server as shown in Lab 1.

To enable end users to send e-mails from their devices, we need to make sure that the BESAdmin account can authenticate to the Exchange Server and has Send As permissions for all the end users that will be sending e-mails from their device.

The preceding two steps must be carried out prior to installing the BES, as it creates an account we can use to authenticate our BES to the messaging server, and allows end device users to be able to send e-mails from their BlackBerries via the BESAdmin account.

We need to ensure that we have local administrator privileges on the server that we are going to install the BES software on, so that we can log in to the server and run the BES services as a Windows Service—remember that the software will be installed using the account we have created—BESAdmin. We need to make sure that the BESAdmin account is not a member of the *Domains Admin Group* in the Microsoft Active Directory. Some groups are periodically reset by the system, even if they have been manually configured by the administrator, so it is best practice not to have the account in a group where it does not need the elevate permissions associated with the Domains Admin group—this also ensures a safer secure network.

> Note that the BESAdmin account in BES version 5.0 is purely a service account used for administrative tasks by the BES. We can create and use any account to log in to the BlackBerry Administration Service as shown in Lab 1.

The BlackBerry Enterprise Server system requirements vary based on the number of users supported and the additional services running on the BES. For detailed minimum requirements for BES please see: `http://us.blackberry.com/support/preinstallation/exchange.jsp`.

Lab 1—installing BlackBerry Enterprise Server 5.0

Creating the service account—besadmin

We need to create our service account, which must have a mailbox associated with it.

1. Log on to the Microsoft Exchange Server or the Active Directory Server with an admin account.
2. Open **Active Directory Users and Computers**.
3. Right-click on the Organizational Unit (OU) or the **Users** container where you want to create the Service account and select **New | User**, as shown in the following screenshot:

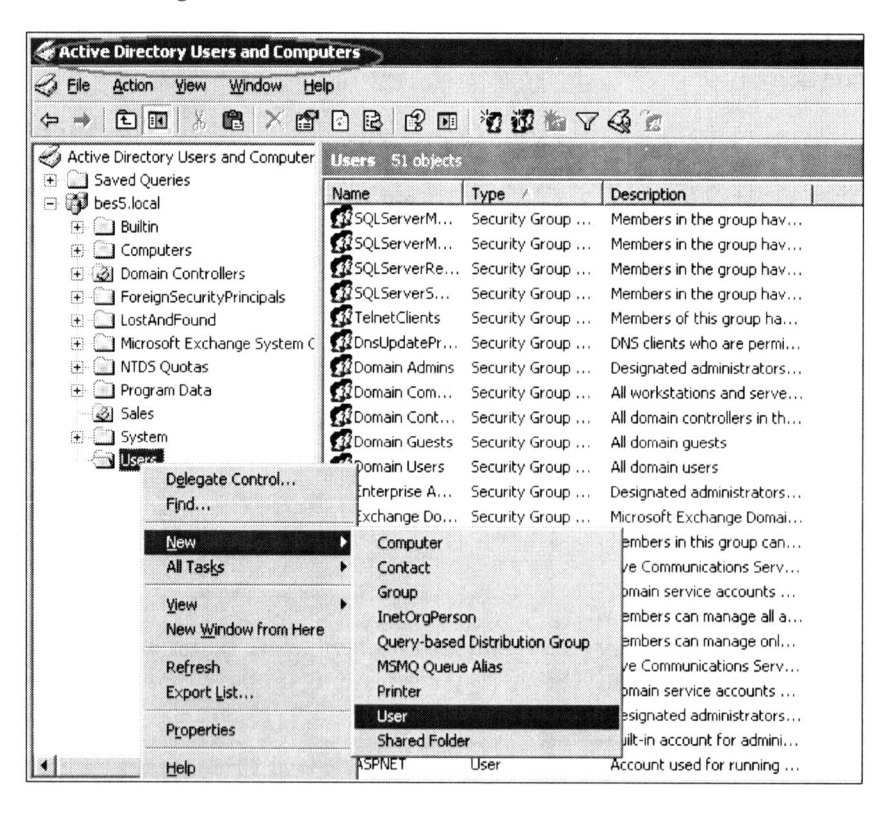

4. Ensure **User logon name:** is `besadmin` and create a strong password that never expires.

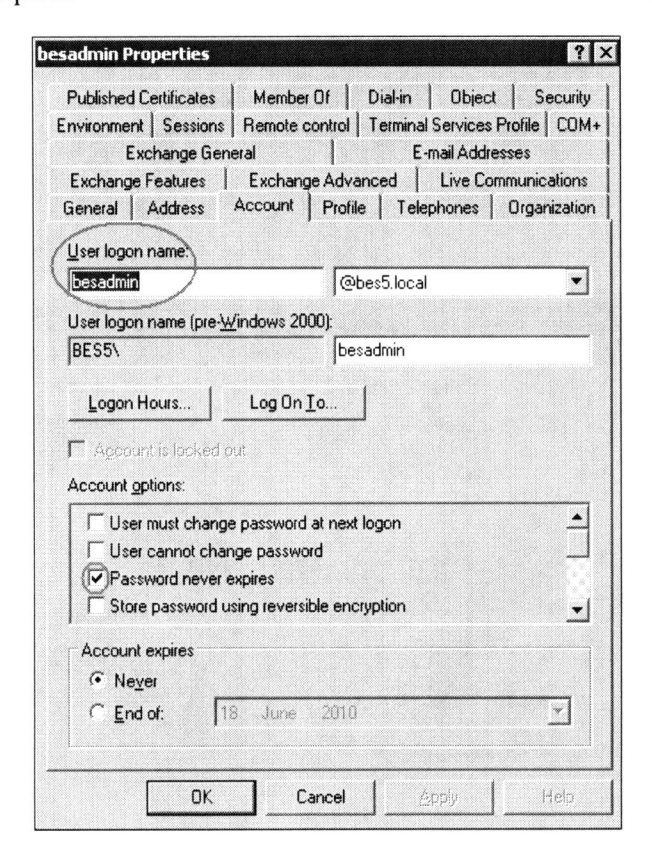

Assigning a mailbox to the besadmin user

1. Open **Microsoft Exchange Management** console.
2. Select **Recipient Configuration** and click the **New Mailbox...** action.
3. Select the **User Mailbox** radio button and click **Next**.
4. Select the **Existing user** radio button and click **browse**, select the **besadmin** service account.
5. Accept the defaults for the new mailbox and click on **New** to create the mailbox.

Assigning Microsoft Exchange permissions to the service account

As mentioned, the service account needs to be able to send e-mails on behalf of the users so that they can send messages from BlackBerry handhelds.

1. Open **Active Directory Users and Computers**.
2. Click on the **View** menu and select **Advanced Features**.
3. Right-click on the OU or the **Users** container and click on **Properties**.

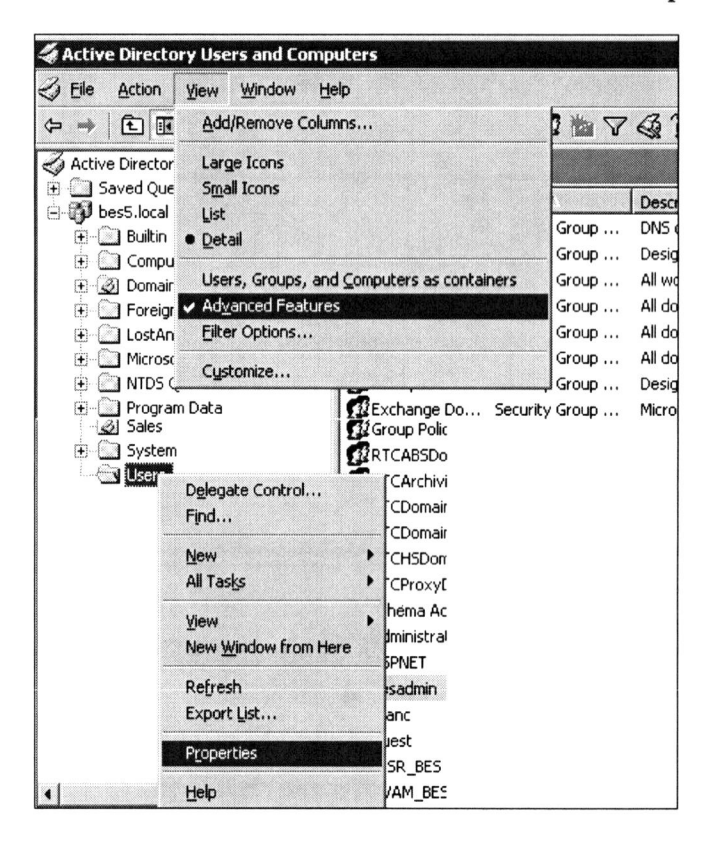

4. Select the **Security** tab.
5. Click the **Add** button and enter the name of the service account (`besadmin`) and click **OK**.

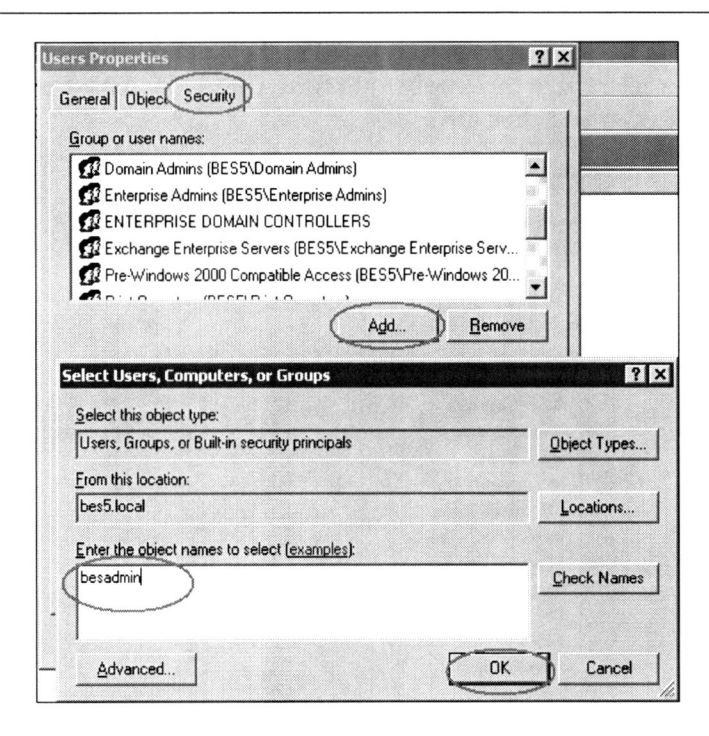

6. Click on the **Advanced...** button, select the **besadmin** account and click on **Edit**.

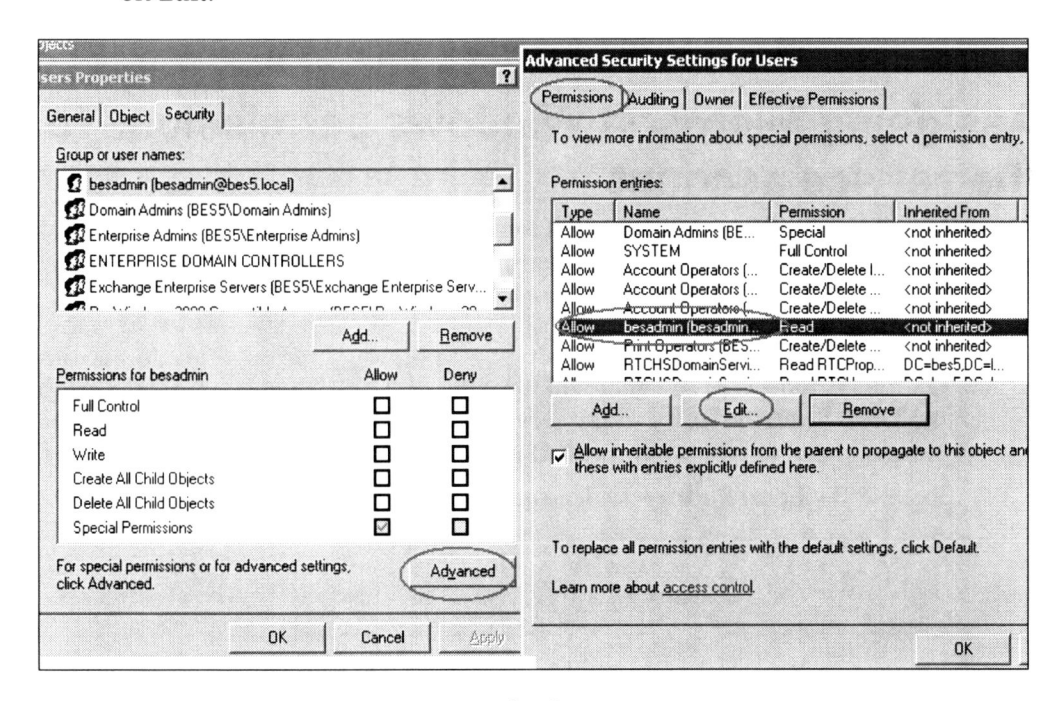

Introduction to BES 5

7. Verify that the service account is listed in the **Name** field, and that the **User objects** is selected in the **Apply onto** field. Check the **Allow** box for the **Send As** permission and click **OK**.

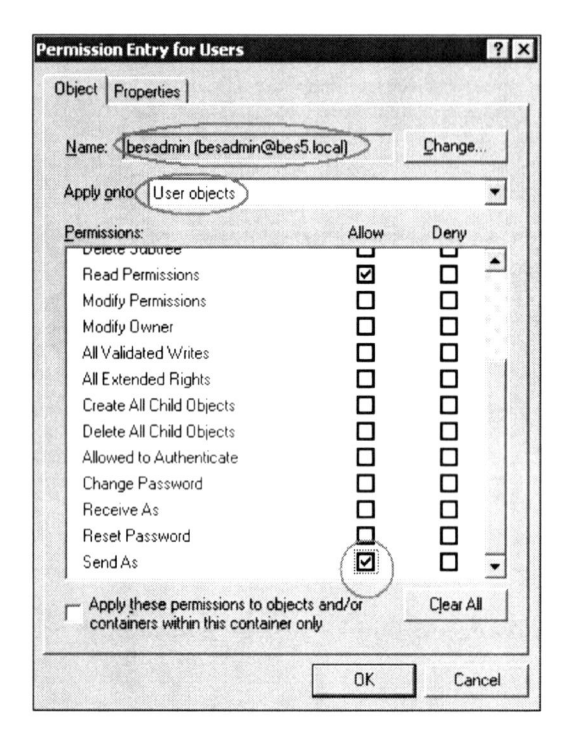

Assigning Microsoft Windows permissions to the service account

We now need to grant the service account local admin rights on the Windows Servers. Remember, if you are going to distribute your BES components, the service account will require local admin rights on each server that has a BES component installed. Follow these steps:

1. On the Windows Servers that will have the BES components installed, open the **Local Security Policy** (if the server is acting as a Domain controller then you will need to edit the **Default Domain Controller Security Settings**).

2. Expand the **Local Policies** folder and select **User Rights Assignment** folder.

3. Right-click **Log on as a service** and select **Properties**.

Chapter 1

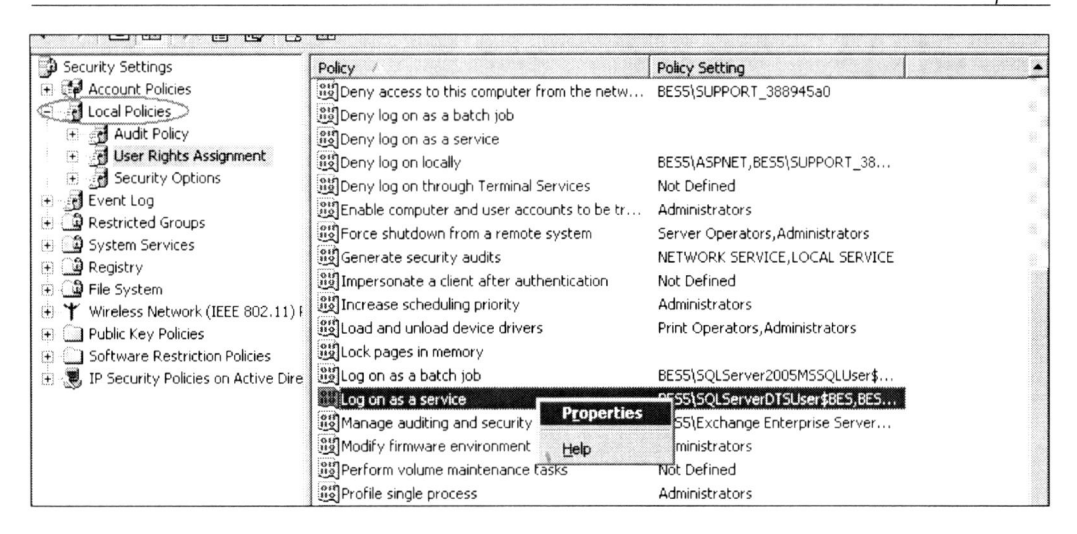

4. Click **Add User or Group** and enter the name of the service account and click on **OK**.

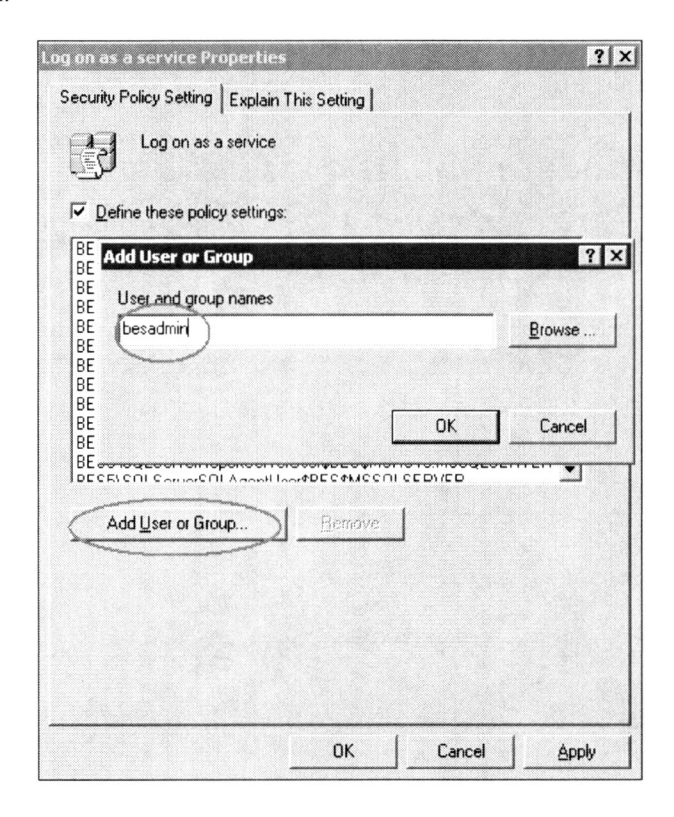

5. Repeat the preceding steps for the allow **Log on Locally** properties.

[21]

6. Open the **Computer Management** console (skip this step if the BES component is on a Domain Controller (DC), as **Local Users and Groups** are disabled when in DC mode).
7. Expand **Local Users and Groups**, and select **Groups**.
8. Right-click on the **Administrators** group and select **Add to Group**.
9. Click on **Add** and enter the name of the service account and click on **OK**.

Configuring Microsoft Exchange permissions for the service account

The service account must be granted additional Microsoft Exchange permissions in order to send and receive messages as other users and to administer the Exchange Information Store. The following procedure describes how to assign this permission for Microsoft Exchange Server 2007:

1. On the Exchange Server, open the Exchange Management Shell and type the following:

   ```
   add-exchangeadministrator "BESAdmin" -role ViewOnlyAdmin
   ```

2. The preceding command gives the service account (besadmin) the view only permission, which is required. Type the following:

   ```
   set-mailboxserver "<Exchange_server_name>" | add-adpermission -user "BESAdmin" -accessrights ExtendedRight - extendedrights Send As Receive-As, ms-Exch-Store-Admin.
   ```

3. Substitute the name of your Exchange Server for <Exchange_server_name>.

   > The preceding command ensures that end users are able to send and receive messages from their devices.

Enabling the database server

We have the following options when it comes to selecting the database system we are going to use to store and create the BlackBerry configuration database.

We can create the BlackBerry configuration database from a file and store the database on a Microsoft SQL Server. We would need to then set permissions for the service account, besadmin, to have access to the database, so it can read and write information to it during and after the installation. See *Creating the BlackBerry configuration database* and *Setting permissions for the Service account manually* in the following sections.

Alternatively, we can create the BlackBerry configuration database during the installation automatically by pointing to our Microsoft SQL Server to create the database. We would need to ensure prior to installation that the SQL Server has the correct permissions for the service account, besadmin, to have access to create the database, so it can read and write information to it. See *Setting permissions for the service account automatically* in the following sections.

If we choose to install the freeware Microsoft SQL Server 2005 Express during the installation, then all the required authentication roles and privileges are assigned automatically, and there is no need for any of the preparation work highlighted earlier.

Some organizations have strict policies on the SQL server. Therefore, it is advisable to create the database prior to installation. If there are no restrictions on creating databases, it is best to create it on the fly during the installation as we will do in our installation of the BES, remembering in both cases that we still have to assign permissions for the service account.

Creating the BlackBerry configuration database

1. Log on to the Microsoft SQL Server with the correct administrative privileges that allow you to create a database.
2. Insert or copy the extracted BlackBerry Enterprise Server media to the SQL computer.
3. Browse to the `Database` folder.

Introduction to BES 5

4. Open the `BesMgmt.cfg` file in a notepad.
5. The following screenshot shows the `BesMgmt.cfg` file:

```
; NotifyInstall - install the database notification service
; NotifyUnInstall - removes the database notification service
; CatalogDatabase - used for DB2 only.  Catalogs remote db locally
; AddOn - used to install additional tables to existing db.  ADD_ON_NAME needs to be set.
; Restore - restores a previously backed up db using RESTORE_FILENAME below
CMD=Install

DATABASE_NAME=BESMgmt

;
; Name of Server to install the db
; Local machine can be specified as local
; Applies only to SQLServer
SERVER=local


;
; The userid/password to use to create/update to the database.  If not set, then the userid will be
; the user executing this program
USERID=
PASSWORD=


;
; Everything is logged to DB_Installv<timestamp>.log but you can also
; get info/error msgs dumped to console by setting this to true
VERBOSE=false


;
; Database version to create/migrate to
; Format is 3.5, 3.6, 4.0 etc
; If left blank, most recent version will be used
VERSION=
```

6. **CMD** should be set to **Install** as we are going to install a fresh copy of the BES server (for those of you who are looking at doing an upgrade please see *Chapter 8, Upgrades*).
7. **DATABASE_NAME** is set as the default instance name of **BESMgmt**.
8. **SERVER** is the name of the server, which can be kept as local.
9. If the **USERID** and **PASSWORD** is left blank then it will use the credentials of the account we are currently logged in as when we execute the setup.
10. Ensure the **VERSION** is left blank, so we create the latest version.
11. We can specify where we want log files, database files, and backup files to be stored, if these are left blank then the default locations are chosen.

So once the preceding file is executed on the SQL Server, we will have our BlackBerry configuration database ready to point to during our installation. To execute the file use the `createdb.exe` command followed by the full path of the `BesMgmt.cfg` file.

Chapter 1

Setting permissions for the service account manually

We now need to make sure that the BES database has the right permission, so the service account besadmin, can access it. Follow these steps:

1. Log on to the SQL Server.
2. Expand the **Security** option.
3. Right-click on **Logins** and select **New Login...**.

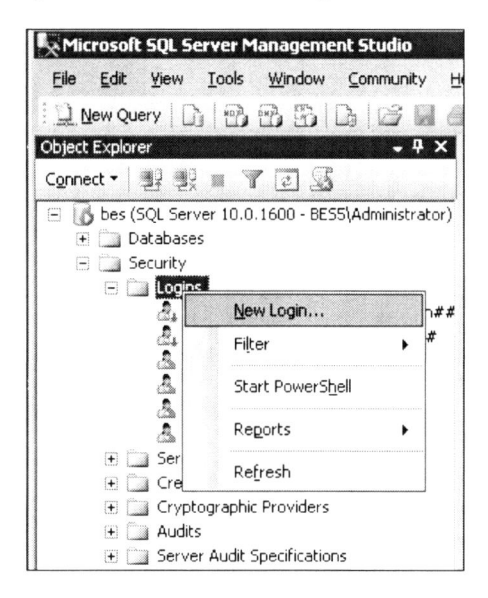

4. Ensure the radio button is selected to **Windows authentication**.
5. Enter the name of the service account in the **Login name** field ensuring the format is `DOMAIN\username`.

[25]

Introduction to BES 5

6. Change the **Default database** to the **BESMgmt** and click **OK**.

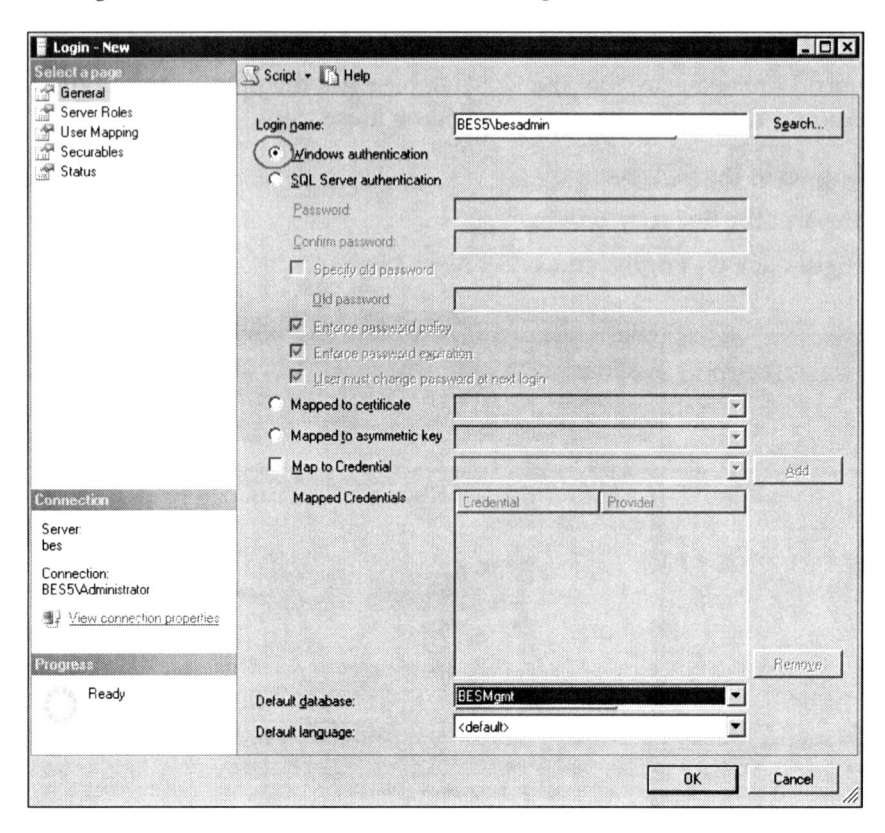

7. Then select **Server Roles**, click the checkbox for the following roles:

    ◦ **serveradmin**
    ◦ **sysadmin**

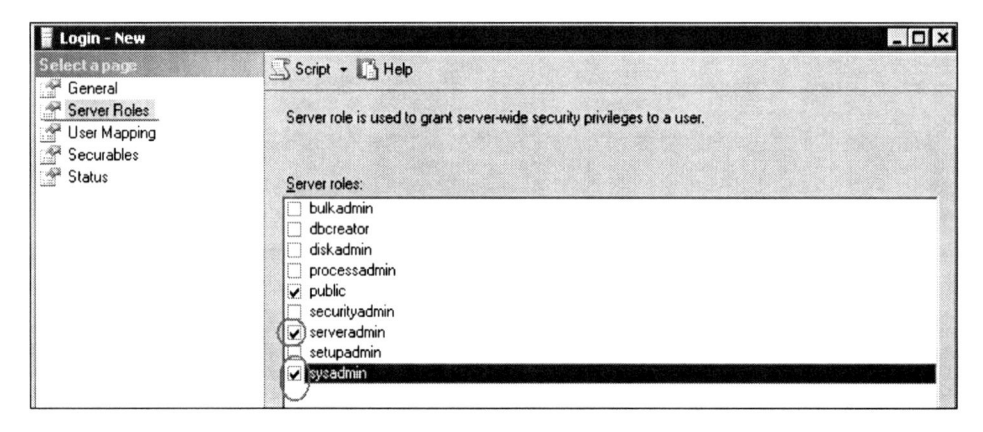

You can also select SQL Server authentication instead of selecting Windows authentication. Follow these steps:

1. Log on to the SQL Server.
2. Expand the **Security** option.
3. Right-click on **Logins** and select **New Login...**.
4. Ensure the radio button is selected to **SQL Server authentication**.
5. Enter a name in the **Login name** field such as Besadmin_DB.
6. Change the **Default database** to the **BESMgmt** and click **OK**.

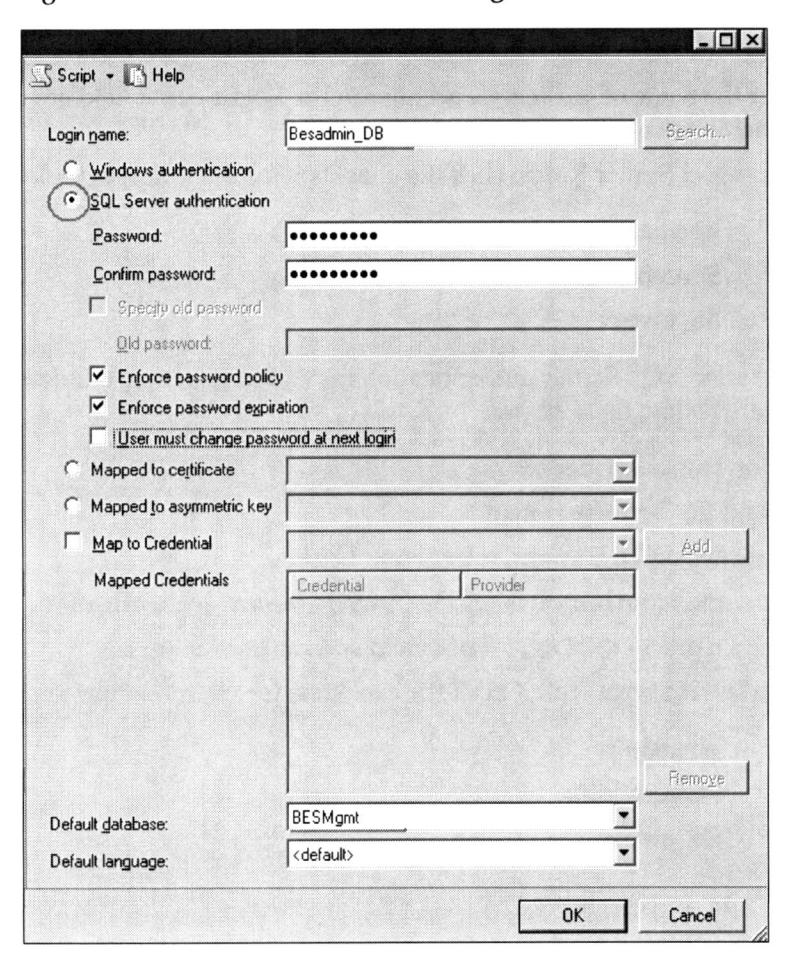

7. Then select **Server Roles**, click the checkbox for the following roles:
    - serveradmin
    - sysadmin

Setting permissions for the service account automatically

In this scenario, we also need to make sure we assign the service account the right privileges, so it can actually create the database along with admin access to the database.

1. Log on to the SQL Server.
2. Expand the **Security** option.
3. Right-click on **Logins** and select **New Login...**.
4. Ensure the radio button is selected to **Windows authentication**.
5. Enter the name of the service account in the **Login name** field ensuring the format is `DOMAIN\username`.
6. Then select **Server Roles**, click the checkbox for the following roles:
   - **dbcreator**
   - **Serveradmin**
   - **db_owner**

You can also select SQL Server authentication instead of selecting Windows authentication. Follow these steps:

1. Log on to the SQL Server.
2. Expand the **Security** option.
3. Right-click on **Logins** and select **New Login...**.
4. Ensure the radio button is selected to **SQL Server authentication**.
5. Enter a name in the **Login name** field such as `besdbadmin`.
6. Then select **Server Roles**, click the checkbox for the following roles:
   - **dbcreator**
   - **Serveradmin**
   - **db_owner**

> Please make sure that the same type of authentication method is used on all the databases, that is, they all use Windows authentication or they all use SQL authentication.

Final checklist prior to installation

Before we head into installing our BES server, it is best to run through the checklist to ensure that we have not missed out on anything. Check for the following:

- Create the service account (`besadmin` account).
- Assign Microsoft Exchange permissions to the service account (Send As permissions).
- Assign Windows permission to the service account (local login).
- Configure the Microsoft Exchange permissions for the service account (view admin rights and rights to the Information Store).
- Database choice (MSDE or SQL).
- Install the MAPI and CDO objects. These need to be installed on the server that will be running the BES software as explained in the *MAPI and CDO files* section of this chapter.
- Make sure that we can initiate an outbound connection on port 3101 from the firewall and the port is open.
- If you are installing on a Windows 2008 Server platform, it is strongly recommended to disable the IP Version 6 from the registry.

Installing BES version 5

The installation process itself is pretty much straight forward; we need to log on to the target BES server using the besadmin service account. Make sure that you have at hand the license key and SRP information provided when you bought the software and follow these steps:

1. Copy or insert the BlackBerry media on to the target BES server. Extract the software to a folder and run the `setup.exe` icon.

Introduction to BES 5

2. Select the appropriate language. A message will be displayed. Ensure that the account shown is the BES Service account (**besadmin**) and click on **Continue Installation**.

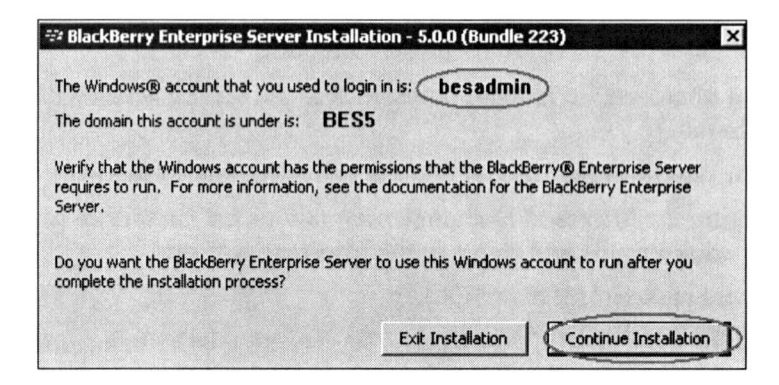

3. Enter details in the EULA and click **Next**.
4. We now have the option to create a new BlackBerry database or choose an existing one. For this lab we are going to create a new BlackBerry configuration database, as shown in the following screenshot. If you created one already using the `BesMgmt.cfg` file then the following steps will differ.

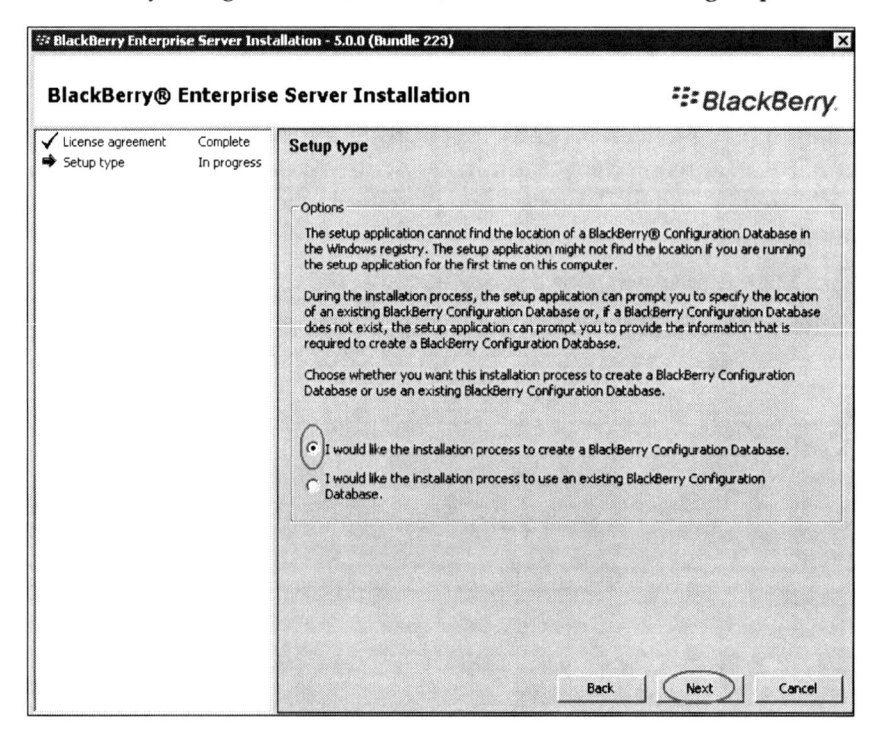

5. Then select to install a **BlackBerry Enterprise Server** with all the components selected, as shown in the following screenshot:

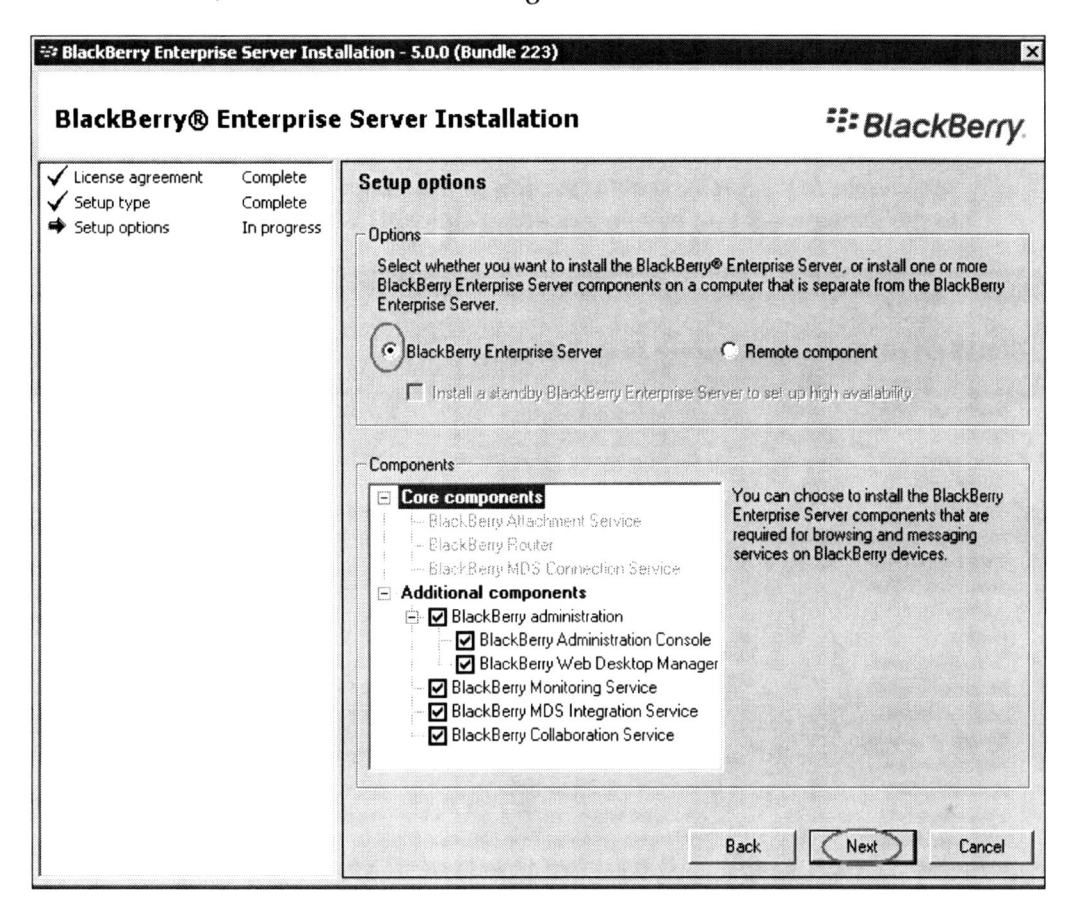

6. The next screen will bring up the EULA for the Apache Service. Accept the license and click **Next**. BlackBerry Enterprise Server does not use **Microsoft Internet Information** (**IIS**) to house the BlackBerry Administration websites, it uses the Apache platform.
7. You will also need to agree to the **CPL license** and click **Next** to continue.
8. The setup will run through a **Preinstallation checklist** so that any software components that the BES needs will be updated. If it's not the latest version or if the software is missing, it will be installed during the setup process.

Introduction to BES 5

9. Also ensure that the **Exchange server permissions** have been applied and there are no errors. The setup will prompt to say that the Send As permission for the service account is not set at the domain level. If you have set it at an OU level, such as the users container then it is fine to carry on with the installation, but bear in mind that only users in that OU will be able to send and receive messages via the BlackBerry Enterprise Server. You can follow the same procedure as specified in the *Assigning Microsoft Exchange permissions to the Service account* section of this chapter for changing the OU to the Domain—if you have users in multiple OU within the domain.

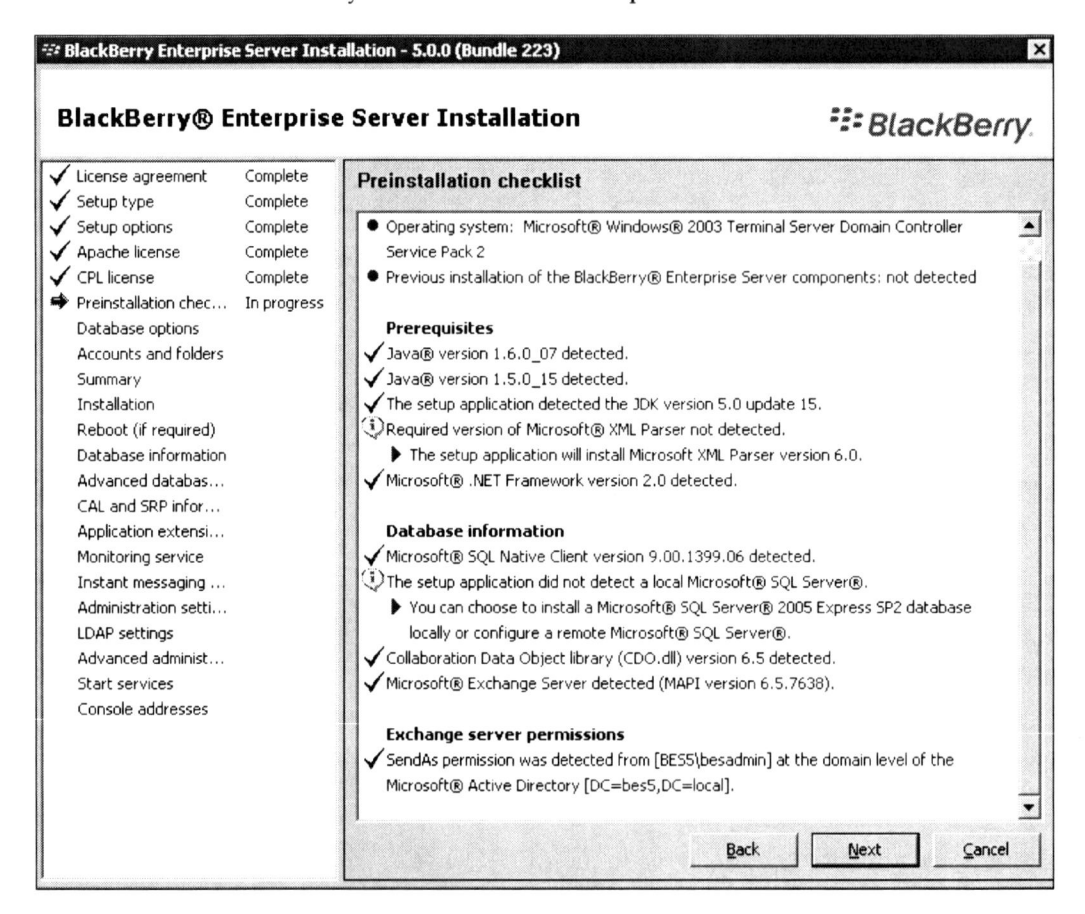

Chapter 1

10. Next, we have to select our database option. We can install a lightweight MSDE on to the same server or we can point to an SQL server to house the BlackBerry database. We will—for the purpose of this lab—choose to house the BlackBerry database on a remote SQL Server, as shown in the following screenshot:

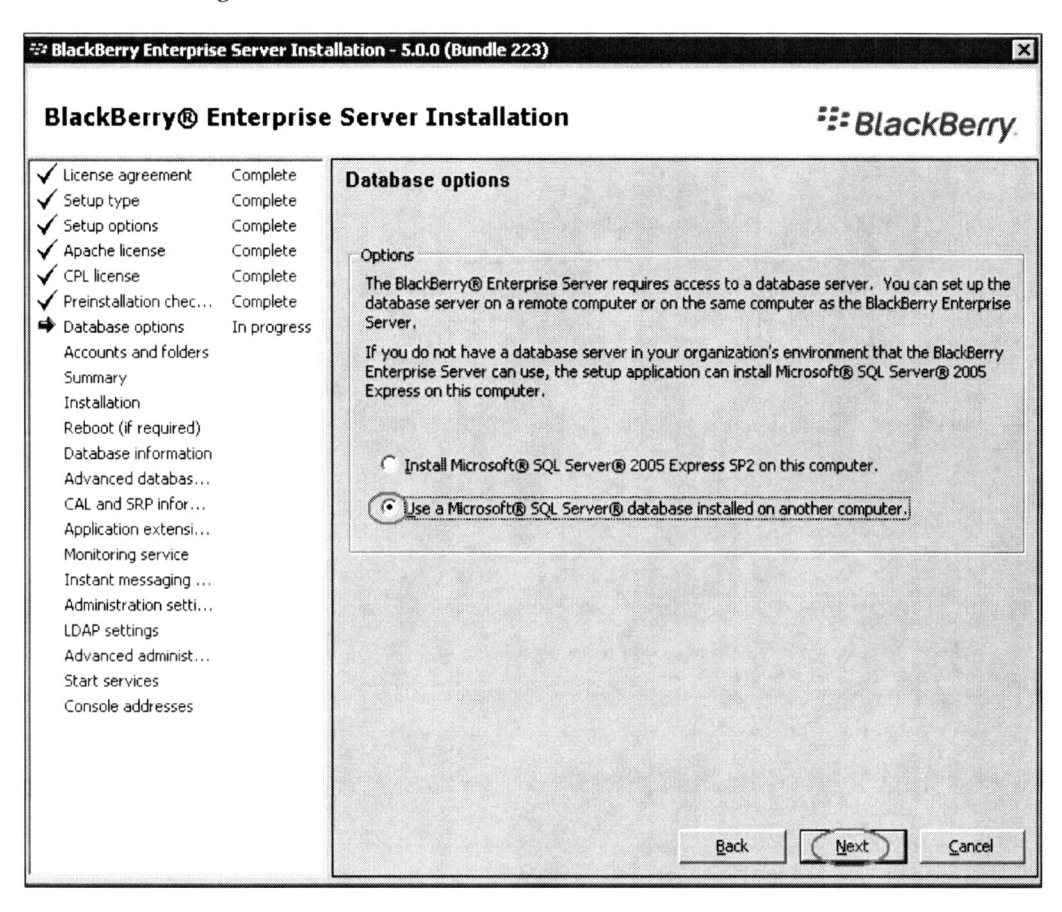

[33]

Introduction to BES 5

11. In the following screenshot, we need to enter the password for the service account. Select the path for the BlackBerry Server installation and the installation log files. We also have to enter the name for the BlackBerry Enterprise Server:

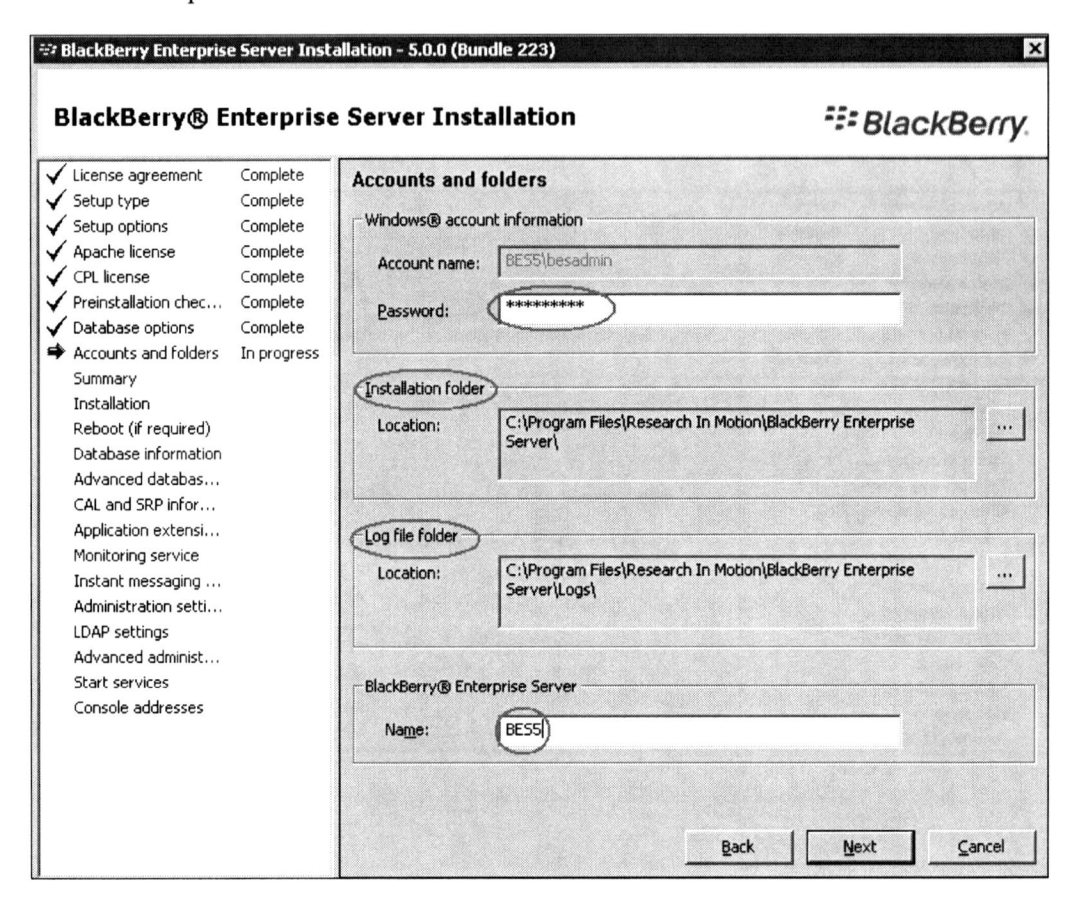

12. You will be presented with an installation summary. View to make sure the settings are correct and click on **Install**. Once the software has carried out the first install part, it will prompt you to reboot the server. Log back in with the **besadmin** service account.

Chapter 1

13. Select **Local** if the SQL Server is housed on the same server as the BES install or select **Remote** if the SQL server is on a different machine.

14. Enter the SQL Server name and the name of the BES configuration database. In our case, BESMgmt, the default name is fine and select **Windows authentication**, as shown in the following screenshot:

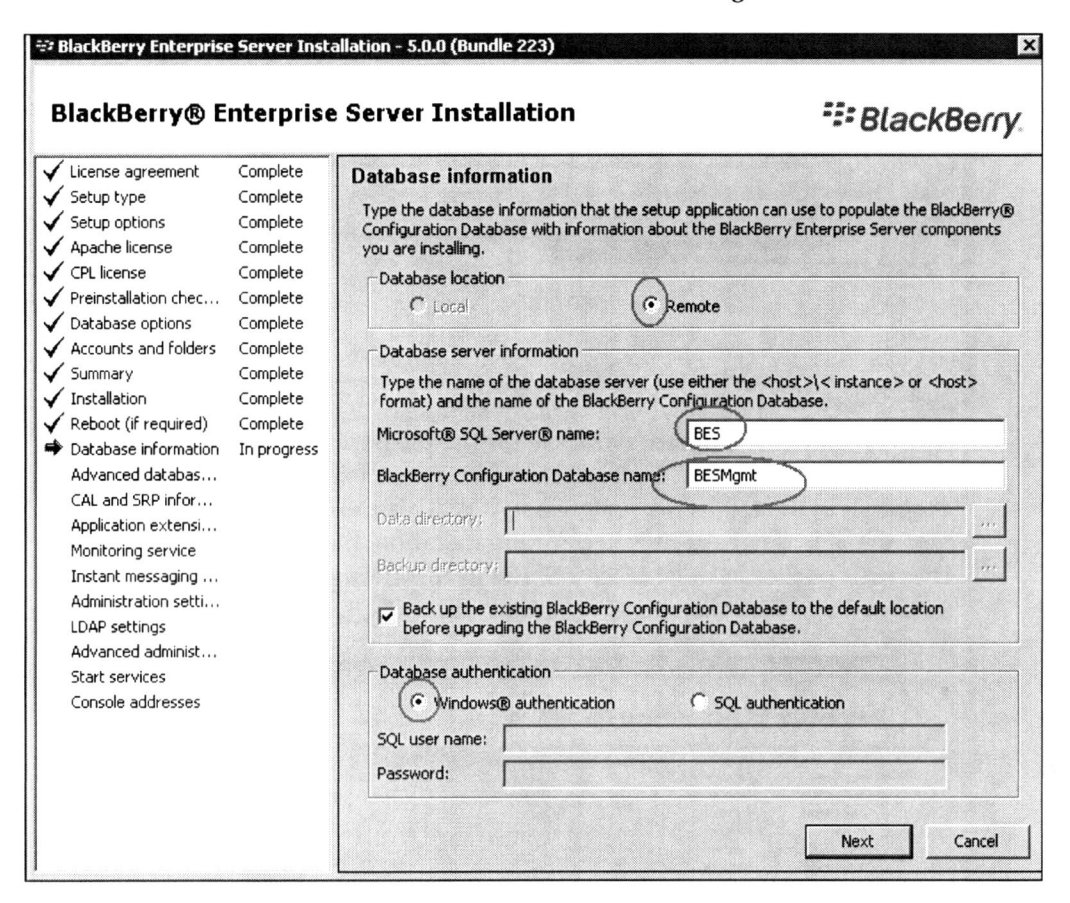

Introduction to BES 5

15. It will prompt you to create the database and as long as all the permissions and roles are set up correctly—as shown earlier in this chapter—the installation will go ahead and create the database for us, as shown in the following screenshot:

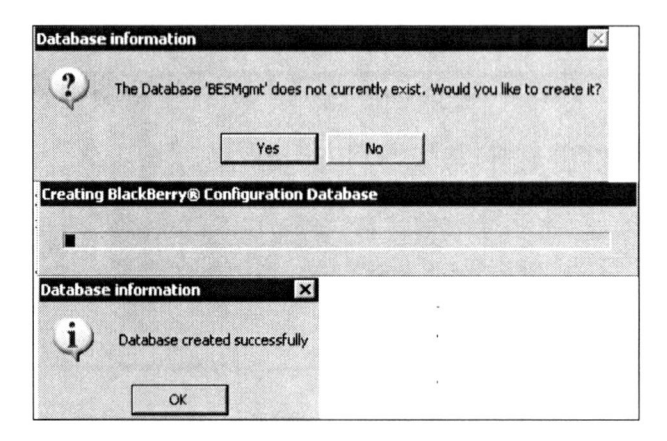

16. It will prompt for a mirror database for the purpose of this lab. We will be coming back to this in *Chapter 8, Upgrades*, so we will leave it unchecked, as shown in the following screenshot. It will also ask you to select the port type the SQL database uses in your organization; the type can either be a **Dynamic port** or in most cases a **Static port** running on **1433**. Please amend these settings according to your organization's SQL setup.

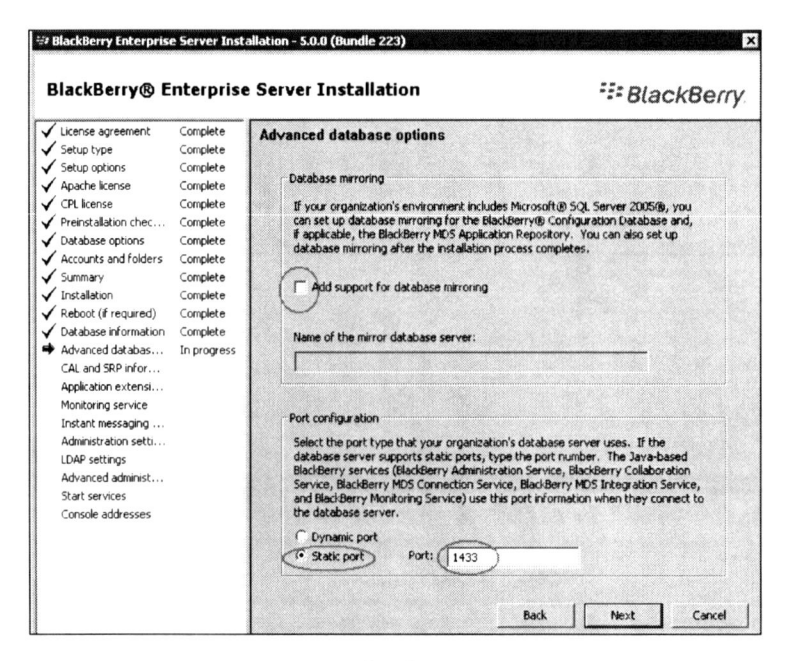

17. It will then prompt you to enter the licensing information for the BES server. Enter the CAL, followed by your SRP host details where the port number should be 3101. You can click on the **Verify** button to make sure the host details are correct.

18. Type in the SRP authentication information provided when you purchased the BES and click the **Verify** button to test the connectivity to the BlackBerry infrastructure.

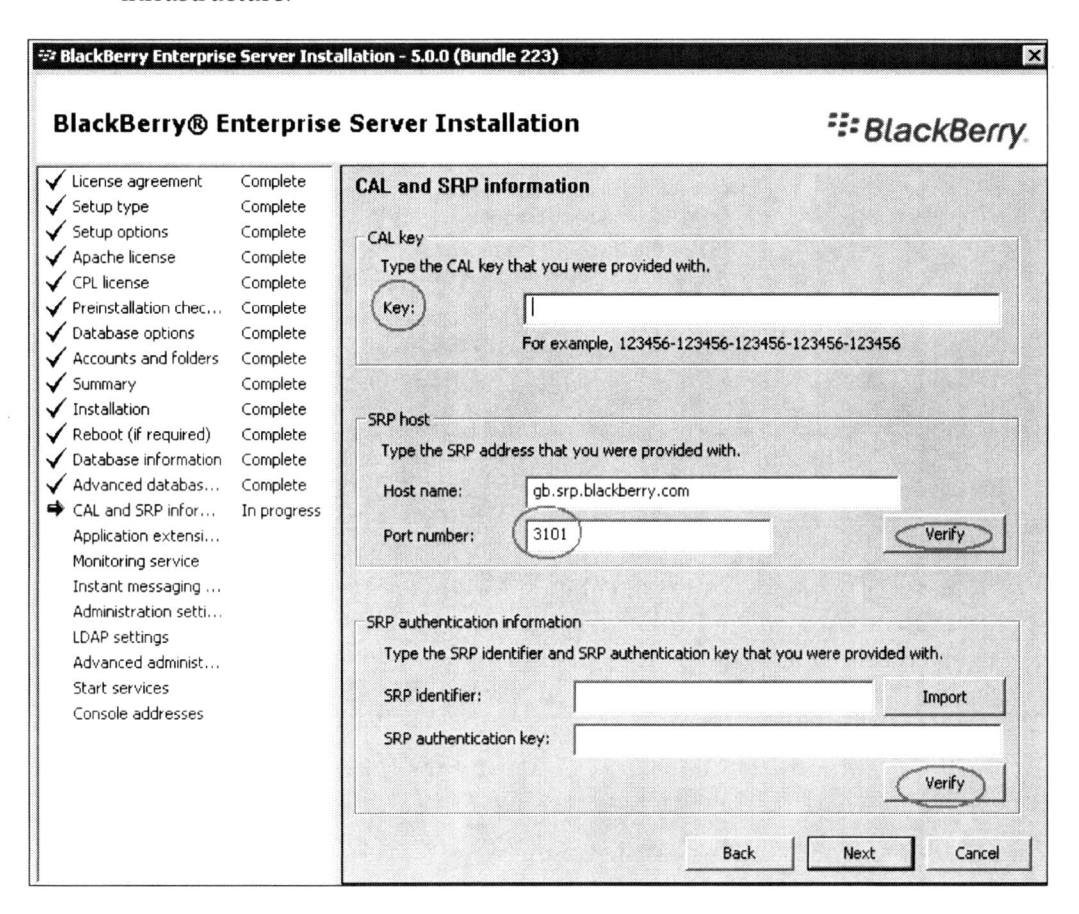

Introduction to BES 5

19. Once you click on **Next**, it will prompt you to check the Exchange Server name and the service account. Enter the name of your Exchange Server and the besadmin account.

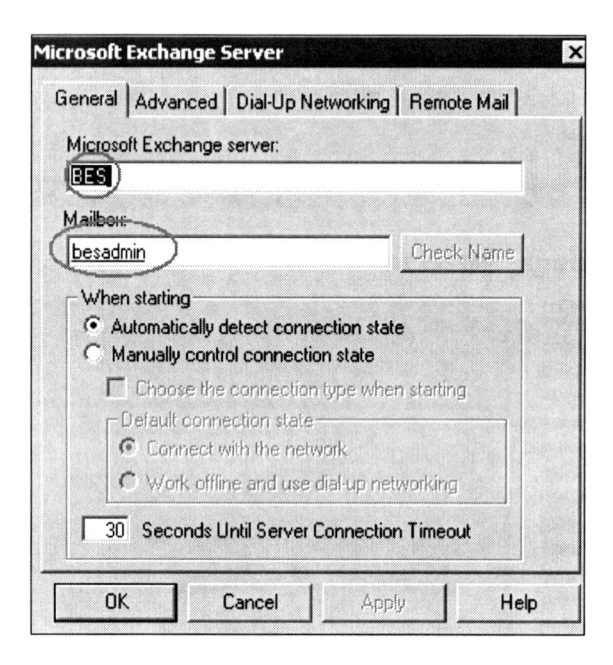

20. Once we have clicked **OK**, it will go back to the **Application extensibility settings** screen. For MDS Integration Service Pool enter a Fully Qualified Domain name in the **Pool name**. This is important so that we can utilize DNS and ensure high availability when we do set up a fail over structure. The binding IP address will be of the BES server.

21. We need to set up the MDS Integration Service database, which will use Windows authentication. Enter a name for the MDS database or you can accept the default one.

22. Verify the port numbers and ensure they don't conflict with any pre-existing port numbers in your infrastructure.

Chapter 1

23. We have to set passwords for two accounts that are used with the MDS integration service—the administrator credentials and the publisher credentials; both accounts are created during installation. Once the passwords are entered, click on **Next**. It will then prompt you to create the MDS database, select **yes**.

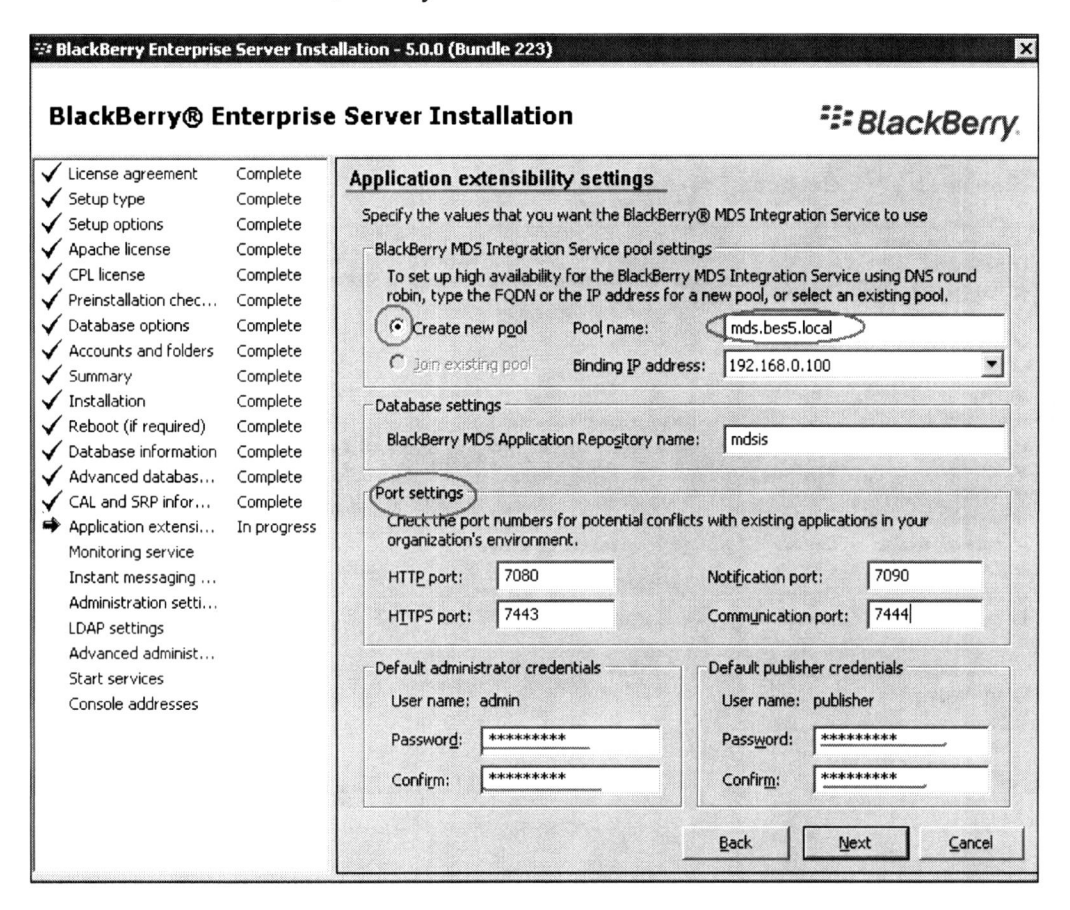

Introduction to BES 5

24. We now have to enter information regarding our **Monitoring service**. We can choose to have the monitoring database on the same SQL server as the BlackBerry configuration database or select a different SQL server. We are going to leave the database server on the same SQL server by placing the tick in the first box, as shown in the following screenshot. We have to give the database a name and by clicking **Next** it will go ahead and create the database for us:

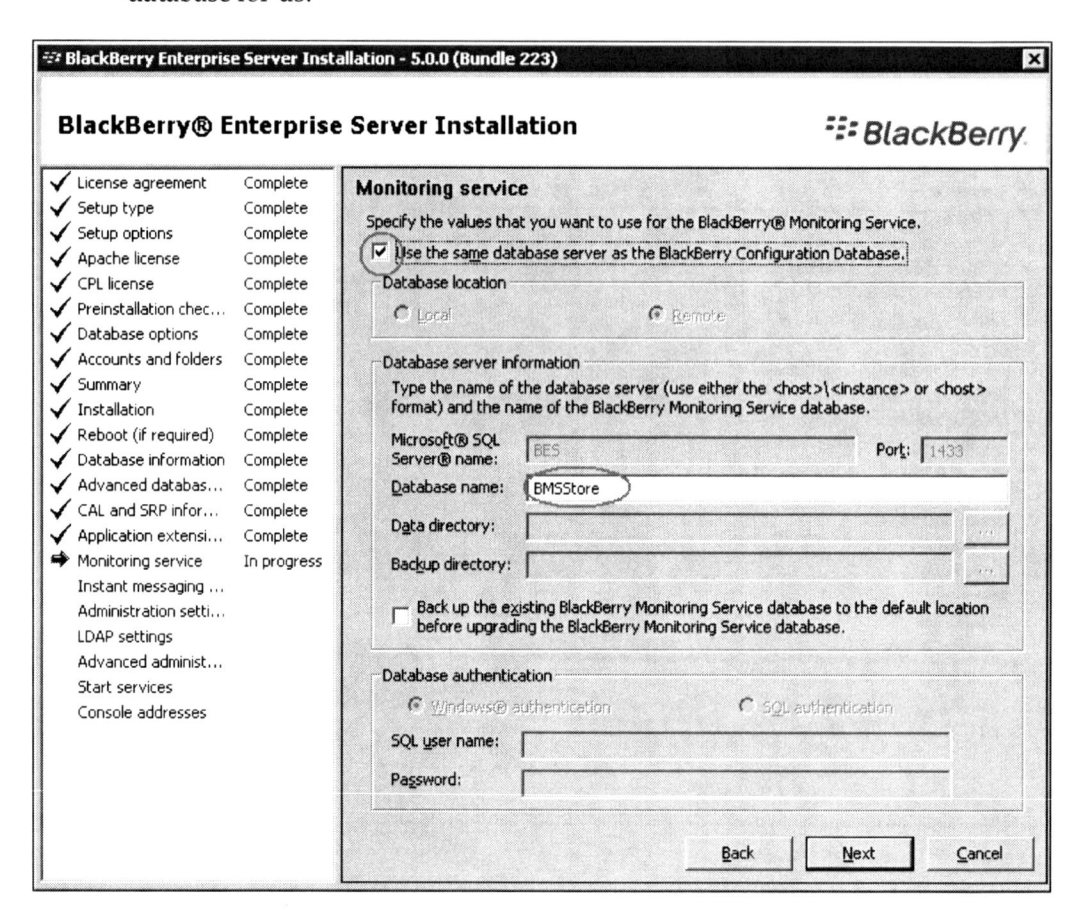

Chapter 1

25. The **Instant messaging settings** now appears, from the **Blackberry Collaboration Service** drop-down. Select Microsoft Office Communication Server 2007 and in the host name type the name of the instant messaging server followed by the port number it uses, as shown in the following screenshot:

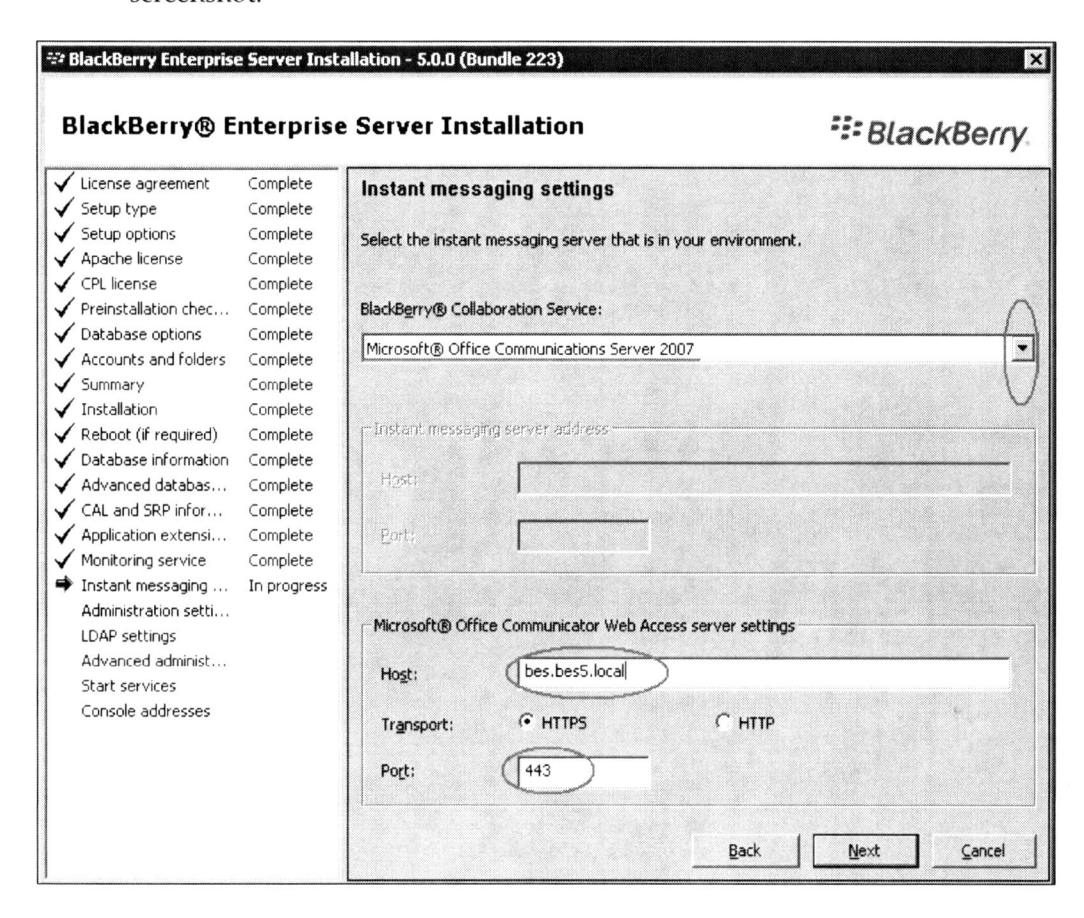

26. We are then presented with the Administration settings page. This is the new system that we will be using to administer the BES server (it has replaced the old BlackBerry Manager). We need to type a FQDN that the BlackBerry Administration Service can use to host the site.

Introduction to BES 5

27. Ensure that the default port numbers don't conflict with any existing applications on your network and then type a password that will be used for the SSL certificate to authenticate with the browsers.

28. In the Active Directory screen, as shown in the following screenshot, type in the name of the service account, `besadmin`, followed by the domain name and the password and verify the settings:

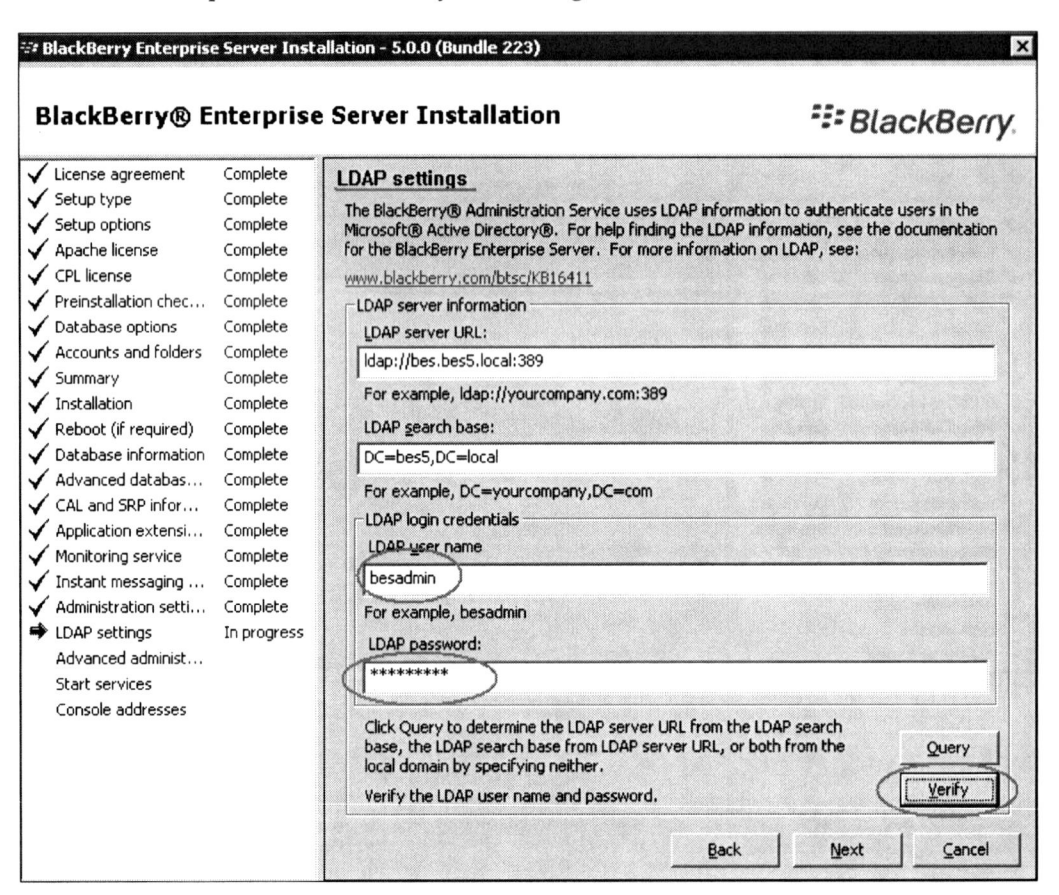

Chapter 1

29. In the **Advanced administration settings** we need to decide how we are going to log into the BlackBerry administration site. We have two options: **Windows authentication** or to use the **BlackBerry Administration Service authentication**—which has a default **User name** of **admin**. We are going to choose the option of using the BlackBerry Administration Service authentication.

30. Enter and confirm the password for the **BlackBerry Administration Service authentication**, as shown in the following screenshot:

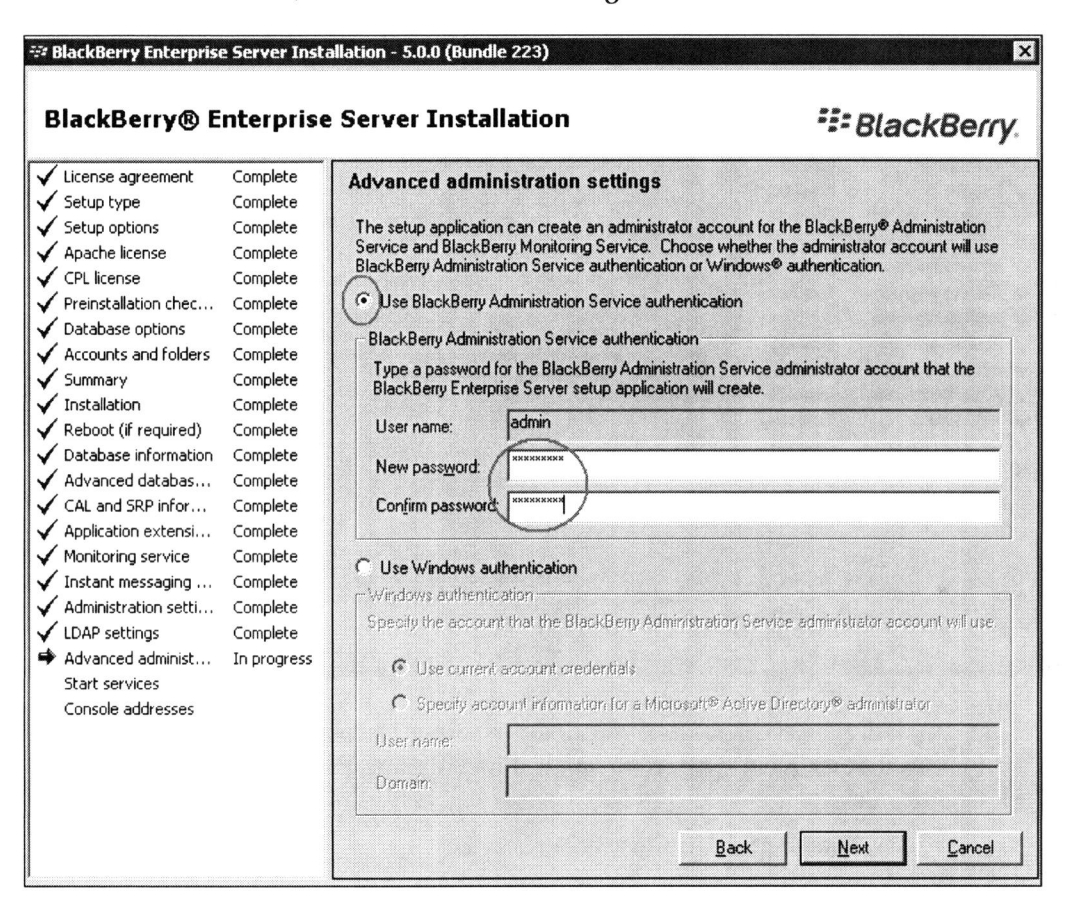

Introduction to BES 5

31. It will now prompt us to start the BlackBerry services, click on **Start services**. Once all the services have started successfully click on **Next**.

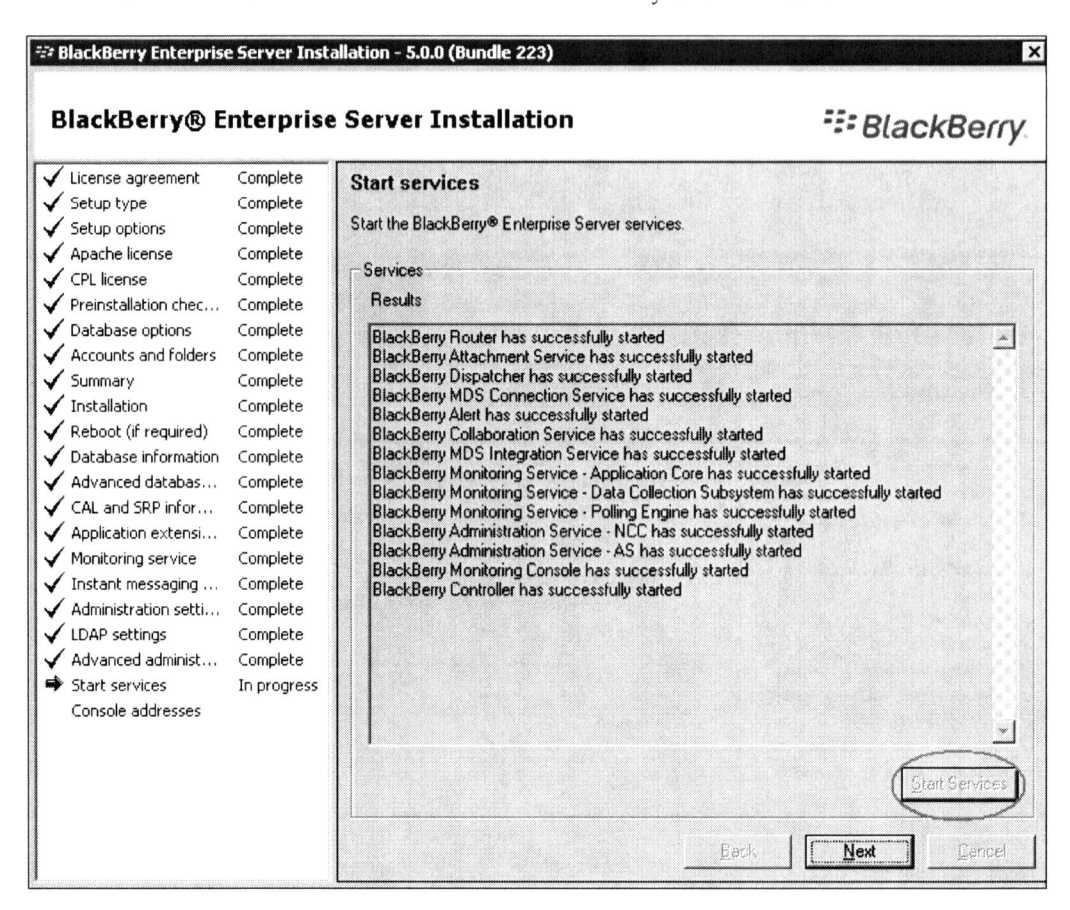

32. We will then be presented with a list of web addresses to access various sites that we have created during our installation. Please make a note of these sites:
    - BlackBerry Administration Service
    - BlackBerry Monitoring Service
    - BlackBerry MDS Integration Service
    - BlackBerry Web Desktop Manager

Chapter 1

[BlackBerry Enterprise Server Installation screen showing Console addresses with all steps Complete and "Console addresses" In progress. Addresses shown:
- BlackBerry Administration Service address: https://BES.BES5.LOCAL:443/webconsole/login
- BlackBerry Monitoring Service address: https://BES.BES5.LOCAL:8443/webconsole/app
- BlackBerry MDS Integration Service address: https://BES.BES5.LOCAL:443/mdsisconsole/app
- BlackBerry Web Desktop Manager address: https://BES.BES5.LOCAL:443/webdesktop/login]

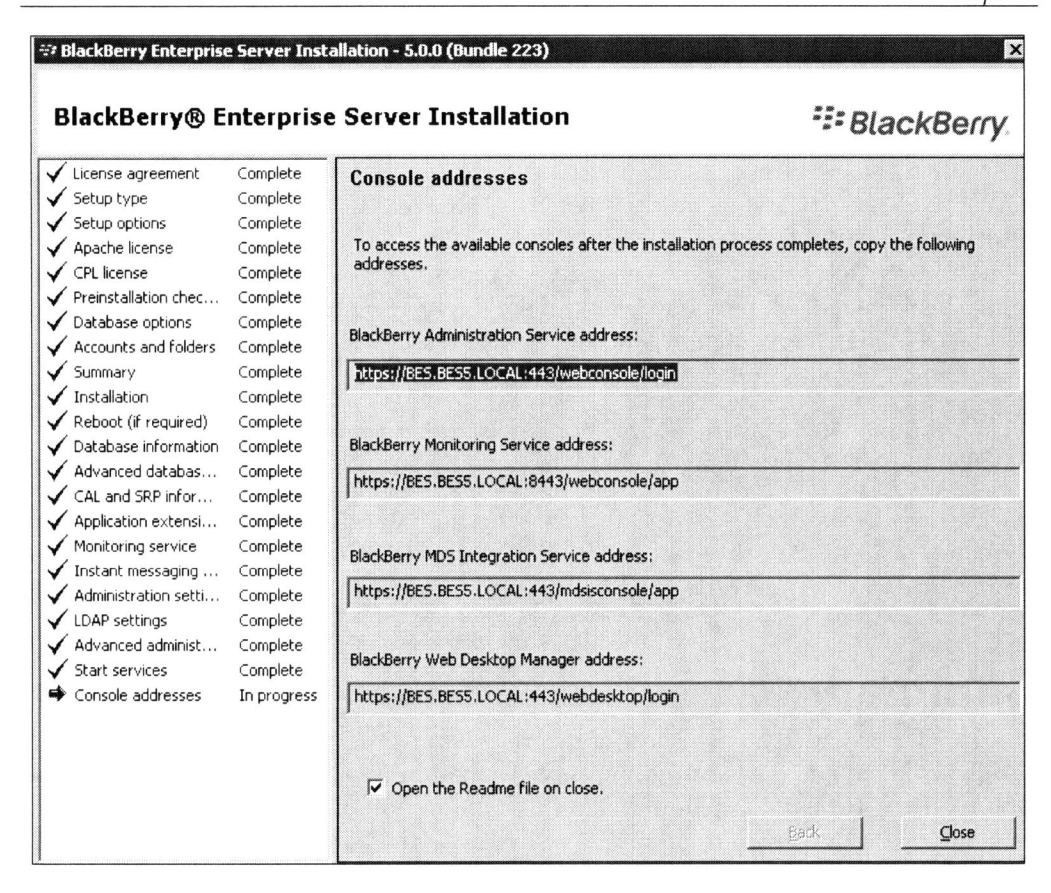

33. Click on **Close**. We have now successfully installed our BES 5!

Applying the Maintenance pack

It is vital that we now go to the BlackBerry website and download the latest Maintenance pack (same as a service pack) for the BES 5 installation. Without installing the latest service pack, you will not be able to carry out certain practicals in Lab 2. The Maintenance pack addresses among other issues the ability to be able to log into the BlackBerry Administration Service site with a Windows domain account. Without MR1 (Maintenance Release 1) if you try to log in with a Windows account, such as the Service account besadmin more than likely you will get an error message along the lines of "*the username, password, or domain is not correct. Please correct the entry*". This issue occurs because the **LDAP (Lightweight Directory Access Protocol)** password stored during the installation is hashed for additional security measures when placed in the BlackBerry Configuration Database, and the BlackBerry Administration Service site then has trouble reading the password.

Download the latest service pack and MR (Maintenance Releases) for the BES and install them before we proceed.

During the installation of the service pack, the software will check if the database—BESMgmt needs to be updated and also perform any updates required on the database. Please note, when you are installing Service Pack 1, it does seem like the fresh install we carried out earlier, except the settings we inputted would have been captured and should not be changed. If prompted, upgrade the BESMgmt configuration database and continue with the upgrade. The installation of the service pack does require a reboot. Once the system has rebooted, log back in with the besadmin account to continue the update.

When prompted join existing application pools already created, and if you have installed the MDS component, select to upgrade the database when prompted.

During the stage entitled Active Directory settings, enter the password of the Service account (this time, the password will be stored correctly in the right readable hash format). We can then start the services and we are ready for the next chapter!

Summary

This chapter provided an overview of the BlackBerry Enterprise Server version 5.0 environment and the features and services that are available within that environment. We also compared and discussed the components involved in the BES version 5.0 and the previous versions. We looked at the requirements needed to start a BlackBerry implementation, followed by a lab whereby we created our service account and installed our BlackBerry Enterprise Server.

In the next chapter, we will be looking at understanding and configuring our newly installed BES.

2
Understanding and Administrating BES 5

In this chapter, we will delve more deeply into the technical architecture of BES. In order to provide you with an understanding of what's under the hood, we will have a look at the information needed to get your users started on the BES. Specifically, we will cover administrative user roles, how messages are delivered, and other key elements of the BES. We will conclude the chapter with Lab 2, which will give a practical insight on how to use the BlackBerry Administration Service console and key elements we need to configure before activating users on our BES.

Delivering messages

Firstly, we are going to look at how the BES delivers messages and in return how a user can reply or forward a message using the end device—a BlackBerry handheld.

In the following scenario, our director Jim needs to send an e-mail to his PA, Susan. Jim is sitting on his computer in the office while Susan is out on the field armed with her corporate BlackBerry.

The following figure shows the components of the BES distributed on different servers for the ease of the diagram, but they can be installed all on one server as discussed in the previous chapter:

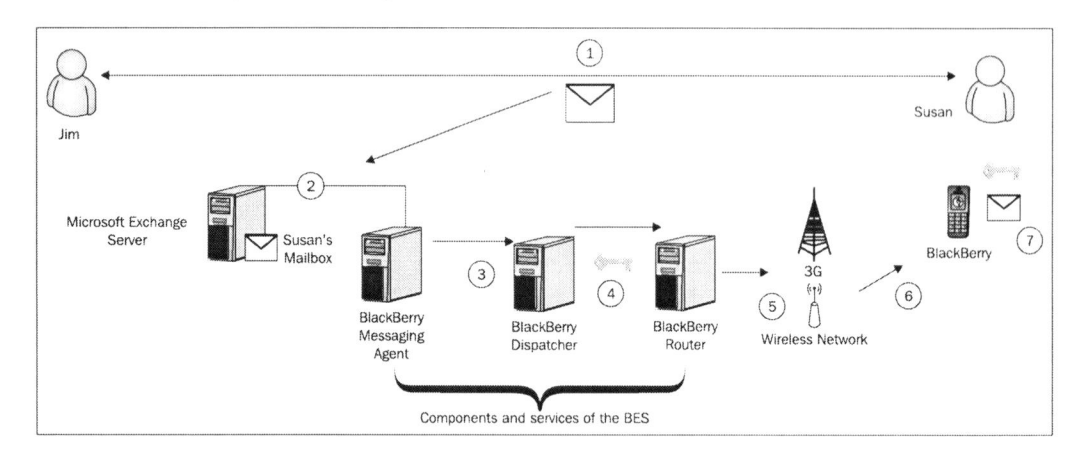

Sending a message to a BlackBerry device

1. Director Jim sends an e-mail to his PA, Susan. The e-mail arrives in Susan's mailbox on the **Microsoft Exchange Server**.

2. Microsoft Exchange notifies the **BlackBerry Messaging Agent** that a new message has arrived for Susan.

3. The **BlackBerry Messaging Agent** retrieves the message from the exchange mailbox then sends the first portion of the message (the first 2 KB) to the **BlackBerry Dispatcher**.

4. The **BlackBerry Dispatcher** compresses the first portion of the message, and encrypts the message with first a randomly generated session key (the session key is also referred to as a message key) and then the device transport key of Susan's BlackBerry device and passes the encrypted data to the **BlackBerry Router** to be delivered to the BlackBerry device.

5. The **BlackBerry Router** sends the first portion of the message to the RIM infrastructure over port 3101. The RIM infrastructure is also known as **RIM NOC (Research In Motion Network Operation Centre)**. The RIM NOC will validate the SRP ID of the incoming BES and will route the message accordingly.

Chapter 2

6. The wireless network locates the BlackBerry device and delivers the message. The BlackBerry device sends a delivery confirmation to the BlackBerry Dispatcher, which passes it on to the **BlackBerry Messaging Agent**. If the BES does not receive confirmation within four hours, it resubmits the message to the wireless network.

   [This is not a delivery report, it does not confirm that the user has received and opened the e-mail; it confirms that the wireless network has delivered the message.]

7. The BlackBerry device decrypts and decompresses the message so that Susan can view it, and the BlackBerry device notifies Susan of the arrival of the message. Only the first 2 KB of the message is delivered to the BlackBerry device initially. To view the full message, the user will need to click on the **get more** option at the end of the initial message, which will download the remaining message to the BlackBerry device, generating a new session key for each new data packet sent to the BlackBerry device to ensure that confidentiality of the data is intact.

Sending a message from a BlackBerry device

Now, we are going to have a look at the process involved in sending a message from a BlackBerry device.

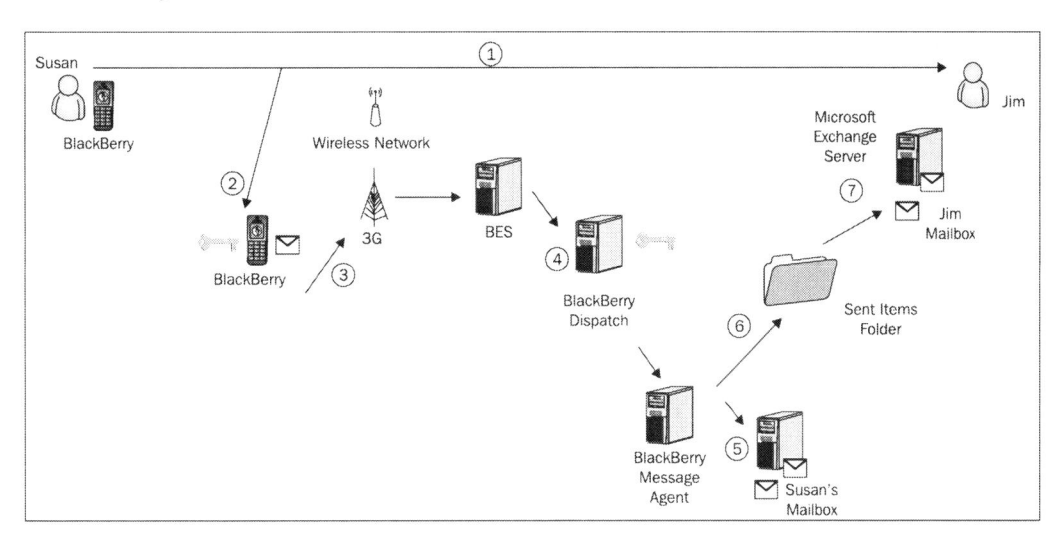

1. Susan reads the message from Jim and needs to reply to him immediately. Using her BlackBerry device, she types out her reply and sends it to Jim. The BlackBerry device assigns the message a REFID. It is important to note that the original message is not sent back across the wireless network to the BES when Susan replies (or forwards the message). Only the content that Susan has added in her message is sent across the network—the original message contents are retrieved from the Inbox and appended to the message before sending it off. This is shown by noticing that you cannot modify the forward or reply content before sending.
2. The BlackBerry device compresses and encrypts the entire message.
3. The BlackBerry device sends the message over port 3101 to the wireless network, which in turn delivers it to the BES. The BES will ONLY accept messages that have been encrypted by the BlackBerry device. If the message is not encrypted with the correct value keys, it will reject it.
4. The **BlackBerry Dispatcher** first uses the device transport encryption key from Susan's device to decrypt and decompress the message, and secondly the session (or message keys) to decrypt the e-mail and display it. If the message cannot be decrypted using these unique key values then the BES rejects the message and sends an error message back to the BlackBerry device.
5. The **BlackBerry Message Agent** sends the message (on behalf of the user) to Susan's Microsoft Outlook mailbox.
6. The **BlackBerry Messaging Agent** copies the message to the `Sent Items` folder (unless there is a prior IT policy in place, which prevents messages from being copied/saved to the `Sent Items` folder).
7. The **Microsoft Exchange Server** then routes the message to Jim's mailbox.

Setting security options

As with any critical network service, we need to focus on and set robust security measures. We are now going to explore the security mechanics that are built into the BES, including encryption of messages and device contents, as well as device authorization.

Understanding encryption

When talking about wireless data, the question on everyone's mind, from the Chief Executive Officer to the Network Administrator, is how secure is the data flying through the air and across the Internet. RIM has developed a solid answer to that question, with strong encryption protecting your data as it traverses through the BlackBerry world. It should also be noted that the data is still kept encrypted with even more layers of encryption when it traverses through the mobile operators data network, such as T-Mobile.

From the moment a user sends a message from his/her BlackBerry until it arrives on the BES, the data is encrypted using transport level encryption. Before the BlackBerry device sends a message, it compresses and encrypts the message using symmetric key algorithms in the form of either **Triple Data Encryption Standard (3DES)** or **Advanced Encryption Standard (AES)**. 3DES with its 112-bit key provides a strong minimum level of protection, whereas AES encryption uses 256-bit keys, providing a stronger level of protection and better prevention from brute force attacks, as well as enhanced performance.

Symmetric key algorithms by default provide:

- **Confidentiality**: The BES ensures that only intended recipients can view the content of e-mail messages.
- **Integrity**: Only the BES and the devices know the value of the keys that are used to encrypt messages. The BES or the device will automatically reject any message that is found to be using a different value of the keys.
- **Authenticity**: Before any data is sent, the BlackBerry device authenticates with the BES to prove that the BlackBerry device knows the transport layer keys in use and its value.

It should be noted here that the BES and the BlackBerry device discard the key pair after they generate the transport keys. So with this encryption architecture there is no way a third party—including RIM itself—will get access to the transport keys. So there is a unique device transport key generated for every BlackBerry device, which changes every 30 days by default.

These transport keys are stored in three areas of our BlackBerry infrastructure; they are never sent between the BES and device during the generation of the transport keys or when messages are exchanged between the two.

The transport keys are stored in:

- The BlackBerry configuration database
- A hidden folder in the root of the users mailbox on the Microsoft Exchange Server
- The flash memory of the BlackBerry device

> The key that is held on the flash memory of the BlackBerry device can be further protected by enabling content protection, which we will see further on in this chapter.

These transport keys are regenerated by default every 30 days. If you feel that these keys have been compromised then they can be manually regenerated, as shown in Lab 2.

The BES also generates a session key (sometimes referred to as a message key), which further protects the data that is sent and received by the BlackBerry device. Each message that is sent or received by the device is first encrypted using the session key and then the transport key.

While the transport key protects the integrity by verifying the sender of the message, the session key, which is randomly generated for each message sent and received, protects the confidentiality of the data by using a random session key to encrypt the data. These session keys are not stored and once the message has been decrypted they are deleted. A session key is randomly generated for each 2 KB of the message. So if a message exceeds 2 KB and consists of several data packets, the BES and the BlackBerry device generate a unique session key for each data packet.

Each session key consists of random data, which makes it difficult for a third party to intercept and decrypt or duplicate the message key.

By default, the BES generates encryption keys using AES. If AES is chosen as the encryption method, your organization must be using BlackBerry desktop software version 4.0 or higher and your BlackBerry devices must have operating software at version 4.0 or higher. The BES does support a mixed software environment, allowing 3DES for older devices and software and AES for more current installations and devices.

The encryption method, 3DES or AES, can be set to an instance-by-instance basis. So if you have several BES servers operating in your BlackBerry domain, each instance server can have different encryption levels assigned to it, as shown next.

Setting the BES encryption method

1. Log in to the BlackBerry Administration Service, on the **Servers and components** menu, expand **BlackBerry Solution topology**, **BlackBerry Domain** and then **Component view**.

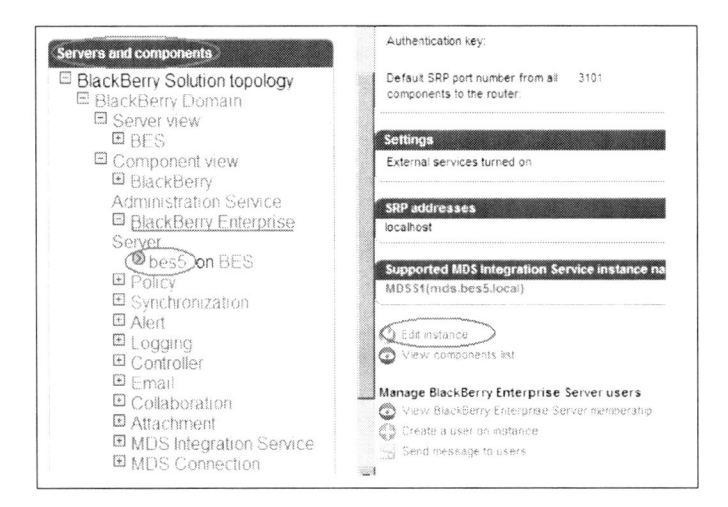

2. In the **BlackBerry Enterprise Server** section, click on the instance you want to change and on the right hand pane, select **Edit instance**.

3. In the **Security information** section, in the **Encryption algorithm** drop-down list, select the Encryption algorithm that you want the BlackBerry Enterprise Server to use.

Protecting content

Content protection is a mechanism that protects the data on BlackBerry devices when the device is locked. If a device has content protection enabled, it will encrypt specific data stored on the device using 256-bit AES encryption, and a public **Elliptical Curve Cryptography** (ECC) key to encrypt data that is received while the device is locked. Specifically, content protection is used to encrypt sensitive e-mails (subjects, title, and body of the message), calendar (meeting locations, subject), memo, tasks, and contact data as well as AutoText entries and BlackBerry browser data, including third-party data that is pushed or saved to the device and the browser cache. We can also use the content protection to encrypt the transport key, which is stored in the device's flash memory. Content protection can be turned on directly by the user on the device or via an IT policy—see *Chapter 4, IT Policies*.

Sending PIN-to-PIN messages

BlackBerry devices allow you to send messages between BlackBerry devices via the **PIN (Personal Identification Number)** function, which is similar to text messaging; every BlackBerry device is given a PIN at the time of manufacturing that identifies the device on the RIM wireless network. All BlackBerry devices have a common global peer-to-peer encryption key by default. This means that BlackBerry devices on your corporate network can send messages to any BlackBerry device. As there is a common peer-to-peer encryption key, the message can be decrypted by any BlackBerry device. If you wish to limit PIN messaging to devices within your organization, you can generate a corporate peer-to-peer encryption key that is only available to devices within your BlackBerry domain. If necessary, you can update this key if you think it has been compromised.

Regardless of the type of peer-to-peer key that is used, corporate or global users should be aware that the PIN messages are not encrypted but scrambled, which means that anyone with access to the peer-to-peer key would be able to read the message, unlike true encryption where a unique session key is generated for each message. Nevertheless, this is better than sending messages in clear text, but PIN messages should not be used for sensitive information, due to their relative insecurity compared to other BlackBerry communications. We will address in Lab 2 how to create a corporate peer-to-peer key. PIN messages sent and received from devices can be logged by altering the IT policy (discussed in *Chapter 4, IT Policies*) sent out to devices. It should be noted that when changing the setting in the IT policy for "Disable PIN Message Wireless Synchronization" all PIN messages will be logged in an unencrypted format.

In addition to the security mechanism described above, BlackBerry Enterprise Server supports the use of S/MIME and PGP technology to provide extra security for e-mail messages and PIN messages. When using the standard encryption methods provided by the BES, messages are encrypted between the BES and the BlackBerry device, but they are not encrypted when they are sent to the Microsoft Exchange Server and beyond. S/MIME and PGP provide a higher secure messaging technology by utilizing sender-to-recipient security in the form of digital signatures and encryption. Both methods require additional support packages and configurations.

The BlackBerry Enterprise Server has the ability to govern which devices are allowed to activate and join the BES environment. This ability is provided through the Enterprise Server Policy, which provides a "whitelist" (approval list) of device characteristics; if a BlackBerry device does not meet a characteristic, then it will not be allowed to join the BlackBerry Server. This policy can be used to heighten the security of the BES in terms of which devices can join the BES environment.

Administrators can specify four different types of characteristics, as described in the following table:

Whitelist	Description
Personal Identification Number (PIN)	This specifies individual PINs that are authorized to access services on the BES—ensuring that no rogue devices can join the BES.
PIN Range	This specifies one or more PIN ranges for devices that are authorized to access the BES—again helping to ensure that no rogue devices can join the BES.
Manufacturer	This specifies the device manufacturer, disallowing connections from the devices that are manufactured by companies that are not on the list—as you will see this only has the option of RIM; the option was related to the BlackBerry built-in program, which never took off.
Model	This access can be restricted to specific BlackBerry device models—ensuring that only devices that your organization has deployed can join the BES.

If a device being activated meets any of the specified criteria, it will be allowed to activate and access the BlackBerry Enterprise Server. Because this policy comes into effect only once it has been activated, it is advisable to set this from day one if you need control on devices that join your BlackBerry server. For example, if devices are already activated on the BES then they will remain activated even after the policy is applied.

The Enterprise Server Policy is flexible as it is possible to allow specific user accounts to override the policy as we shall see in *Chapter 4, IT Policies*.

Now that we have installed our BES, you will have to start dealing with the day-to-day tasks of managing those mobile users and their associated devices. Hopefully, all that work will not fall on the shoulders of one person, especially if you're planning a large BlackBerry rollout. RIM has developed BES with the assumption that enterprises have many different roles in their IT organization, ranging from helpdesk personnel to application server administrators. To support complex IT organizations the BES includes role-based administration, which provides greater flexibility. By default during the installation, six pre-defined administrative roles are created—each with a specific set of permissions and capabilities. The following table lists the default administrative roles that are created:

Administrative role	Description
Security role	This is the overarching administrative role, with the permissions to administer all aspects of the BES environment.
Enterprise role	The most privileged role after the security role, users in this role are delegated the ability to perform all administrative functions except security tasks such as creating, editing, and deleting a role.
Senior helpdesk role	This role can administer Users and Groups, but can only view IT policies and set activation passwords. It can also administer user's devices.
Junior helpdesk role	This role can only view Users and Groups, device settings, and set activation passwords.
Server only role	This role manages server tasks related to the BES environment.
Users only role	This role can perform and manage tasks relating to users and end user devices.
Monitoring system administrator	This role can configure and manage monitoring jobs.
Monitoring view administrator	This role can view monitoring information.

As you can see from the preceding table, each role consists of a set of permissions, which governs what the administrative account can do using the BlackBerry Administration or Monitoring site.

You can add multiple roles to a single administrative account—the account will inherit all the permissions that are turned on for all the roles the administrative account is assigned.

We can create our own roles with the appropriate permissions, or we can go in and manipulate the pre-configured default roles to meet our needs. By default, when we create a new role all the permissions are turned off.

We can also create additional administrative accounts to assign these roles to help distribute the administration of the BES to various users in your IT organization.

The BlackBerry Enterprise Server allows us to create groups; this helps us to simplify the administration of user accounts. When user groups can belong to more than one group, for example, a user called Jane belongs to the Sales group and also to the Managers group. If this happens to be the case then the user will inherit the least restrictive role.

We will explore the above in more detail during Lab 2.

At the end of Lab 1, we took a note of the websites created for various admin tasks concerning the BES. Next, we are going to look at logging into the BlackBerry Administration Service; this is the main tool to administer and control the BlackBerry Enterprise Server.

Logging into the BlackBerry Administration Service

For previous users of BES this is the new BlackBerry Manager.

1. Open a Microsoft Internet Explorer browser (must be Microsoft Internet Explorer as the site uses ActiveX controls that are only supported by Microsoft Internet Explorer).

2. Navigate to the site name, in the format of:

    `https://[FQDNserver_name]:443/webconsole/app`.

    For example, `https://bes5.beslocal:443/webconsole/app`, where the `[FQDN server_name]` is the computer that hosts the BlackBerry Administration Service—the BES service.

3. If you get a "page cannot be found error", please run through the following steps.

Understanding and Administrating BES 5

4. Check the binding order of your network cards—if your machine has more than one NIC, we need to make sure that the binding order is correct by going through the following steps:
   - Click on **Control Panel**
   - Double-click **Network Connections**
   - On the tool bar, select **Advanced**
   - Then click on **Advance Settings...**

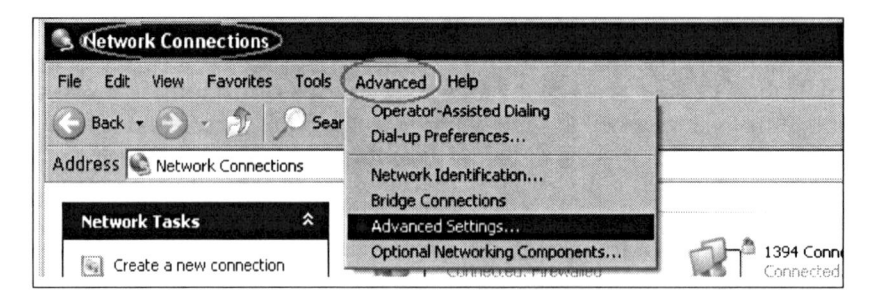

5. Ensure that the binding order is correct with your primary NIC showing first in the list.

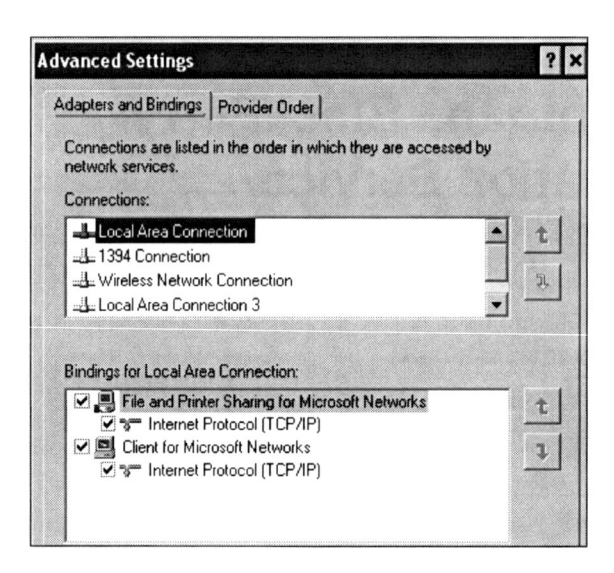

6. We need to make sure that our SQL Server is listening on the right ports and that correct protocols are enabled for the SQL Server.
7. Launch **SQL Server Configuration Manager**.
8. Expand **SQL Server Network Configuration**.

Chapter 2

9. Click on **Protocols For MSSQLSERVER** — or your SQL instance name.
10. On the right hand pane ensure **TCP/IP** is enabled, select its **Properties** and click on the **IP Addresses** tab.

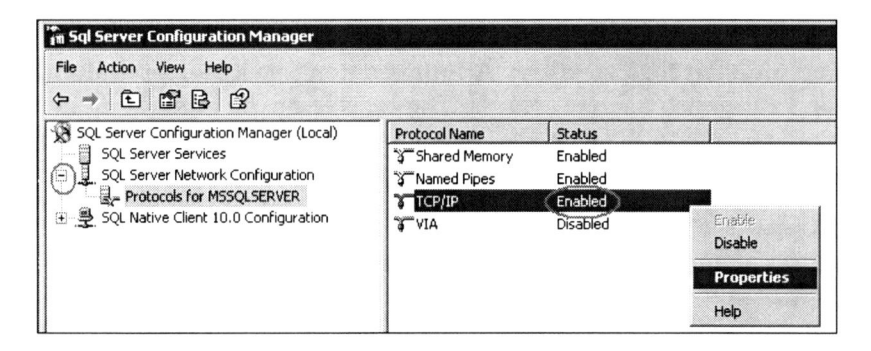

11. On this tab, ensure the port is set to use **1433** (or whichever port or method (dynamic or static) you specified during installation).

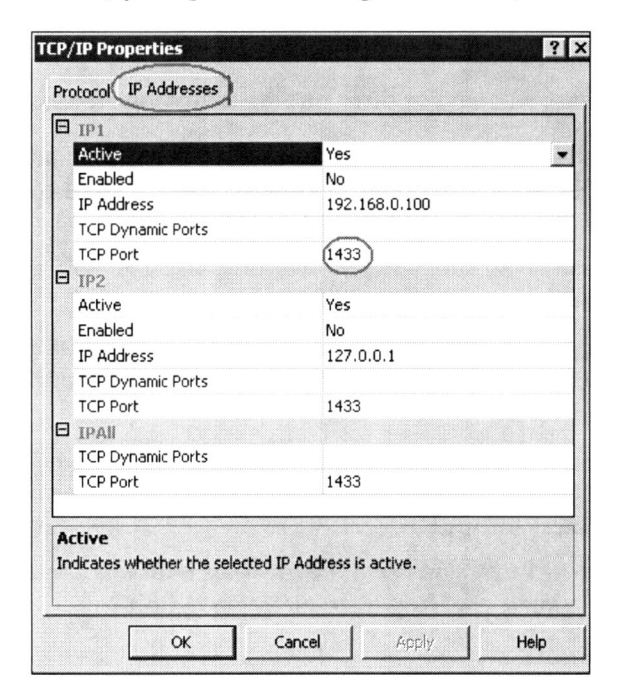

[59]

12. Check to make sure there are no stale records in DNS from redundant or wrongly bound Network cards to ensure the correct FQDN is resolved when we launch the site. This can be done by launching DNS console and deleting any DNS records that point the server name to the wrongly bounded IP address.

13. Finally, restart the BlackBerry Administration Service – Application Server using the `services.msc` console. The console can be brought up by typing `services.msc` in the **Run** box, selecting the service, and then clicking on **Restart**.

You should now be able to log into the site without getting the "page cannot be displayed error". Some servers may require a reboot rather than just a restart of the BlackBerry Administration Service. Also note that once you restart the BlackBerry Administration Service, there is a time delay for the DNS pool to kick in before the page is displayed.

Next, we are going to get an error associated with the SSL certificate that we created during the installation, as the SSL certificate is self-signed (if using IE 7 or the later versions).

To overcome this issue, we need to carry out the following steps:

1. Add the URL to the trusted websites in IE options, then add the self-signed SSL certificate to the trusted root of the local computer from which we are trying to access the site.

2. Navigate back to the site, where a warning message will appear. Select the option to **Continue to this website (not recommended)**.

3. In Internet Explorer, click on **Tools** menu followed by **Internet Options**. On the **Security** tab, click **Trusted sites**, click on **Sites** and add the console to the list of trusted sites.

4. In the browser window on the toolbar, you will see a symbol for Certificate error – click on that followed by **view certificates**. Click on **install certificate** and choose **local computer**.

5. We should now be able to open the browser with the console address without any issues, enabling us to move on to Lab 2.

Lab 2

In this lab, we are going to look at the following features:

- Overview of the BlackBerry dashboard.
- Settings for the BlackBerry Administration Service.
- Creating and setting administrative roles and groups.
- Activating the Enterprise policy — to provide the heighten security measures discussed earlier on in this chapter.
- Generating a peer-to-peer encryption key — we want to ensure that PIN-to-PIN messages can only work within our corporation and not outside. This will ensure devices can only use PIN-to-PIN messaging with other devices within our network and not outside.
- Resetting the transport keys.

Logging into the console

We have two options to log into the console. We can use Active Directory Authentication or we can use the BlackBerry Administration Service to log on. The first uses an AD account, while the second option uses the admin account that we created during the installation. As we chose to use the admin account during the installation, we will enter the details for the admin account to log in.

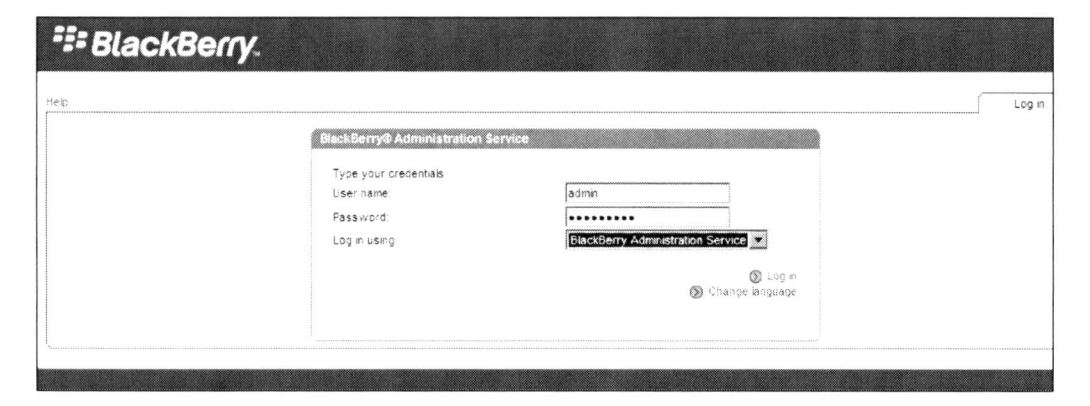

Understanding and Administrating BES 5

Once you have logged in, you will see the new BlackBerry dashboard management system, as shown in the following screenshot:

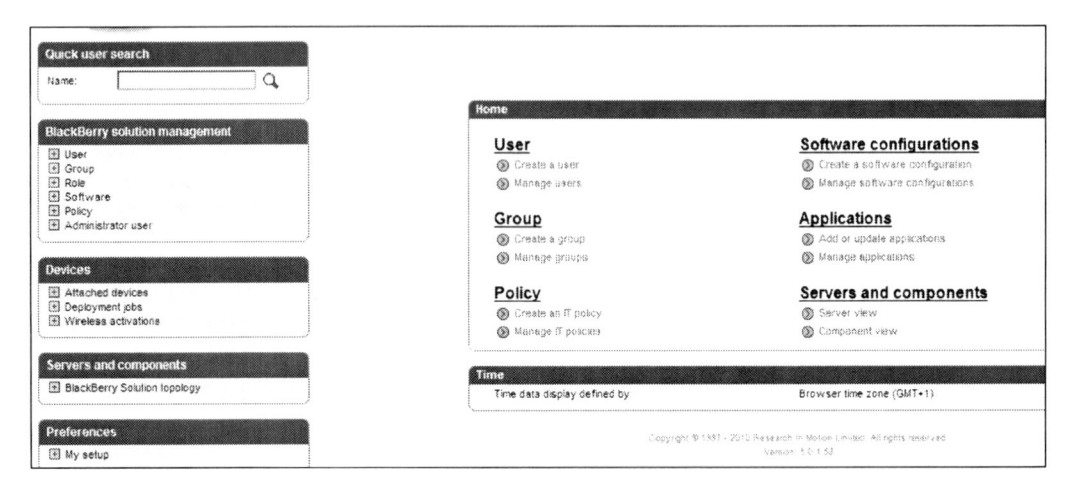

Settings for the BlackBerry Administration Service

1. Under **Servers and components**, expand **BlackBerry Solution topology**; expand **BlackBerry Domain** and then **Component view**.

2. Click on **BlackBerry Administration Service** and on the right hand pane we can see the settings for our main admin interface.

3. With the **Component information** tab, select scroll down and click on **edit component**.

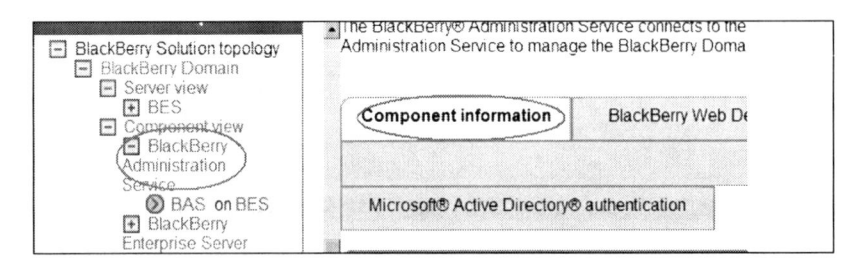

4. Under **Security settings**, we can change the minimum password length; for the BAS login accounts default is set to **4**.

5. We can also set the expiry time of the password by specifying the number of days; default is set to **365**. These can be changed to keep in line with your organization's security policies.

If required, we can add the company logo and change fonts using the other tabs.

Creating administrators and administrative roles

If we are going to create a role that suits our company needs we are looking to create two roles: a junior helpdesk role and a senior helpdesk role. You might recall from the table under the PIN-to-PIN messages section that the two roles mentioned are pre-configured roles within the BES environment, so why would we need to re-create these two roles?

The reason is that if we are going to use groups in our BlackBerry organization to make admin tasks and management easier, we need to be aware that when we use the two default roles, they by nature have the ability to add themselves to groups, which could have higher, more elevated permissions than you would expect.

For example, if we create a group called Senior Helpdesk, which has the default senior role assigned to it, then add the following administrative user accounts to it: Tim and Jo.

We then create a Junior Helpdesk group, which has the default junior role assigned to it and add our two junior administrative accounts to the group: Tom and Harry.

When Tom or Harry log on to the BlackBerry Administration Service they could add themselves to the Senior Helpdesk group, because by nature the Junior Helpdesk role has the ability to grant access to groups!

So I would prefer to create my own groups, roles, and administrative users from scratch as shown next.

Creating a role

We have the option of creating the role from fresh or we can copy an existing role and change the permissions we need for our organization. For our Junior Admin role, we are going to copy the Junior Helpdesk Administrator role and modify it, so members of it cannot elevate themselves to higher levels of permissions (when we use groups in our organization to carry out administrative tasks).

1. Under **BlackBerry solution management**, expand **Role** and click on **Manage roles**.
2. Click on the **Junior Helpdesk Administrator** role.

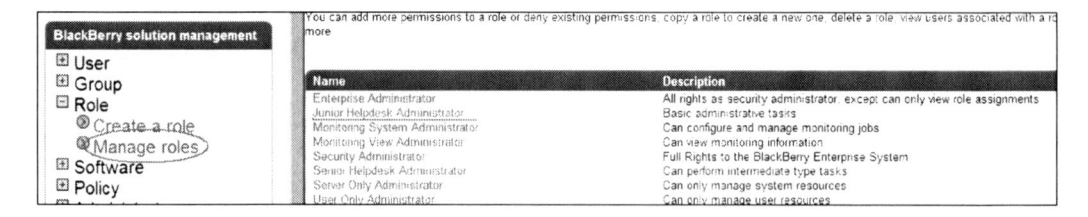

3. Select **Copy role**.

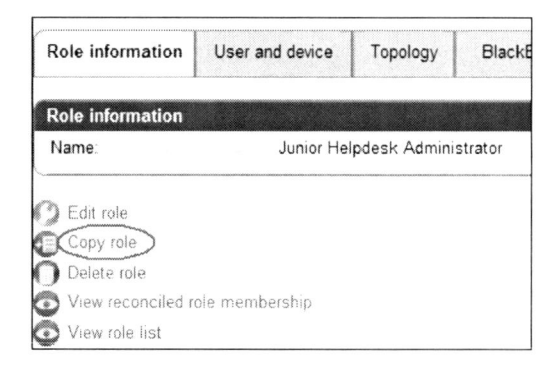

4. Enter the name **Junior Admin Role** and a description and select **Copy role**.

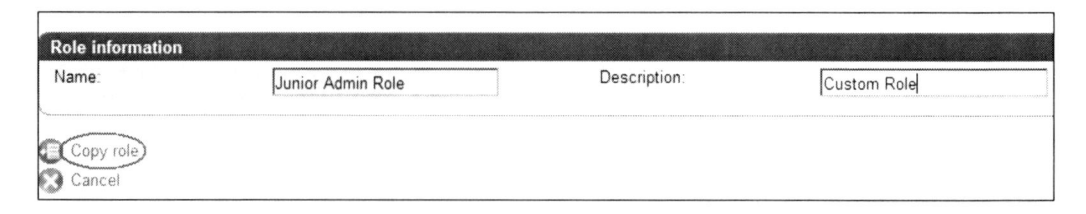

5. Click on **View role list** and select **Junior Admin Role**.

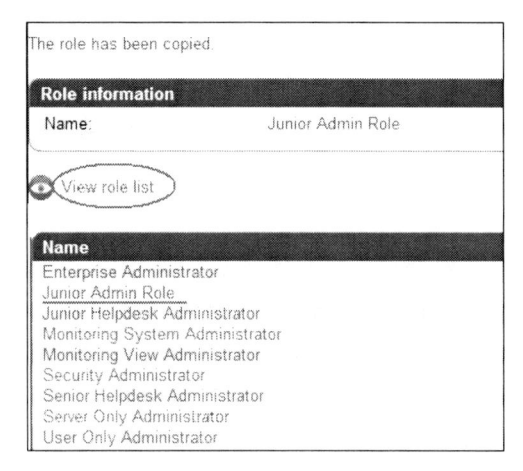

6. Click on **Edit role**.

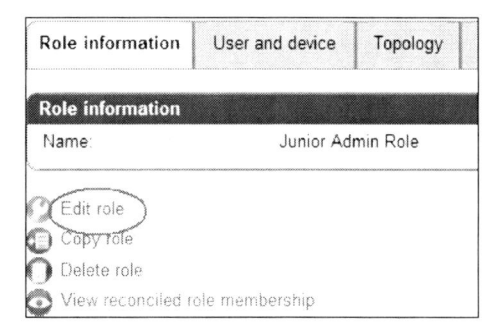

7. Click on **User and device** tab.
8. Change the drop-down for **Edit a group** to **No Access**.

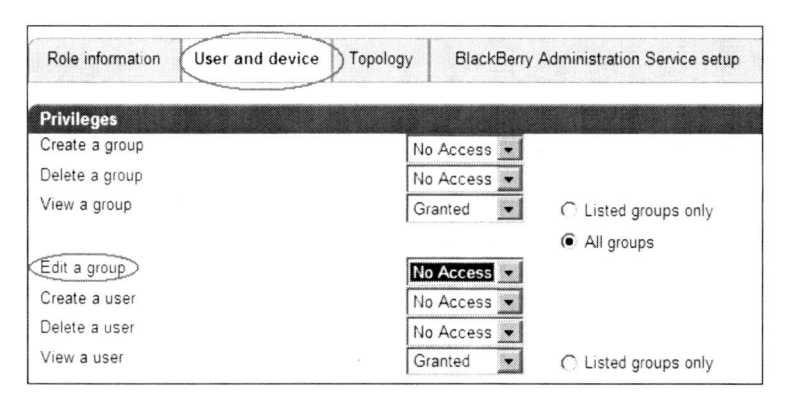

Understanding and Administrating BES 5

9. Check to see if the other permissions are within your organizational policy and then select **Save all**.

Next, we are going to create a group called Junior Admins and assign it the role we have just created. We envisage in our network that there will be several Junior Admins; therefore having a group will make our management easier.

Creating a group

1. Under **BlackBerry solution management**, expand **Group** and click on **Create a group**.
2. Enter the group name — Junior Admins and a description and click on **Save**.

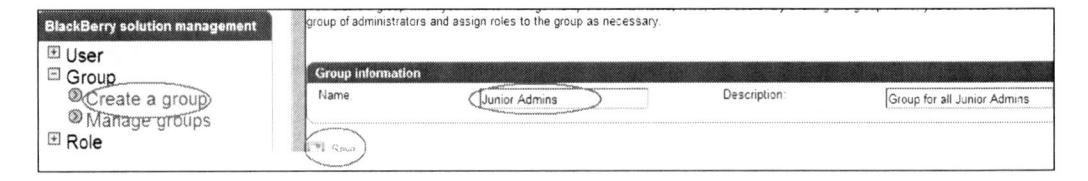

3. Click on **Manage groups**.
4. Select **Junior Admins** group.

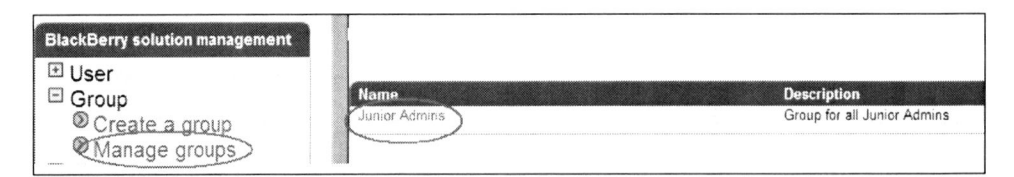

5. Click on the **Roles** tab, and then click on **Edit group**.

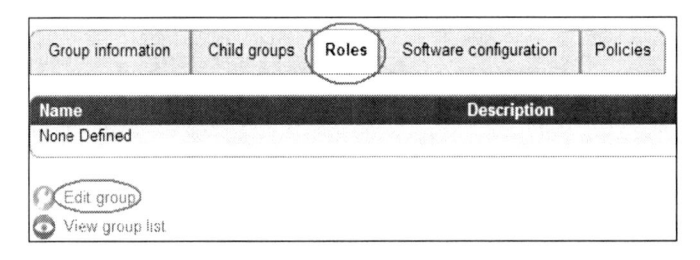

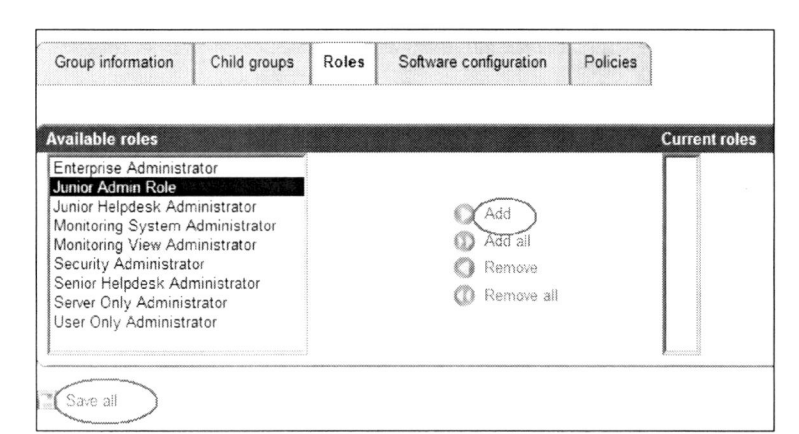

6. Then add the **Junior Admin Role** and select **Save all**.

> When you add a role to a group all the accounts in the group become administrative accounts even if the accounts are user accounts for BlackBerry devices. So it's important to understand at this stage that we are creating groups for pure administrative purposes.

Next, we are going to create our administrative users—who have just joined our company as junior admins.

Creating an administrative user

1. Under **BlackBerry solution management**, expand **Administrative user** and click on **Create an administrative user**.
2. In the **Display name**, enter a friendly name for the user—Howard.
3. Select the **Authentication type** for the user to log in—**Active Directory** or **BlackBerry Administration Service**.
4. Enter the appropriate details. If using BAS, the username is not linked to any accounts and therefore can be anything with a strong password (remember we set the minimum length for this password earlier in the lab). If using Active Directory, you will need to specify the Active Directory account username and the domain name.
5. Select the **Role**, which we just created for this user—**Junior Admin Role**.

Understanding and Administrating BES 5

6. Click on **Create an administrator user**.

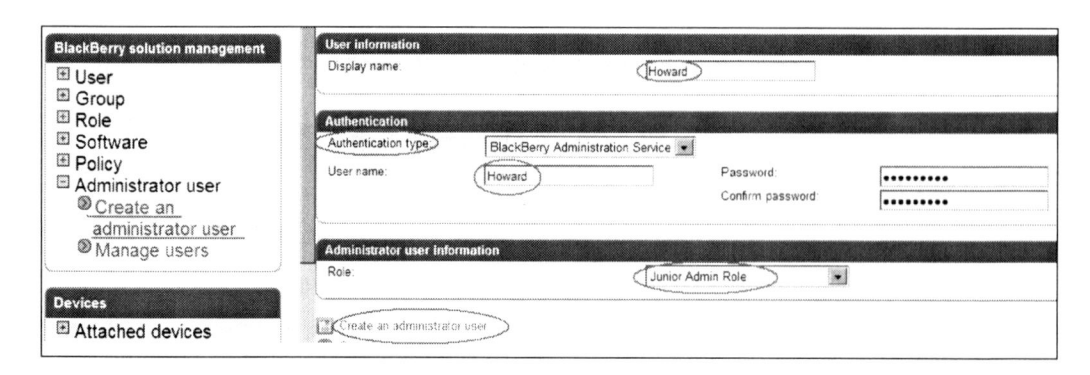

7. Finally, we are going to add our newly created user to the group Junior Admins.
8. Under **BlackBerry solution management** expand **Administrative user** and click on **Manage users**.
9. Click on **Howard** (or the user you have created).

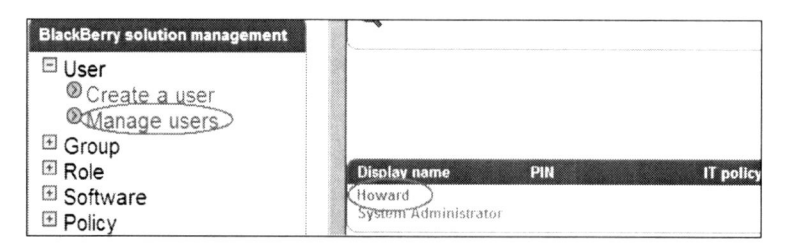

10. Then click **Edit user**.

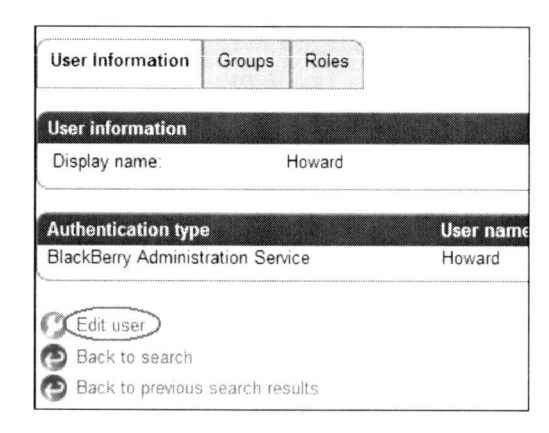

11. Select the **Groups** tab.
12. Add the **Junior Admins** group.
13. Select **Save all**.

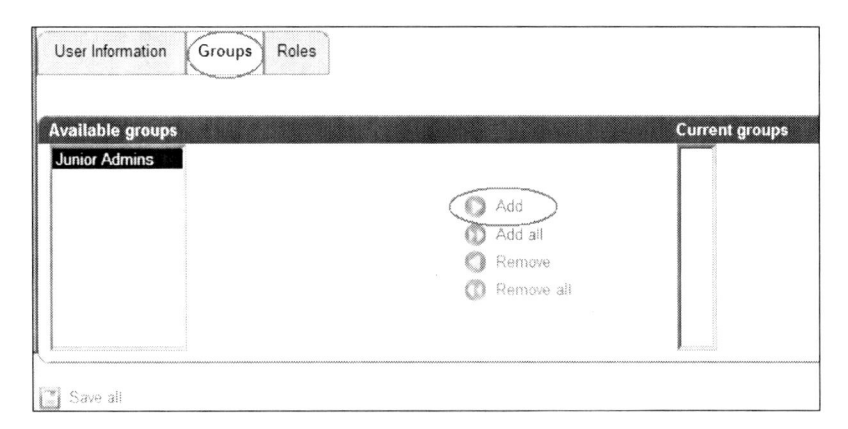

So to recap on the above, when you create an administrative user you need to assign the user a role to start with. It is always advisable to assign the user the role with the least permissions to start with. The user can then be placed in appropriate groups, bearing in mind that a user can belong to more than one group. If this happens then the user is given the least restrictive role.

There are two more aspects we would like to set from the off on our BES, one is the Enterprise policy as discussed earlier in the chapter and also the ability to limit BlackBerry Messaging to our corporate network. We will look at activating the Enterprise policy first, remembering that it is a whitelist of devices that are allowed to join our BlackBerry infrastructure.

Activating the Enterprise policy

1. Under **Servers and Components**, expand **BlackBerry Solution topology**, expand **BlackBerry Domain** and then **Component view**.
2. Click on **BlackBerry Enterprise Server**, and on the right hand pane select **Turn on Enterprise Service Policy**.

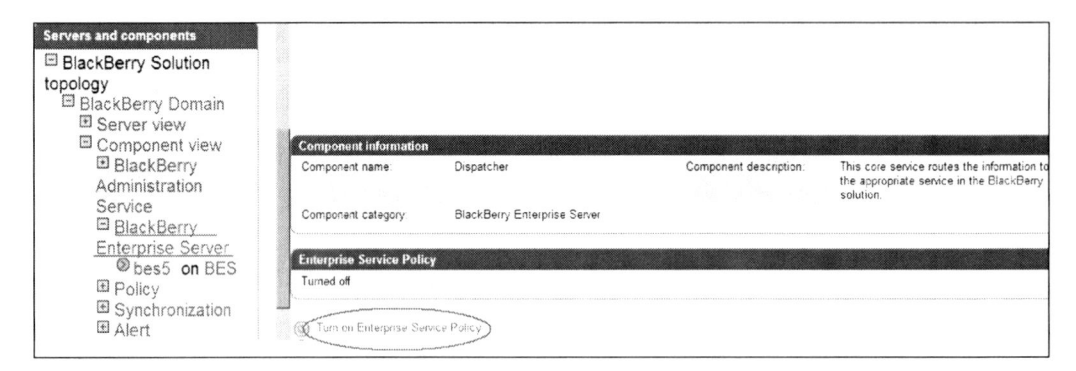

3. It will prompt you to make sure that you want to turn the service on—click on **Yes**.

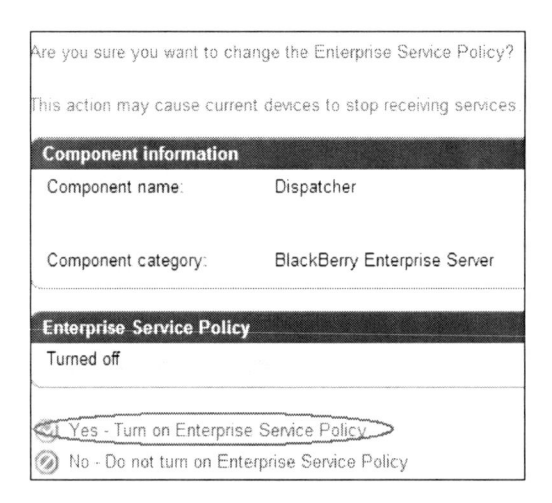

4. It will then display a page where we can set the rules for our whitelist-scroll down and click on **Edit Component**.

Chapter 2

5. We can enter a PIN range or we can manually add the new device's PIN when we receive new devices by clicking on the **Add new allowed PINs** tab.

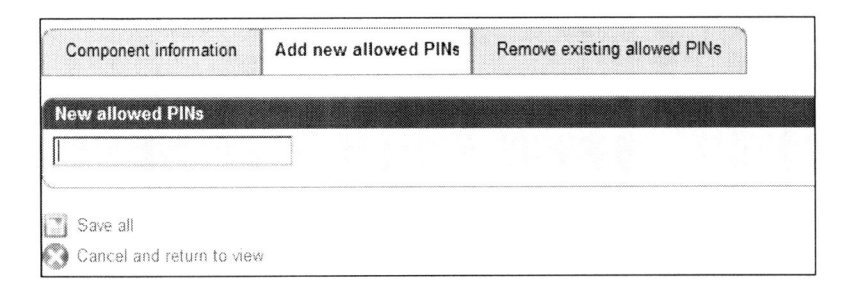

6. We can select which BlackBerry models are allowed to join our BES. Once we have made the changes, we can select on **Save all**.

> Now, each time a new device needs to be activated, we need to make sure that we manually enter the PIN in the tab and also allow for that model to join the BES if not already selected.

We can also override the Enterprise setting when activating a user as shown in *Chapter 4, IT Policies*.

[71]

Setting a corporate peer-to-peer key

1. Under **Servers and components**, expand **BlackBerry Solution topology**. Click on **BlackBerry Domain** and then on the right hand pane select the **Update peer-to-peer encryption key** under **Additional tasks**. As mentioned before, setting this option will ensure that PIN-to-PIN communication is restricted to devices/users within the same BlackBerry domain. Once we have enabled this option, users will only be able to send PIN messages to users that are in our organization — users that are a part of our BlackBerry domain. Users would not be able to send PIN messages to external devices/users outside of our BES domain.

2. Select **Create new key**.

3. Click on **Update peer-to-peer encryption key**.

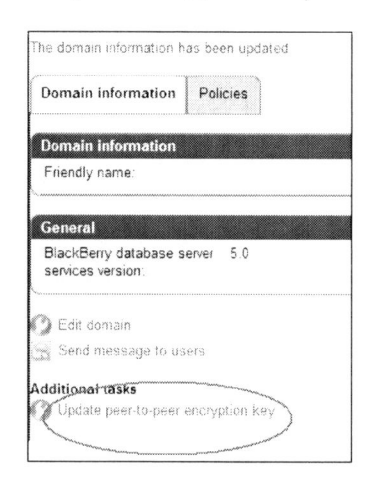

4. Then select **Set new key**.

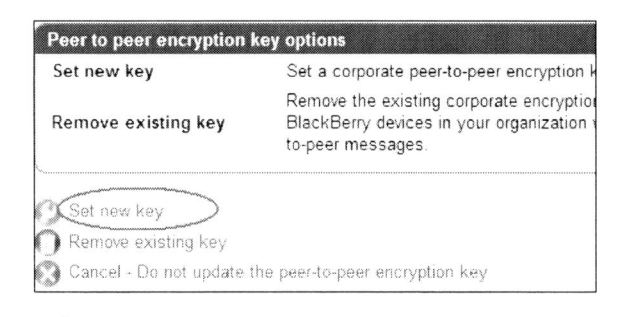

5. We have two options, select the first one—**Set new key and store existing key** if the corporate key has NOT been compromised.

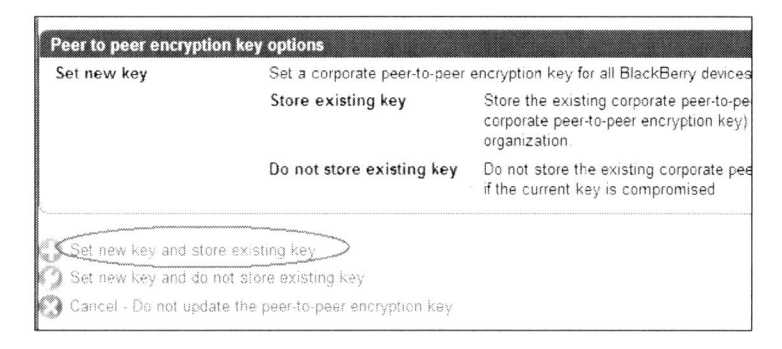

6. Select the second option if the key has been compromised.

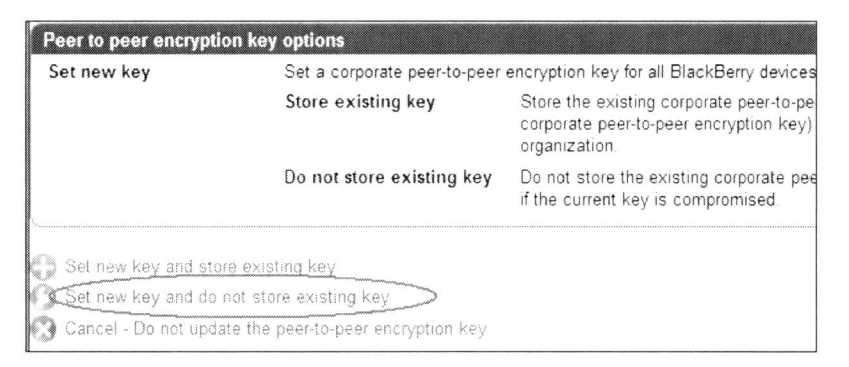

> After setting all the above, PIN-to-PIN messages will be limited to devices within the company BlackBerry infrastructure.

Regenerating the transport keys—main encryption keys

This can be done via Desktop Manager or on the device itself, to regenerate the keys on a device:

1. Go to **Options**, **Security options** and then **General Settings**.
2. Under **Services**, select the default BES service and select the option to regenerate the encryption key.
3. It can be done using Desktop Manager. When the device is connected, a message will pop up allowing you to move the cursor of the mouse randomly-this will generate the encryption key.
4. As we approach the end of Lab 2, now we should be more comfortable with the workings of the BlackBerry service and the main interface to administer the BlackBerry Server. As you can see, there are a lot more options and settings we need to go through!
5. It is advisable to create more administrative user accounts, roles, and groups to ensure you get familiar with the interface system.

Summary

In this chapter, we have examined the main management console to administer the BES. We have looked at role based administration for users and groups and their capabilities. We have also walked through the process of setting encryption and phase one of security measures to our BES environment. We have looked at the underlining principles that make the BES work, and reinforced the encryption techniques and methods that the BES uses.

In *Chapter 3, Activating Devices and Users*, we are going to look at creating users and activating devices, as we now have a broad understanding of how BlackBerry Enterprise Server works.

3
Activating Devices and Users

Now that we have a clear understanding of the BlackBerry Enterprise Server and have established some administrative roles and administrative users, we are ready to provide our Microsoft Exchange users access to the BlackBerry Enterprise Server. In this chapter, we will be looking at activating devices and the various methods that are available to do so. We will be looking at created users on our BES system, and then assigning them Smartphone devices.

BlackBerry Enterprise users must already exist on the Microsoft Exchange Server. The purpose of creating a BlackBerry Enterprise Server user is so that you can assign a device to the user and then manage that device via policies as we will see in *Chapter 4, IT Policies*. As with the administrative users, to make tasks and management of device users easier, we can create groups and add users to the groups, and then assign policies to the whole group rather than individual users. Again, users can be part of multiple groups and we will see how the policies are affected and applied when users are in more than one group.

We will look at creating a single user account so we become familiar with the settings, but in a practical environment we would need a quicker way to create the users, especially if we have over 500 users in our organization. In Lab 3, we will look at importing users to the BES.

Creating users on the BES 5.0

We will go through the following steps to create users on the BES 5.0:

1. Within the BlackBerry Administration Service, navigate to the **BlackBerry solution management** section.
2. Expand **User** and select **Create a user**.

Activating Devices and Users

3. We can now search for the user we want to add either by typing the user's display name or e-mail address. Enter the search criteria and select **Search**.

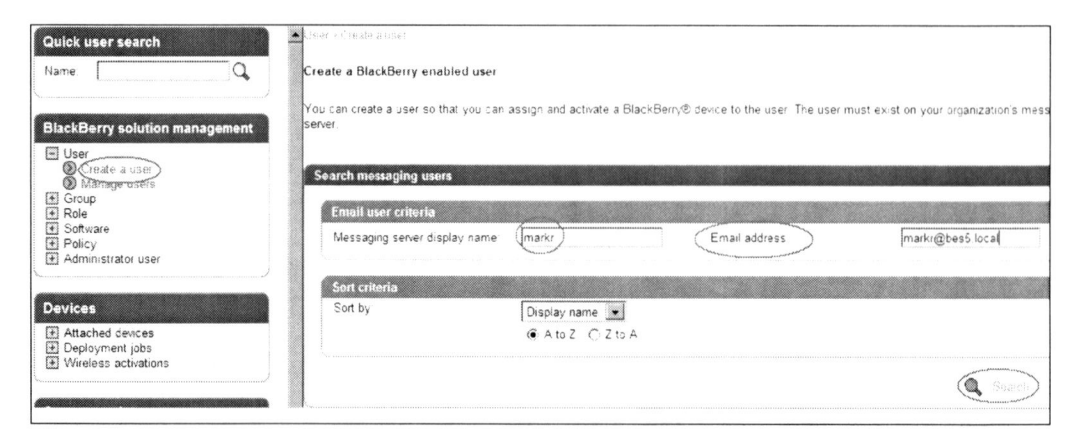

4. We then have the ability to add the user to any group we have already created; in our case we only have an administrative group. We have three options on how the user will be created, with regards to how the device for the user will be activated:

    ○ **With activation password**: This will allow us to set an activation password along with the expiry time of the activation password for the user

    ○ **With generated activation password**: The system will autogenerate a password for activation, based on the settings we have made in our BlackBerry Server (shown further on in this chapter)

    ○ **Without activation password**: This will create just a user who will have no pre-configured method for assigning a device

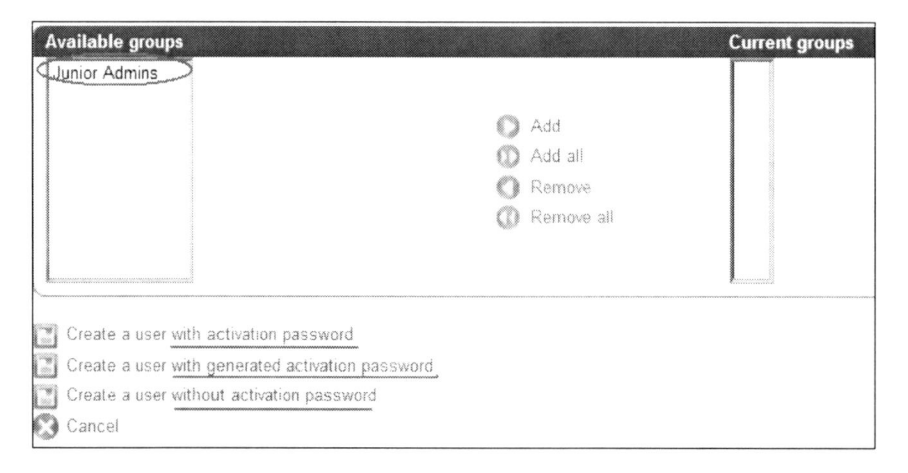

5. For this example, we will select **Create a user without activation password**. Once we have covered the theory and explored the settings within this chapter regarding activating devices, we will return to the other two options.

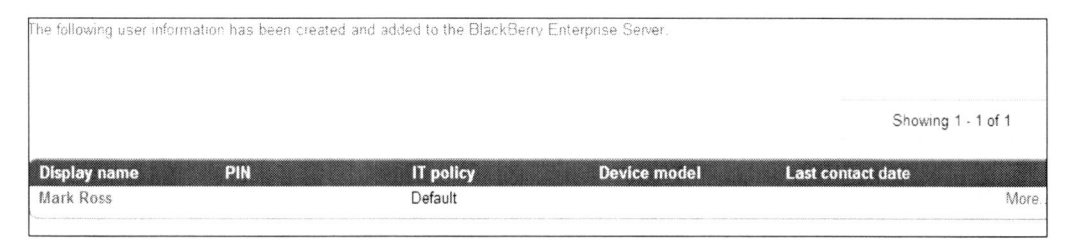

We can create a user even if the search results do not display the user — generally this occurs when the Exchange Server has not yet synched the user account to the BlackBerry Configuration Database, typically when new users are added. This method is shown in Lab 3.

Groups can be created to help manage users within our network and simplify tasks. Next we are going to look at creating a group that will house users — all belonging to our Sales Team.

Creating a user-based group

To create a user-based group, go through the following steps:

1. Expand **Group**, select **Create a group**, in the **Name** field enter `Sales Team`, and click on **Save**.

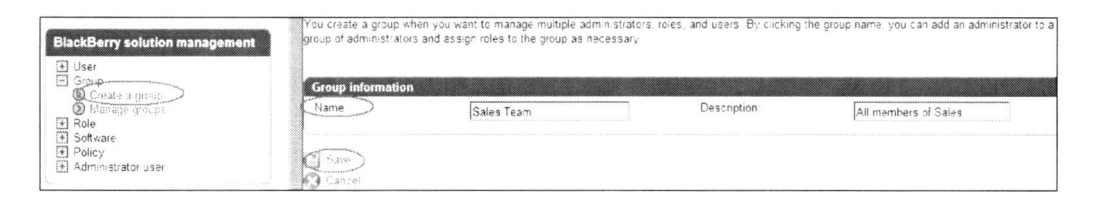

Activating Devices and Users

2. Select **View group list**.

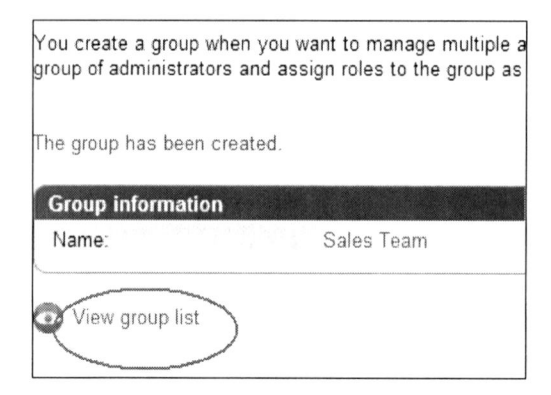

3. Click on **Sales Team**.

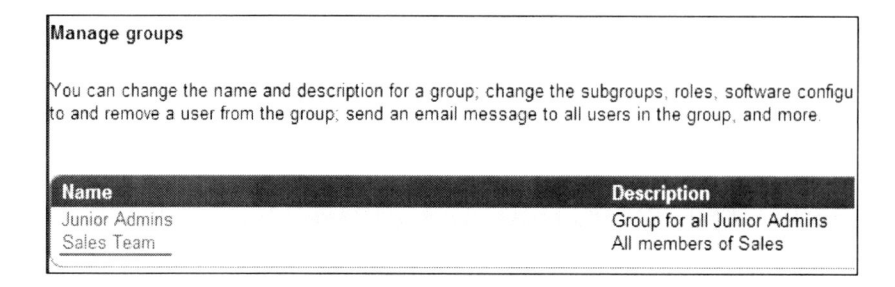

4. Select **Add users to group membership**.

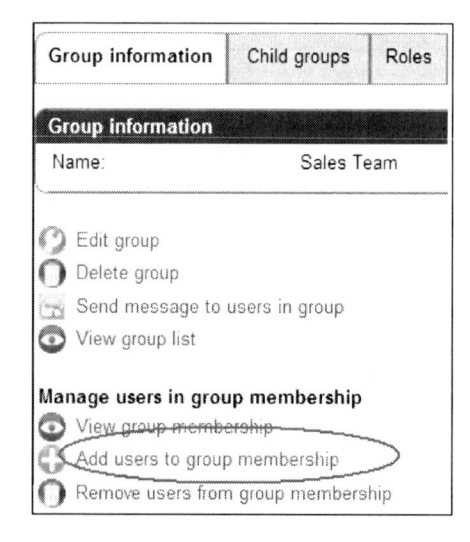

[78]

5. Select the user we have just created by placing a tick in the checkbox next to the user's name, and click on **Add to group membership**.

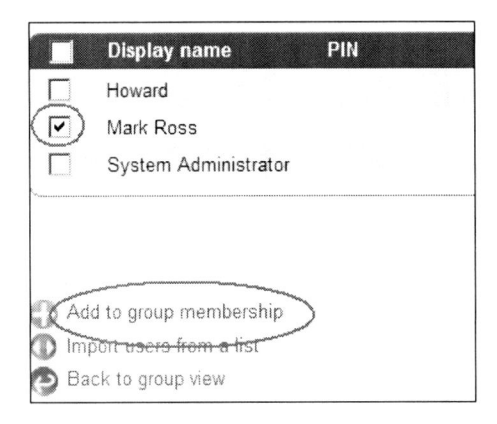

6. We can click on **View group membership** to confirm the addition of our user to the group.

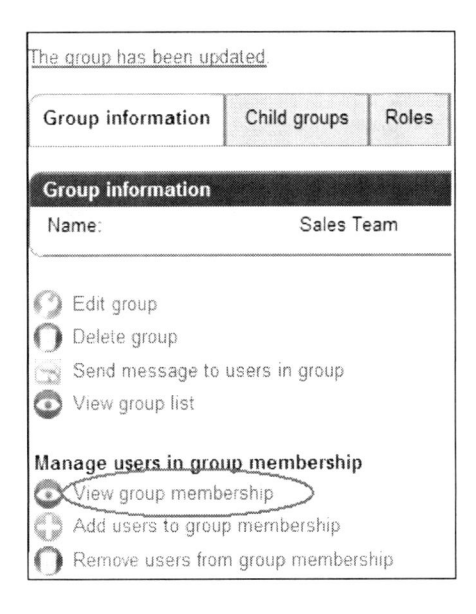

We will be adding more users to this group later on in Lab 3 when we import the users via a text file.

Preparing to distribute a BlackBerry device

Before we can distribute a BlackBerry device to a user using various methods, we need to address a few more settings that will affect how the device will initially be populated. By default when a device is activated for a user, the BlackBerry Enterprise Server will prepopulate/synchronize the BlackBerry device with the headers of 200 e-mail messages from the previous five days. We can alter these settings so that headers and the full body of the e-mail message can be synched to the device for up to a maximum of 750 messages over the past 14 days.

1. In the BlackBerry Administration Service, under **Servers and components** expand **BlackBerry Domain | Component view | Email** and select the BES instance. On the right-hand pane select the **Messaging** tab.

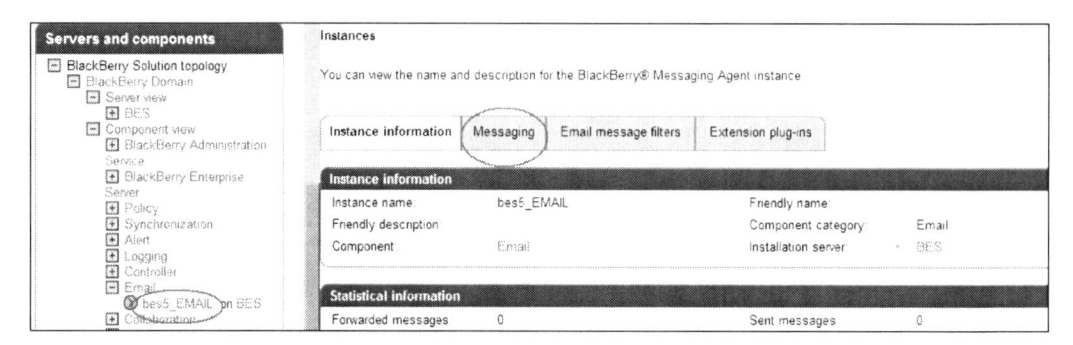

2. Scroll down and select **Edit instance**.

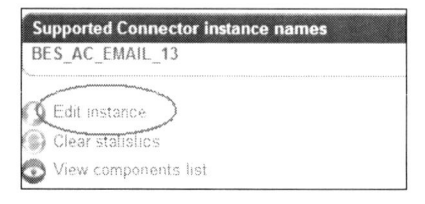

3. To ensure that both headers and the full e-mail message is populated to the BlackBerry Device, in the **Message prepopulation settings**, change the **Send headers only** drop-down to **False**.

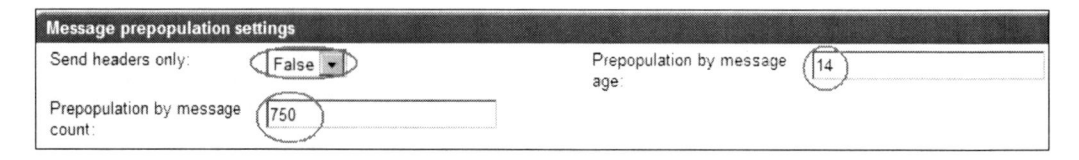

4. Change the **Prepopulation by message age** to a max of 14 days, by entering `14`.
5. We can change the number of e-mails that are prepopulated on the device by changing the number of **Prepopulation by message count**, again a max of `750`.

By making the preceding two values to zero, we can ensure that no previous e-mails are populated on the device.

Within the same tab, we can set our **Messaging** options, which we will examine next. We have the ability to set:

- A Prepended disclaimer (goes before the body of the message)
- An Appended disclaimer (goes after the user's signature)

We can enter the text of our disclaimer in the space provided, then choose what happens if there is a conflict. The majority of these settings can also be set at a user level (settings made on the server override any settings made by the user, that's why it is best practice to have these set on the server level), which we will see later in Lab 3. If user setting exists then we need to notify the server how to deal with a potential conflict. The default setting is to use the user's disclaimer first then the one set on the server.

Bear in mind, the default setting will show both the user's disclaimer and then the server disclaimer on the e-mail message.

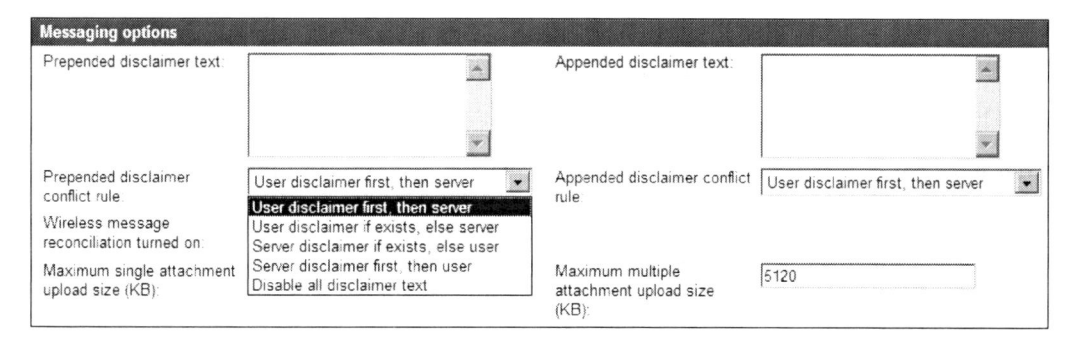

Activating Devices and Users

Wireless message reconciliation should be set to **True** — the BlackBerry Enterprise Server synchronizes e-mail message status changes between the BlackBerry device and Outlook on the user's computer. The BES reconciles e-mail messages that are moved from one folder to another, deleted messages, and also changes the status of read and unread messages. By default the BES performs a reconcile every 30 minutes; the reconcile is in effect checking that for a particular user the Outlook and the BlackBerry have the same information in their databases. If this is set to False then the above mentioned changes will only take effect when the device is plugged in to Desktop Manager or Web Desktop Access.

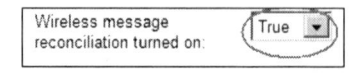

We have the option of setting the maximum size for a single attachment or multiple attachments in KB. We can also specify the maximum download size for a single attachment.

Rich content turned on set to **True** allows e-mail messages that contain HTML and rich content to be delivered to BlackBerry devices; having it set to False would mean all messages are delivered in plain text. This will save a lot of resources on the server(s) housing the BES components. We can set the same principle for downloading inline images.

Remote search turned on set to **True** — this will allow users to search the Microsoft Exchange server for e-mails from their BlackBerry devices.

In BES 5, we have a new feature that allows the user, when on his device-prior to sending out a meeting request — to check if a potential participant is available at that time or not. (Microsoft Exchange 2007 users need to make some changes to support this feature; see the BlackBerry website for further details on the hot fixes required.) **Free busy lookup turned on** is set to **True** if you want the above service. If system resources are being utilized heavily, this feature can be turned off by selecting False.

Hard deletes reconciliation allows users to delete e-mail messages permanently in Microsoft Outlook (by holding the *shift* + *del* keys). You can also configure the BES to remove permanently deleted messages from the user's BlackBerry device. You must have wireless reconciliation turned on for this to work.

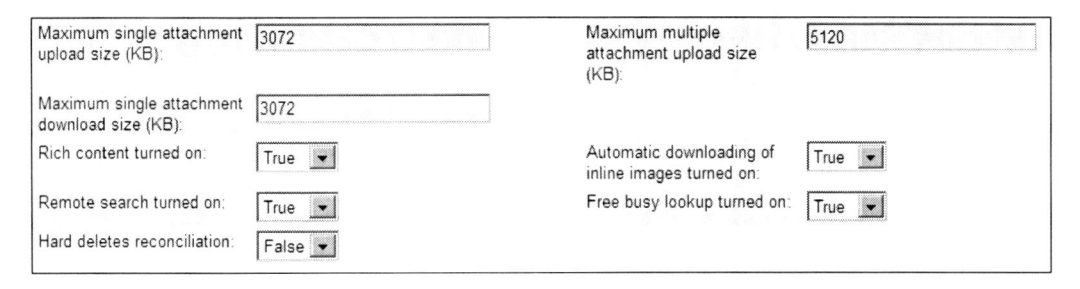

Maximum single attachment upload size (KB):	3072		Maximum multiple attachment upload size (KB):	5120
Maximum single attachment download size (KB):	3072			
Rich content turned on:	True		Automatic downloading of inline images turned on:	True
Remote search turned on:	True		Free busy lookup turned on:	True
Hard deletes reconciliation:	False			

The other settings will be visited later on in this book. Now that we have prepared our messaging environment, we are ready to activate our first user.

Activating users

When it comes to activating users, we have five options to choose from:

- **BlackBerry Administration Service**: We can connect the device to a computer and log on to the BAS to assign and activate a device for a user
- **Over the Wireless Network (OTA)**: We can activate a BlackBerry to join our BES without needing it to be physically connected to our organization
- **Over the LAN**: A user who has BlackBerry Desktop Manager running on his or her computer in the corporate LAN can activate the device by plugging the device into his or her machine and running the BlackBerry Desktop Manager
- **BlackBerry Web Desktop Manager**: This is a new feature of BES 5 that allows users to connect the device to a computer and log in to the BlackBerry Web Desktop Manager to activate the device, with no other software required
- **Over your corporate organization's Wi-Fi network**: You can activate Wi-Fi-enabled BlackBerry devices over your corporate Wi-Fi network

Before we look at each of the options available to us, let's examine what enterprise activation is and how it works along with its settings; this will also help us choose the best option for activating devices for users and avoid errors during the enterprise activation.

Understanding enterprise activation

To allow a user's device to join the BlackBerry Enterprise Server, we need to activate the device for the user when we create a user and assign the user an activation password. The user will enter his or her corporate e-mail address and the activation password into the device in the Enterprise Activation screen, which can be reached on the device by going to **Options | Advance Options | Enterprise Activation**. Once the user types in the information and selects Activate, the BlackBerry device will generate an `ETP.dat` message. It is important that if you have any virus scanning or e-mail sweeping systems running in your organization, we ensure that this type of filename with extension is added to the safe list. Please note that this `ETP.dat` message is only generated when we activate a device over the air. If we use other methods where the device is plugged in via a cable to activate it, NO `ETP.dat` file is generated. The `ETP.dat` message is then sent to the user's mailbox on the Exchange Server over the wireless network. To ensure that the activation occurs smoothly, make sure the device has good battery life and the wireless coverage on the device is less than 100db. This can be checked by pressing the following combination on the device *Alt* + NMLL. The BlackBerry Enterprise Server then confirms that the activation password is correct and generates a new permanent encryption key and sends it to the BlackBerry device. The BlackBerry Policy service then receives a request to send out an IT policy, which we will be covering at depth in *Chapter 4, IT Policies*, and allows service books to access the BlackBerry device.

Service books control the wireless synchronization data. Data is now transferred between the BlackBerry device and the user's mailbox using a slow synch process. The information that is sent to the BlackBerry device is stored in databases on the device, and each application database is shown with a percentage completed next to it during the slow synch. Once the activation is complete, a message will pop up on the device stating 'Activation complete'. The device is now fully in synch with the user's mailbox and is ready to send and receive data.

Now that we have got a general grasp of the device activation process, we are going to look at the five options mentioned previously, in more detail.

Activating a device using BlackBerry Administration Service

This method provides a higher level of control over the device, but is more labor-intensive on the administrator as it requires no user interaction.

Connect the device to a computer that can access the BlackBerry Administration Service, and log in to the service using an account that has permissions to assign devices.

Under the **Devices** section, expand **Attached devices**. Click on **Manage current device** and then select **Assign current device**. This will then prompt you to search for the user's account that we want to assign the device to. Once we have found the user, we can click on **User** and then select **Associate user** and finally click on **Assign current device**.

Activating devices over the wireless network—OTA

The wireless enterprise activation method allows a device to be associated with a user and provisioned to access the BES without connecting the device physically to your network. Using this method, the administrator provides the user with an activation password that they enter along with their e-mail address, into the Enterprise Activation program stored on the device, as described in the previous process. The password is created by the administrator and can be communicated to the user via an autogenerated e-mail or over the telephone.

The wireless activation password is created for each individual user account. It is a single use password, meaning that once the password has been used to activate a device, it is no longer valid. The password is only valid for 48 hours by default and is invalidated if the user unsuccessfully attempts to activate a device with the password five times. Let's have a look at some of the options available regarding this password.

In BlackBerry Administration Service, expand **Wireless activations**, click on **Device activation settings**, and on the right-hand pane select **Edit activation settings**.

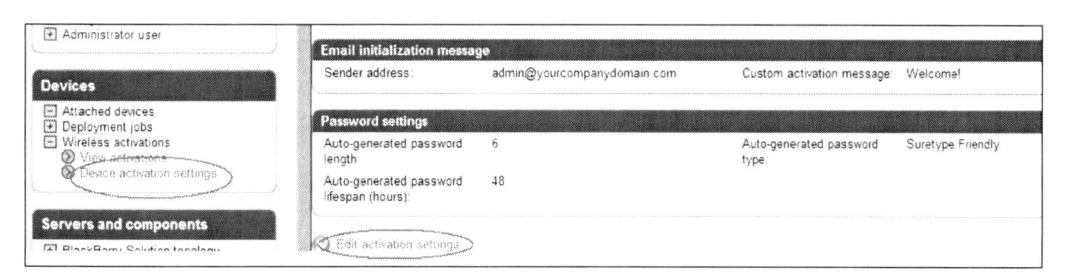

The e-mail initialization section enables us to customize the automessage that is sent to users if we choose to generate and e-mail an activation password to the user. We can change the sender details to match the organization's administrative account and add a message to inform the users of the steps that need to be taken to activate the device, possibly including the helpdesk number and e-mail address, in case users run into any difficulties. In the **Password settings** section, we can enter the length of the password that users have to type into the device, which is by default set to six. We can also depict the type of password—*SureType* passwords help users that have devices, which don't support a full qwerty keyboard, such as the Pearl, making the entering of the password easier. We can also make sure that the autogenerated password is always in lowercase, or we can choose the setting that makes sure that the passwords are all alphanumeric characters. The default lifespan of the activation password is set to 48 hours. Once the 48 hours have passed, the activation password becomes invalid.

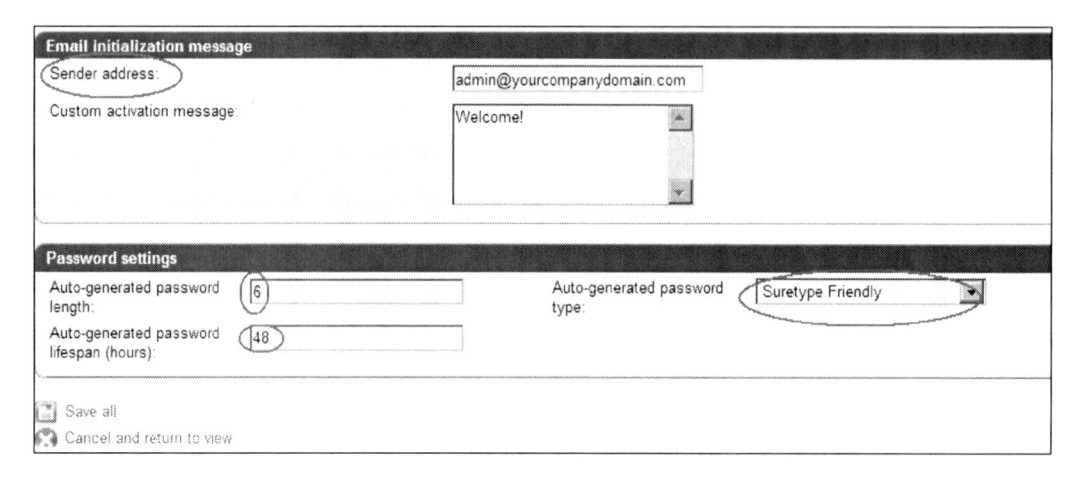

In Lab 3, we will look at generating activation password for users within the Sales group, and also setting activation password manually for a user.

Activating devices over the LAN

Users can activate their device by plugging it into a machine in the corporate LAN and running BlackBerry Desktop Manager. Once the device is connected and BlackBerry Desktop Manager is started, a wizard will pop up asking the user to select the type of account they want the Desktop Manager to function with. The activation process using this method is described further:

1. Connect the device to the PC in the LAN and launch BlackBerry Desktop Manager.
2. From the wizard select the work e-mail account. It will then prompt you to move the mouse cursor, as mentioned earlier-this will generate the transport encryption keys.
3. Once the keys are generated, the BlackBerry router will start the synch process by sending the user's e-mail messages and organizer data to the BlackBerry device; if the device is unplugged then the synch will still continue over the wireless network.

> If you deploy this method as an administrator to activate the devices, create outlook profiles for all your users on one PC, and then when you launch the BlackBerry Desktop Manager, select the user profile for that device — you will need to make sure that the service account has full mailbox rights to read the user's outlook data.

Activating devices using BlackBerry Web Desktop Manager

The principle is the same as the previous one except this option does not need any software installed on the user's PC, and can be used to activate multiple devices by the Administrator by just logging in as the user. This can be done by browsing to the web desktop manager site that was created during the installation, the login page looks the same as the BlackBerry administration site except the fields are coloured green. You can log in as a user and activate the BlackBerry device, without having to install any additional software. To use this site you must be running Internet Explorer as the site will need to install a RIM Active X component that only functions in Internet Explorer. Once you have logged into the site you can select **Activate Device** from the menu, and also select the **Troubleshooting** tab to resend service books which will also force the activation if you are experiencing any issues.

Activating the device over the corporate Wi-Fi

It is vital that when you are carrying out **over-the-air** (**OTA**) activations that the `ETP.dat` file can traverse through your network infrastructure without being dropped or scanned by firewalls, filtering rules, or anti-virus protection. Before starting a corporate-wide wireless activation, it is always good to test by sending a `test.dat` file to a mail account on the Exchange server to ensure nothing is blocking the delivery of the file. Remember that the `ETP.dat` file is the main building block in enterprise activation — it's this file that kick starts the activation process.

Another common issue with activating devices is that they are not provisioned correctly by the wireless carrier to join a BlackBerry Enterprise Server. Each carrier has its own tariffs and options regarding provisioning a device to use a BES. Once you receive the device, before commencing activation download the Enterprise Activation Readiness tool, to see if the device is correctly provisioned by the wireless carrier to join a BES network.

Activating Devices and Users

There is a difference between the device being registered on the wireless network and the provisioning of the device to use a BES. A device that is registered on the wireless network means it can send and receive data—we can check this by sending a PIN message, as shown in Lab 3. If the device is not registered, we can manually register it from the device by carrying out the following:

1. Go to **Options | Advance options | Hosting routing table**, click on the BlackBerry button and select **Register now**.

2. To see if the device is provisioned correctly for the BES, use the readiness tool mentioned, check with the wireless carrier. Also, you can see if the device has been sent the provisioning service book by clicking on **Options | Service books | Provisioning**.

3. Once you download the tool, select the BlackBerry Enterprise Server, enter the PIN and IMEI number of the device (both information can be found on the device by going to **Options | Status**). The tool will indicate if the device is ready to be activated. To activate a device on BlackBerry Enterprise Server 5.0 or higher, you need to make sure that the device is running BlackBerry device software version 4.0 or higher, some features are only available on device software 5.0. *Chapter 5, Software Configuration and Java Applications* describes the process of upgrading the software on devices.

4. It is also advisable to make sure that no instant forwarding is set on the user's mailbox that we are trying to activate—as when the device sends the `ETP.dat` file to the Exchange server and then on to the user's mailbox, if the message is forwarded instantly then the BlackBerry router and other BlackBerry components would not have enough time to process the message and the activation will just hang on the device. It will finally report an error message to contact the System Administrator.

5. As mentioned before, it's important that the service account has the correct permissions so it can tap into the user's mailbox to process the `ETP.dat` file.

6. In our case, we have to also remember that we have set an Enterprise Server Policy, which means that we must whitelist the device on the BES, using its PIN and making sure we have allowed that device model to join the BES.

7. During activation, if the device is hung on 'waiting for services', it usually indicates that the device already has an IT policy applied to it (see *Chapter 4, IT Policies* for an in-depth look into IT policies) or the BlackBerry Policy service is not started. For the latter, check servers on the BES server to see if the BlackBerry Policy service is started and is logged in using the service account we created—BESAdmin. For the first issue, it is best to wipe the device. This can be done by following the procedure:

- Go to **Options | Security options | General settings**, click the BlackBerry button on the device and select **Wipe Handheld**.
- It will then prompt you to enter the word 'blackberry' to confirm the wipe.
- Finally, to avoid slow synch issues when the device is synching the address book, make sure that the contact has at least one of the following three fields populated:
    - First Name
    - Last Name
    - Company Name

8. Content protection is disabled. It can be enabled once the activation is completed. A new feature in BES 5 allows the administrator to view the activations that are taking place. There are three stages of the act.

9. Now that we have activated our BlackBerry device, we need to take a look at what options we have regarding the e-mails, contacts, tasks, and calendars-collectively known as **PIM (Personal Information Management)** or Organizational data.

Messaging environment

We have the option of setting filters to depict what messages the BlackBerry Enterprise Server forwards to the BlackBerry device. After activation, our device will be prepopulated with e-mails based on the settings we defined earlier. What we are looking at next is what types of messages will filter through to the user's device after it has been activated with the initial settings.

When the message comes into the mail messaging environment, the BlackBerry Enterprise Server can apply one of the following filters to the message:

- Forward the message to the device
- Forward the message with priority
- Do not forward the message

Activating Devices and Users

As an administrator, when you create a message filter it overrides any message filter that is set by the users via BlackBerry Desktop Manager or Web Desktop Manager. We can create a global message filter that will be applied to all users on the BlackBerry Server. Users cannot see or change this filter and as mentioned it will override any filter that the user sets. Next, we are going to look at applying a global filter so that all direct messages from the Administrator account are not forwarded to the BlackBerry device.

1. Log on to BlackBerry Administration Service.
2. Under **Servers and components**, expand **BlackBerry Solution topology** followed by **BlackBerry Domain** and then **Component view**.
3. Select **Email** and click on **Edit instance**.

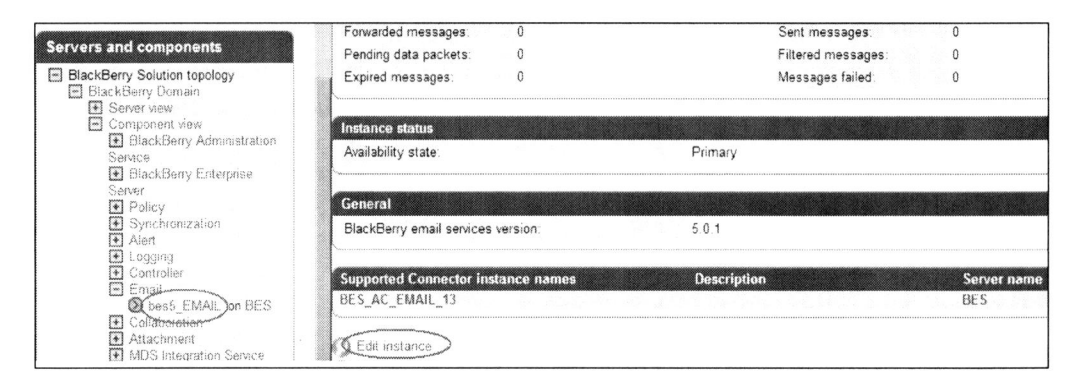

4. On the right-hand pane click on the **Email message filters**. Type a name for the message filter, and select the drop-down to **Enabled—Yes**.

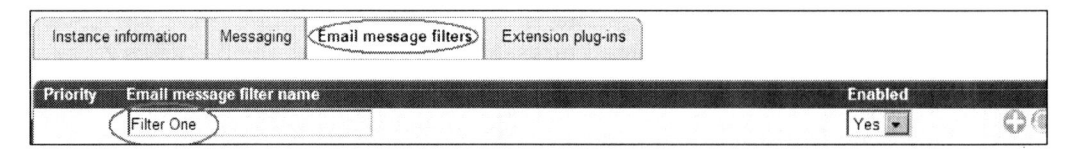

5. Select the **From** checkbox and add the administrator's e-mail address. The **Recipient type** can stay as the default as we want to ensure that all direct e-mail is not forwarded to the user's device.
6. We leave the **Importance** and **Sensitivity** boxes unchecked, so all messages are not forwarded, and place the radio button to **Do not forward email messages to the device**.

7. Select **Save all**.

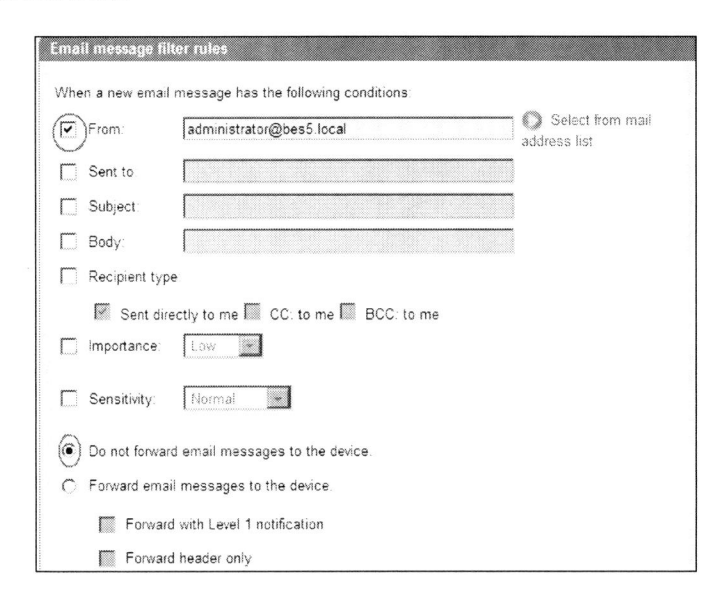

The message filters that we create are applied in the order that they appear in the **Email message filters** section. So we must ensure that the least restrictive message filter is at the top, with the most restrictive message filter appearing at the bottom of the list. Global message filters are applied immediately, as soon as they are enabled. If you don't require a message filter, then you can go back into the settings and from the drop-down select No. Also, please bear in mind that not all the features that you specify for the message filter have to match exactly for the filter to be applied. As long as there is one positive hit on the filter, the message filter will be applied by the BlackBerry Messaging Agent and the action of the message filter will be carried out.

In Lab 3, we will look at applying a message filter to a specific user, whereby the message is forwarded using Level one notification — Level one notification means that the e-mail will appear in bold, or depending on the device's OS, in a different font color. It also gives the option to assign it a different alert tone via the profile settings on the user's device.

> If no message filters are applied then the default setting on all user accounts is to forward e-mail messages to the device. Also remember that global filters — like the one we created — are applied before user filters.

Activating Devices and Users

Synchronizing organizational data

There are a number of settings within the BlackBerry Enterprise Server that relate to the synchronizing of organizer data. The following list details the settings that can be configured for organizer data.

- Enable or disable synchronization for specific organizer data, that is, message filters, address books, tasks, and so on. Synchronization is enabled by default for all organizer data.

> Please note that calendar settings are NOT part of the organizer data; calendar synchronization issues are controlled separately, and is turned on by default.

- Determine how organizer data will be synchronized, either from the device to the server, the server to the device, or both ways (bidirectional).
- Identify the data source to be used in case there is any conflict between the mail server or the user's device, and which data source should be used-either the mail server's database or the user device's database.

These settings can be set at the global level, which will affect all users on the BlackBerry Enterprise Server or they can be set at a specific user level. Again, global settings are applied before individual user settings.

1. Log on to BlackBerry Administration Service.
2. Under **BlackBerry solution management**, expand **User**, and then select **Manage users**.
3. Select a user account.

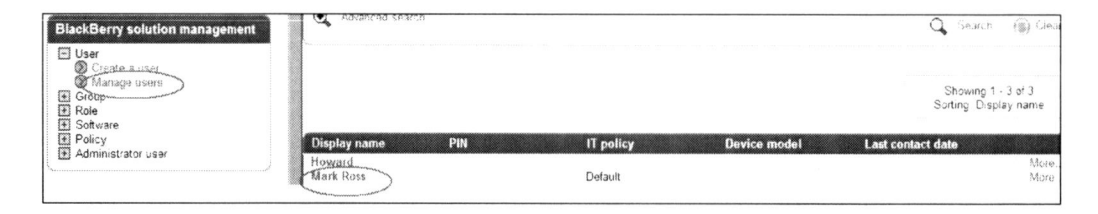

4. Click on **Edit user**.

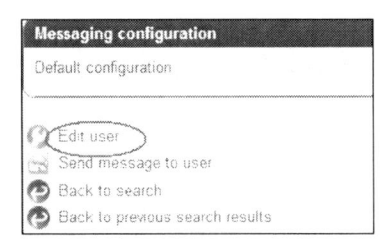

5. Under the **Messaging configuration** section, click on **Default configuration**.

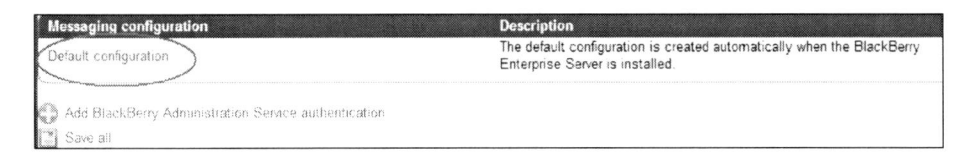

6. Under **General**, select the **Organizer data synchronization** tab. We can for this user:
    - Turn wireless synchronization on or off
    - Allow automatic device management
    - Allow automatic wireless backup — by default this is turned on and will back up the account settings and data from the BlackBerry devices to the BlackBerry Enterprise Server

The remaining settings are similar to those discussed but would be activated for the user we have selected.

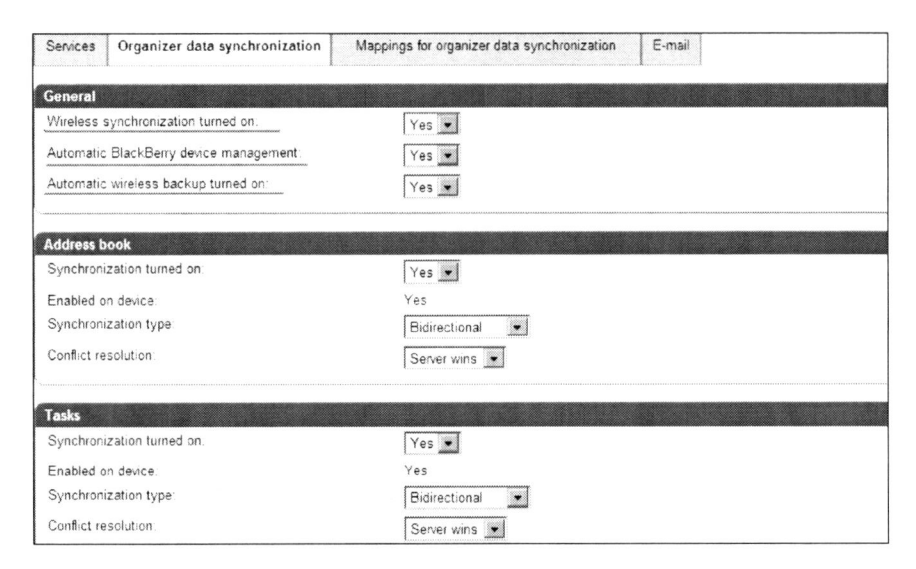

Activating Devices and Users

Up to now, we have looked at activating a BlackBerry device for a user, and we have seen the settings available to us once the activation is completed, regarding organizer data. Before we move on to the lab, we should spend some time looking at the device itself, and what the activation has done to the device and common troubleshooting processes that can be carried out on the device, if synching of data is not happening.

Using one of the activation methods previously explained, a user should have a BlackBerry device that is fully synched with his or her mailbox. Depending on the rules and filters that we have set, messages should have been prepopulated on the device and new messages should be coming into the device, as they are sent.

New features with BES version 5 and device software version 5 or higher also allow us to use Flags for follow-up support. You will get the same flag structure replicated to messages on the BlackBerry device. Also we can synch all of the user's folders, not just the inbox. This can be set by going through the following steps:

1. Log on to BlackBerry Administration Service.
2. Under **BlackBerry solution management** expand **User**, and then select **Manage users**.
3. Select a user account; click on **Edit user**, and under the **Messaging configuration** section click on **Default configuration** (as shown in a previous screenshot).
4. Select the **E-mail** tab, and under the **Settings message redirection**, place a checkbox in the folders that you would like to replicate to the device, along with the user's inbox.
5. Select **Save all**.

The address book should be fully populated—this time the BlackBerry Enterprise Server allows us to synch more than the default address book from the user's mailbox. If the user has more than one address book in his or her mailbox then following is the procedure to ensure that multiple address books are synched. BlackBerry Enterprise Server also allows the synching of public folders, which was not available in the previous versions; this setting can also be enabled at the following same interface:

1. Log on to BlackBerry Administration Service.
2. Under **BlackBerry solution management**, expand **User** and then select **Manage users**.
3. Select a user account; click on **Edit user**, and under the **Messaging configuration** section click on **Default configuration**.
4. Select the **E-mail** tab (as shown in a previous screenshot).

5. Under the setting **Private contact folders**, all contact folders set up for the user will appear and we can select the ones we want by placing a tick in the checkbox. We then can assign which contact folder will be default, by selecting the correct one via the drop-down menu.

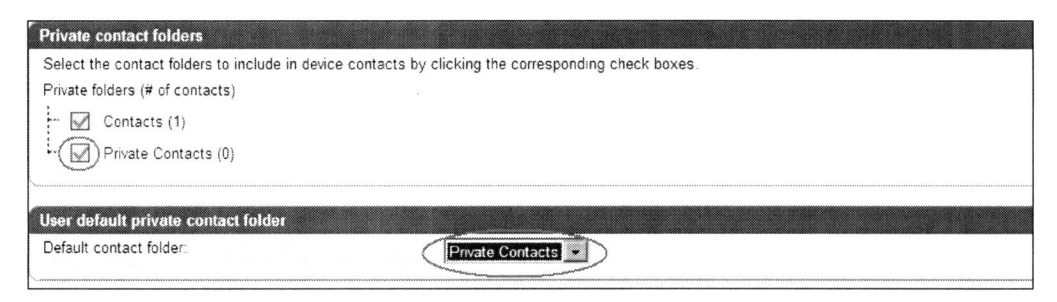

6. Under the **Published public contact folders**, we can select any public contact folders we have-these will then be synched to the device.
7. Select **Save all** once it is completed.

If there are any issues of synching the address book, the following commands can be run from the BlackBerry device that will help to rebuild and resynch the address book:

1. On the device, navigate to the address book.
2. Hold down *ALT* + VALD, this will validate the address book and look for any inconsistencies between the device database and the one stored on the BlackBerry Enterprise Configuration database.
3. *ALT* + RBLD will force a rebuild of the data structure on the device's database.
4. Finally, if we are still facing issues, we can erase and rebuild the address book. The following command will cause the device to delete the current address book and prompt the BES server to resynch the address book. Navigate to **Options**, and type RSET (no need to hold down the *ALT* key, but you must be in the options menu to issue the command.)

On the device, we should also see a fully synched calendar. You have probably noticed that when we were looking at and configuring PIM/organizer data, there were no settings for calendars. Calendar synchronize is turned on by default for all users when their device is activated; we can see this by using the BlackBerry TraitTool.

1. Log on to a server that hosts the BlackBerry Enterprise Instance.
2. Extract the contents of the installation files to a folder on the server.

Activating Devices and Users

3. Open up the command prompt on the server, navigate to the `Tools` folder within the extracted files and locate the `TraitTool.exe`.
4. In the command prompt type:

   `Traittool -global list`

5. If we are having global issues with calendar synch, we can turn off the synch process and start the synch process again by using the following commands:

   `traittool -global -trait smartsyncenable -set false`
   `traittool -global -trait smartsyncenable -set false`

If the issue is isolated to a particular device, we can force a resynchronization of the calendar from the device by following the procedure:

1. On the device, go to Calendar.
2. Click the BlackBerry button and select **Options**.
3. Click on the Calendar and select **Wireless Synchronization** to **No**.
4. Open up Web Desktop Manager or BlackBerry Desktop Manager.
5. Select **Backup and Restore**, select **Advance** button on the right-hand pane, find the database for the calendar and select **Clear**.
6. Repeat the first three steps except this time select **Wireless Synchronization** to read **Yes**. This will perform a resynch of the calendar.

If the device cannot access BlackBerry Desktop Manager, then we can use the following key combination on the device to enable a resynch of the calendar from the BES:

1. On the device go to Calendar.
2. Click the BlackBerry button and select **Options**.
3. Type `SYNC` — for a slow calendar synch.
4. Type `RSET` — to resynch from the BES.

There are several other trait commands that can be used to change calendar synch settings.

Users can now also forward calendar appointments from their devices, a feature that is new to BES version 5. We did mention in *Chapter 1, Introduction to BES 5* that a new feature of BES version 5 is the ability to access documents from the device that are stored on the remote corporate LAN. This will be looked at more closely in *Chapter 6, MDS Applications*.

This brings us to Lab 3, where we will continue to build our BlackBerry Enterprise Environment.

Lab 3

In this section we will be looking at importing bulk users from our existing mail server environment into the BES environment.

Importing users to the BlackBerry Enterprise Server

In most organizations, we would already have a list of users present in our messaging environment (or in Active Directory). Instead of adding a single user at a time—which in a large organization could take up valuable time—we can create a `.csv` file and import a batch of users. When we carry out the import of users, we can specify:

- The names of the groups we want to add the users to
- Details about activation such as type of activation, password, and expiry times
- E-mail address
- Which Blackberry Enterprise Server instance to join, denoted via the SRP ID

For the purpose of this lab, we are going to create a `.csv` file that will create and add six users to our group called Sales Team. Set each one up with a default activation password of 'password', which has an expiry time of 40 hours.

1. Open up Notepad.
2. Add the following column headings, each separated on one line with a comma:
    - E-mail address
    - SRP ID
    - Group names
    - Activation password operation
    - Activation password
    - Activation password expiry

Activating Devices and Users

For each user, specify their e-mail address, the SRP ID for the BlackBerry Enterprise Server instance we want to join, and the group name—in our case it will be "Sales Team". We will set the activation password operation for all users to specify, the activation password for all users will be "password", and the expiry time will be 40, denoting 40 hours before the password expires. Your text file should look similar to the following screenshot:

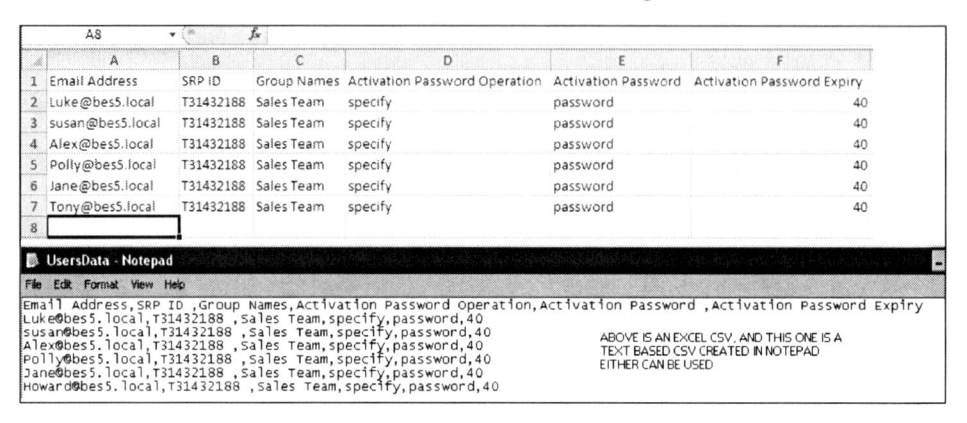

Email Address	SRP ID	Group Names	Activation Password Operation	Activation Password	Activation Password Expiry
Luke@bes5.local	T31432188	Sales Team	specify	password	40
susan@bes5.local	T31432188	Sales Team	specify	password	40
Alex@bes5.local	T31432188	Sales Team	specify	password	40
Polly@bes5.local	T31432188	Sales Team	specify	password	40
Jane@bes5.local	T31432188	Sales Team	specify	password	40
Tony@bes5.local	T31432188	Sales Team	specify	password	40

```
Email Address,SRP ID ,Group Names,Activation Password Operation,Activation Password ,Activation Password Expiry
Luke@bes5.local,T31432188 ,Sales Team,specify,password,40
susan@bes5.local,T31432188 ,Sales Team,specify,password,40
Alex@bes5.local,T31432188 ,Sales Team,specify,password,40
Polly@bes5.local,T31432188 ,Sales Team,specify,password,40
Jane@bes5.local,T31432188 ,Sales Team,specify,password,40
Howard@bes5.local,T31432188 ,Sales Team,specify,password,40
```

ABOVE IS AN EXCEL CSV, AND THIS ONE IS A TEXT BASED CSV CREATED IN NOTEPAD EITHER CAN BE USED

3. Save the file as a normal `.txt` file, if created in a notepad.
4. Within the BlackBerry Administration Service, navigate to the **BlackBerry solution management** section.
5. Expand **User** and select **Create a User**, then select **Import new users**.

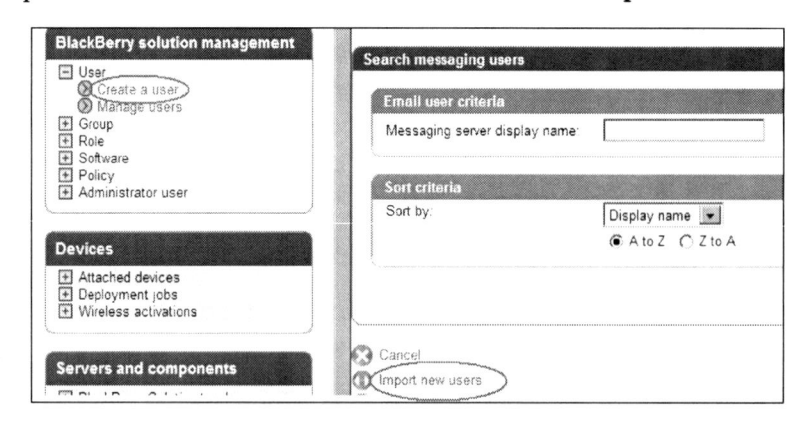

6. Browse to the text file we created previously and select **Continue**.

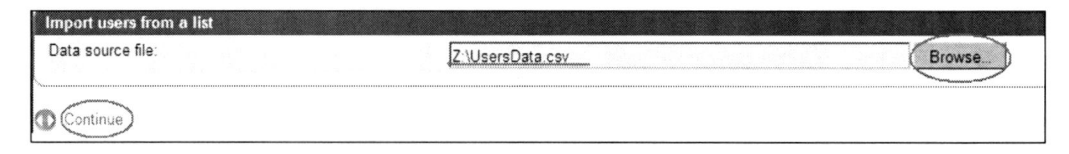

[98]

7. Once the import is finished, you will see the message stating the following users have been created and e-mailed the activation password we set in our CSV file, as shown in the previous screenshot of the CSV file.
8. In the CSV import file settings, we can—under **Activation Password Operation**—choose to type the following keywords, which would have alternative effects on the user activation method:
    - Generate: This would automatically generate and e-mail an activation password to the users
    - None: It will just create the user account
9. We can also check to ensure that the six users are added to the Sales group.
10. Click on **Manage groups**, select **Sales Team**, and then select **View group membership**.

Adding a user when the user is not present in the company directory lookup

As mentioned earlier, sometimes the BlackBerry Mail store does not synch with the contact information database in the BlackBerry Configuration Manager in time, so there could be an instance when a new user is created in Active Directory/Exchange, but is not displaying the user account in the search results within the BlackBerry Administration Service. If that happens, we can follow the steps to add the user account on to the BlackBerry Enterprise Server:

1. Expand **User**, click on **Create a user**, then click on **Add user from company directory**.

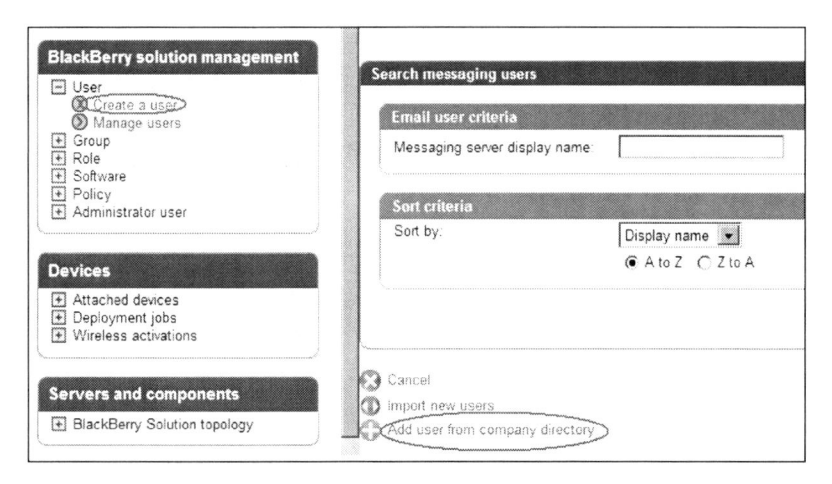

Activating Devices and Users

2. Type in the user's e-mail address in the **Email address** field.
3. Click on **Find user in company directory**.

```
Add user from company directory

You can create a user so that you can assign and activate a BlackBerry® device to the user
The user list from the company directory is automatically updated on a timely basis. The upc
component

Search messaging users
Email address:                                              markr@bes5.local

  ⊕ Add user from company directory
  ⊗ Cancel
```

4. Click on **Save user to available list** and create BlackBerry enabled user.
5. You can now select the BlackBerry instance, add the user to any groups, and create a user with an activation password which you specify, or alternatively one which is generated. You can also create the user with no activation password.

Setting a disclaimer at the server level for all users

To ensure that the integrity of the organization is kept up to standards when users are using the BlackBerry device, we need to ensure that our company disclaimer is attached to the end of each message. This can be done as follows:

1. In the BlackBerry Administration Service under **Servers and components**, expand **BlackBerry Domain | Component view | Email** and select the BES instance.
2. On the right-hand pane, select the **Messaging** tab.
3. Scroll down and select **Edit instance**.

Chapter 3

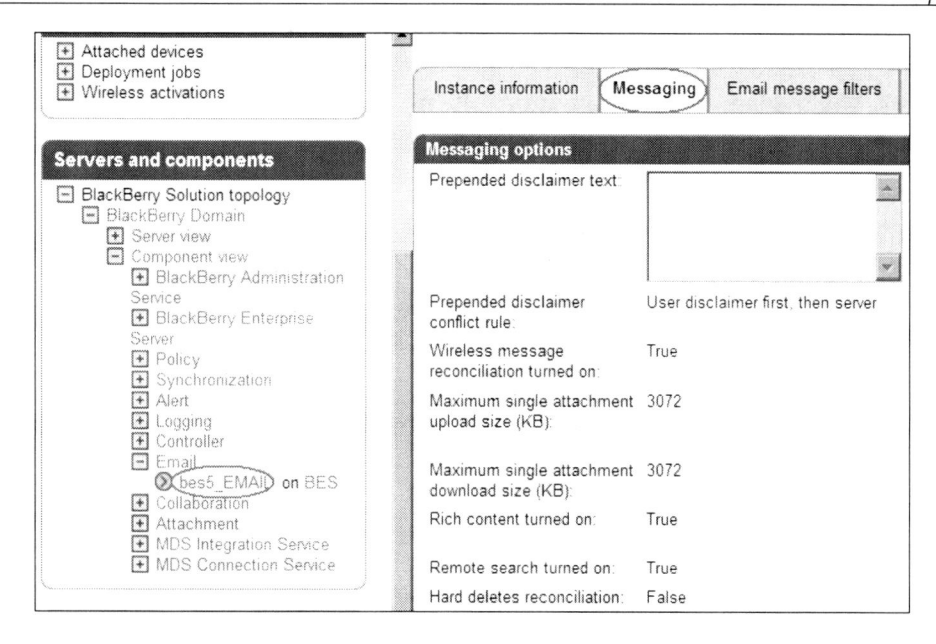

4. Under **Messaging** options, enter the disclaimer in the textbox marked **Appended disclaimer text**.
5. Set the conflict rule so that the Server disclaimer is used first, then the user's, as shown in the following screenshot:

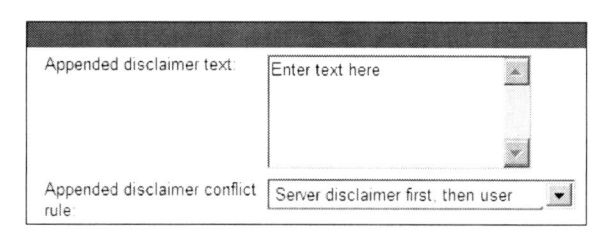

6. Select **Save all**.

Activating Devices and Users

Setting activation passwords

We can set these if we carry out an import such as in the previous section, otherwise we can set the activation passwords for multiple users by carrying out the following procedure:

1. Expand **User**, select **Manage users**, then select **Manage multiple users**.

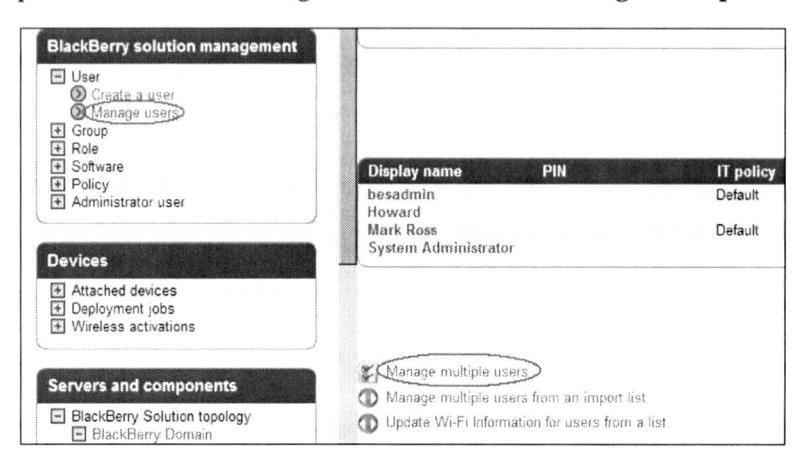

2. Place a checkbox in all the users that we want to set an activation password for.

3. Under **Device activation**, select **Specify an activation password**, and enter an activation password and the time it has before it expires.

4. Then select **Specify an activation password**.

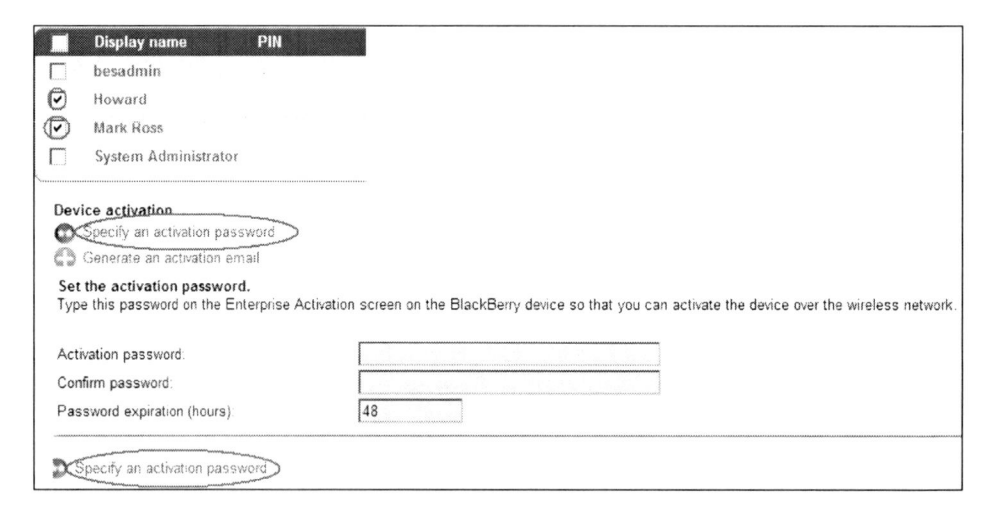

Sending a PIN message

To ensure we have data communication before we activate a device, we can test it by sending a PIN message. Also remember in our setup we have activated the Enterprise Policy, so any devices we try and activate must fit into the policy's type and make, and we must also specify the device's PIN in our policy.

On the device, go to **Options** | **Status** to see the device's PIN number. Go to **Messages**, press the BlackBerry button, and select **Compose PIN**; send a PIN message to ensure you have data connectivity.

Applying a Level One message filter to a user

We will conclude this lab by demonstrating how we can apply a Level One message filter to a user's account. The advantage of this is that if the message matches the criteria we have set up in the filter then we can forward that message on to the user with a level 1 notification. Messages with level 1 notification appear in bold (and if the device has the latest 5.0 software running then they appear in a different font color). They can also be assigned a different tone alarm on the device, so the user knows who the message is from.

We have a user called Howard who needs to know instantly when his Boss Susan e-mails him—when he is on the road—as it usually contains updates on sales figures and prices. For this we can create a message filter and then forward that message on with level 1 notification.

1. Expand **User**, select **Manage users**, then select **Howard**, and then **Edit user**.

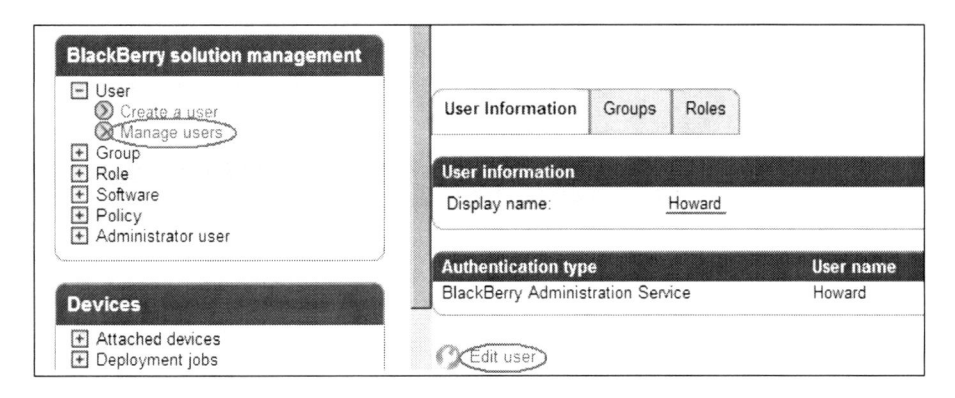

2. Under **Messaging configuration**, click on **Default configuration**.

Activating Devices and Users

3. Select the **E-mail** tab.

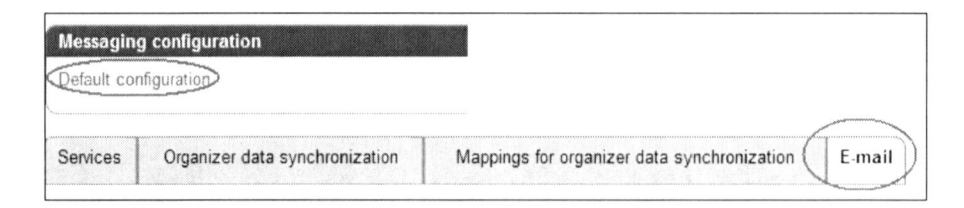

4. Under **Priority**, enter a name for the message filter—`Level One_Susan`.
5. Make sure the rule is marked enabled to **Yes**.
6. Place a tick in the **From** field and select Susan's account.
7. Ensure the radio button is placed in **Forward email messages to the device**.
8. Place a tick in the box marked—**Forward with Level 1 notification**.

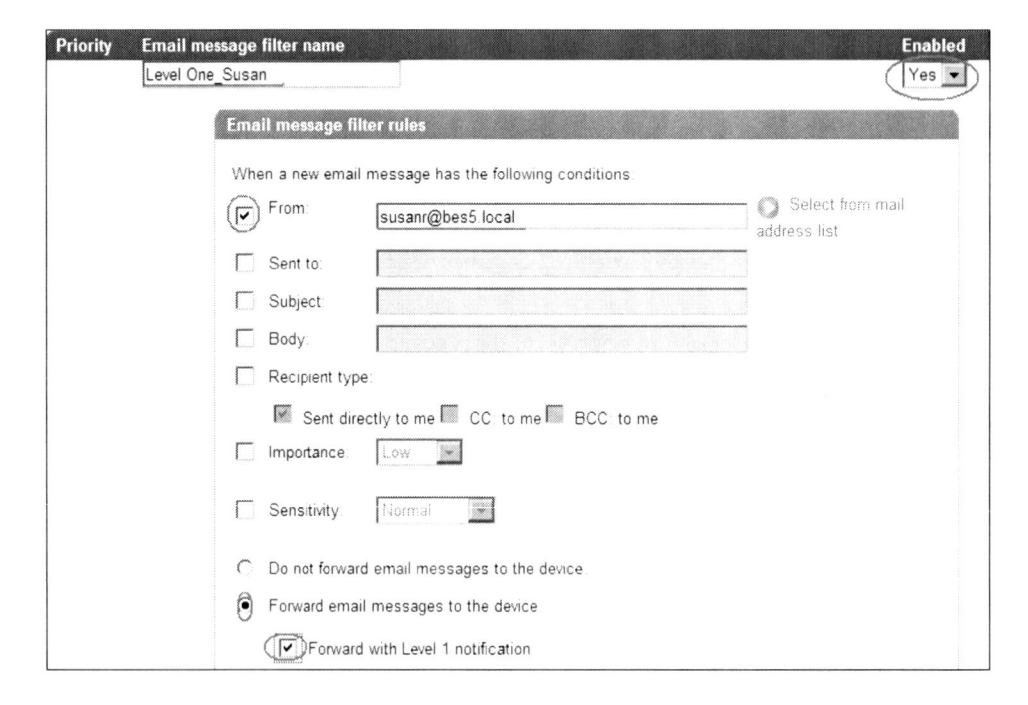

9. Click on **Save all**.

On Howard's device, we can go to **Options | Profiles | Select the active profile | Select Level One** and set a different ring tone.

Now, when Susan sends Howard an e-mail, he will know instantly that it is from Susan and that Howard needs to access it on his device.

Summary

In this chapter, we have covered the methods for creating and managing user accounts, and we have looked at the different ways we can activate a device for a user. We have also examined the settings associated with organizer data. In the next chapter, we will review the IT policy capabilities of the BlackBerry Enterprise Server.

4
IT Policies

In the previous chapter, we covered the steps required to provision users and activate devices within the BlackBerry Enterprise Server environment. As administrators, we want to see users interacting with their devices in accordance with organizational policies. In this chapter, we are going to explore the capabilities provided by the BlackBerry Enterprise Server to configure and enforce a variety of policies for device settings. Administrators have the ability to set over 400 granular IT policies; we will have a look at some of them next.

IT policies

IT policies are used to control the behavior of BlackBerry Devices, BlackBerry Desktop Manager Software, and BlackBerry Web Desktop Manager within your organization. These policies comprise of individual IT policy rules that enforce specific behavior regarding applications on a BlackBerry device or security settings for the BlackBerry Enterprise Solution. IT policies can be applied to individual users or to a group of users within the BlackBerry Enterprise Server. When a device is activated on the BlackBerry Enterprise Server, the default IT policy is pushed out to the device. Many administrators will want to modify the default IT policy or create a new set of policies to apply within their organization.

New IT policies included in BES version 5 allow us to control the BlackBerry Messenger application more efficiently along with other instant messenger services. IT policy rules are grouped based on the type of behavior that is modified, such as password policies, Bluetooth policies, or Wi-Fi policies. Policy rule enforcement is determined based on the rule setting, which is set through pre-defined options such as True, False, and Default for the Allow Peer-to-Peer Messages Rule, or with a string value such as 6 for the Minimum Password Length Rule.

IT Policies

As BES 5 allows us to have users in more than one group and also allows us to nest groups, there is the potential for a user to be assigned more than one IT policy, by the virtue of being in multiple groups. A user can only be assigned one IT policy; later on in the chapter under the conflict section, we will be examining how the BES resolves this issue. As mentioned, in order to configure the IT policy rules for your organization we can either edit the default IT policy or we can create a new policy. In the following section, we are going to look at creating a new IT policy and applying it to an individual user, and then to groups within our organization. In Lab 4, we will be looking at setting the particular options within a policy in more detail, under the *Creating the Sales Team IT policy* section of this chapter.

Creating a new IT policy

1. Log on to the BlackBerry Administration Service.
2. Under **BlackBerry solution management**, expand **Policy**.
3. Click on **Create an IT policy**.
4. In **IT policy information**, enter the name and click on **Save**.

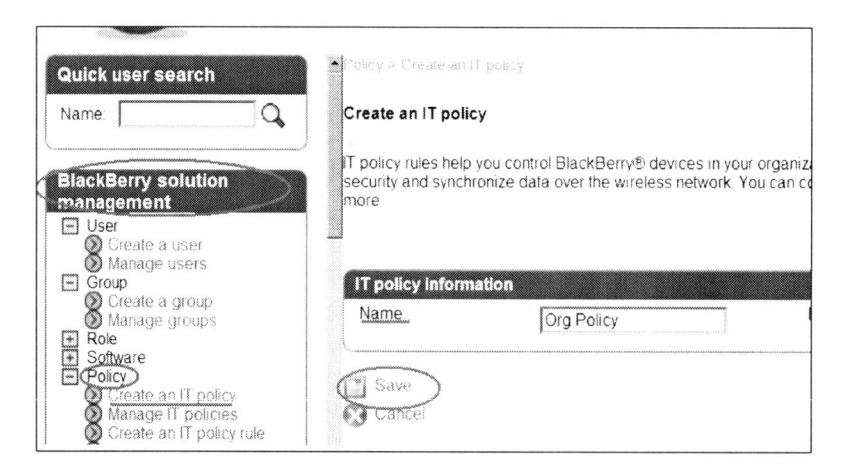

5. To configure the IT policy, click on **Manage IT policies** and select the policy we just created.
6. Click on **Manage IT policies**, select the **Org Policy**, and select **Edit IT policy**.

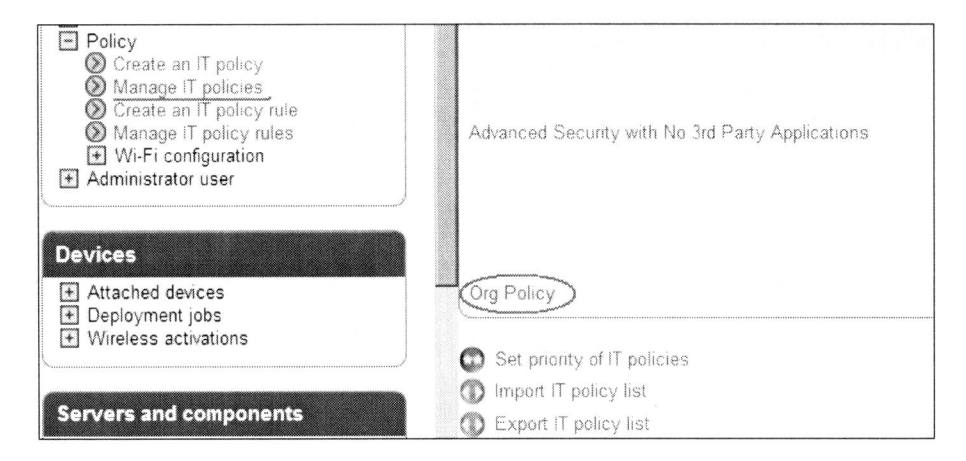

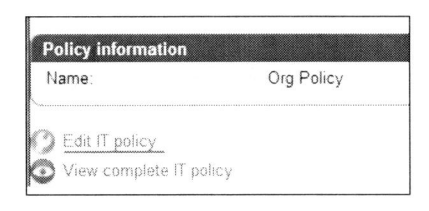

We can now see the group-based policies that we can configure. For example, we can select the tab for Camera and select the option to disable Photo and Video Camera on the BlackBerry device. It should be noted that some policies—to come into effect on the device—require the device to be running a certain version of the BlackBerry device software. For example, for the Video Camera to be disabled, the device must be running Java-based BlackBerry device software version 4.3.0 or higher. This information can be found by clicking the **More links** next to the policy description. Once we have made a change, we can select **Save all**.

We will look at the other options available to configure our policy in Lab 4, where we will be setting a robust policy for our sales team. Next, we are going to look at assigning this policy to a user rather than to a group.

Assigning an IT policy

Now that we have created an IT policy, we need to apply the policy to make it effective. Firstly, let's have a look at applying the policy we have just created to an individual user.

IT Policies

To a user

1. Click on **Manage users**, search or select a user, and click on the **Policies** tab.

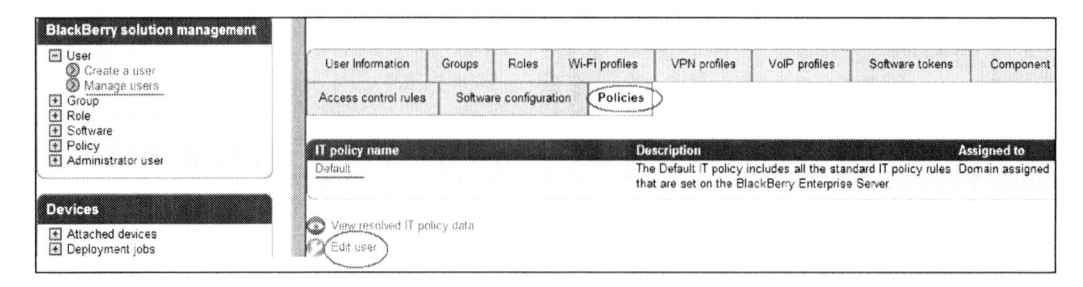

As you can see during the activation the default IT policy has already been assigned to the user. We need to change this so that the user is assigned the Org Policy we just created.

2. Click on **Edit user**.
3. From the drop-down select the **Org Policy**.
4. Click on **Save all**.

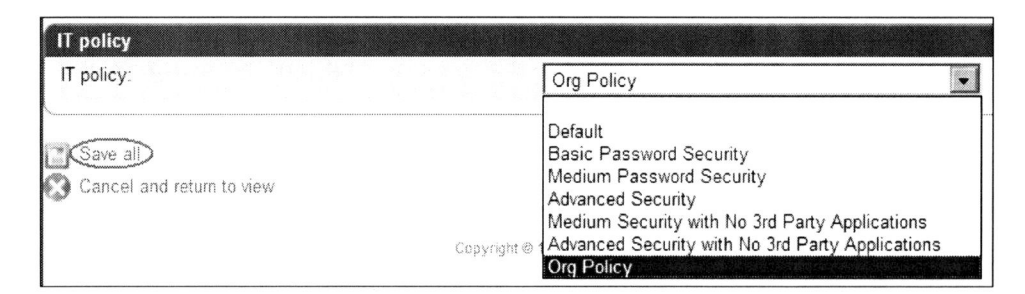

To a group

1. Click on **Manage groups**, select the group which we want to apply the IT policy to.
2. Click on the **Policies** tab, and select **Edit group**.
3. From the drop-down, select the **Org Policy**.
4. Click on **Save all**.

We have now successfully applied the Org Policy to a user and to a group. Any user that joins that group in the future will automatically have the Org Policy pushed to their device. IT policies are pushed over the wireless network any time a policy is changed or when a new policy is applied, automatically. The policy is pushed out over the air and to the device within a 15 minute time frame. Once the IT policy hits the device, the changes are applied immediately. We have the option of sending an IT policy to a device manually, and we can also schedule the BES to send the IT policies to devices at scheduled time intervals whether or not the policy has been changed. We will look at how to do this in Lab 4, under the *IT policy settings* section of this chapter.

Rules for conflicting IT policies

The BlackBerry Enterprise Server can only apply one IT policy per user account, so there is the potential for a conflict to happen, as a different IT policy can be applied to a user, a group, and the BlackBerry Domain. The default conflict resolution rules built into the BlackBerry Enterprise Server state that: An IT policy applied to a user account has the highest priority—so regardless of any group memberships or any BlackBerry Domain IT policy, the user will have the IT policy that was applied to his user account enforced.

Groups—users with no IT policies assigned to them directly will use the highest priority IT policy from any group that they belong to—so if a user finds himself in several groups and has no direct IT policy assigned to him, the IT policy which has the highest priority from the groups will be enforced.

Domain—if no individual or group IT policy is assigned to the user account, the default IT policy is applied; as we saw when we activated the users in *Chapter 3, Activating Devices and Users*, they were all assigned the default IT policy.

Now we have an understanding of the conflict rules, we need to set up the priorities of our IT policies, so when users find themselves in multiple groups, the correct policy is applied.

IT Policies

Setting IT policy priorities

1. Expand **Policy**, click on **Manage IT policies**.
2. Click on **Set priority of IT policies**.

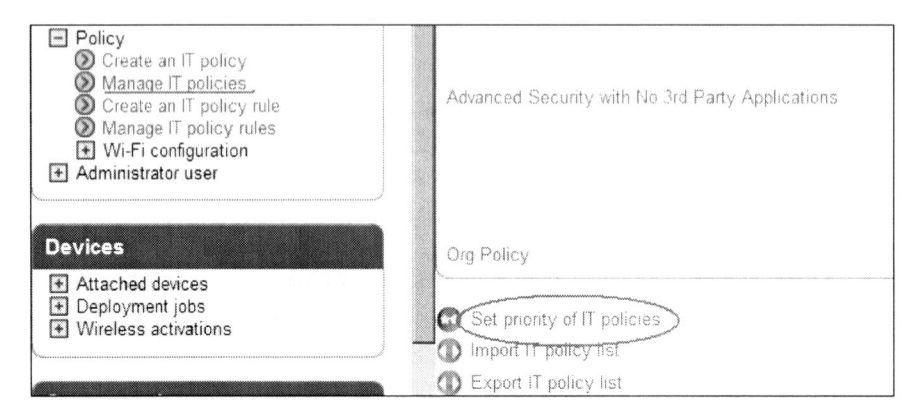

3. Using the up and down arrow, we can position the IT policies higher or lower in the list.

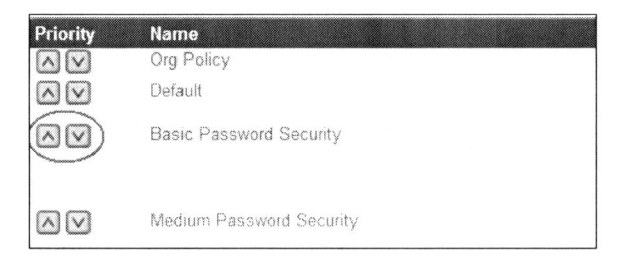

4. Click **Save**.

As the IT policy assignment to a user is automatic, based on these conflict resolution rules, we can double-check which policy has been assigned to a user by following the procedure described next.

Verifying a user's IT policy

1. Click on **Manage users**, and select the user account we want to verify the IT policy for.
2. Click on the **Policies** tab, and select **View resolved IT policy data**.

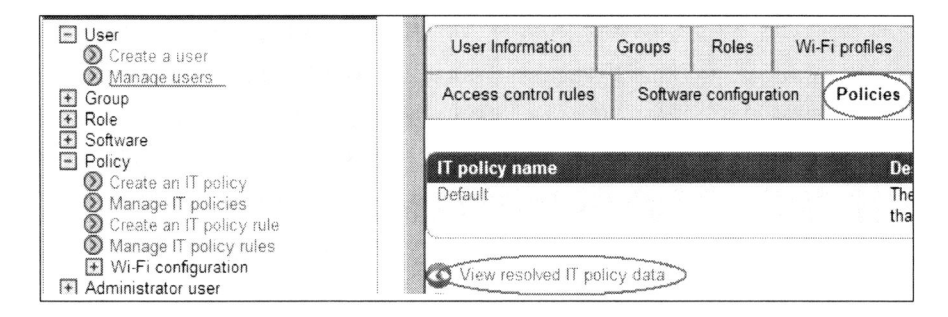

3. The chosen IT policy appears in the **Policy information** section.

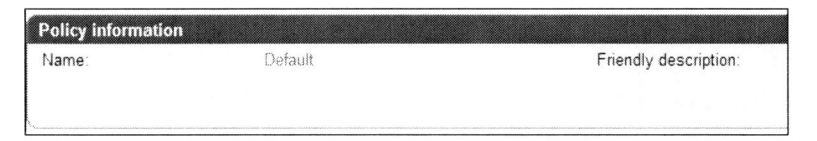

Now that we have seen how crucial IT policies are within our setup, we need to ensure that all devices have an IT policy applied to them at all times; this will ensure that the device is operated within our organizational policy. Therefore, there is a setting discussed in Lab 4 under the *Deactivating devices that do not have an IT Policy* section of this chapter, which allows us to deactivate from our BlackBerry Enterprise Solution any device that does not have an IT policy assigned to it.

We also have the ability in BES 5 to create new IT policy rules for third-party applications that we could be running in our organization that are available on users' devices. We can create the new rules for the third-party applications and add the rules to an existing IT policy such as the Org-the one we created or the default IT policy-or we can create a new IT policy. Please note you cannot create new rules to control already existing BlackBerry features and applications.

To set a new rule for a third-party application that your organization is using, the following options are available to us:

1. Expand **Policy**, click on **Create an IT policy rule**.
2. Type a name for the policy.

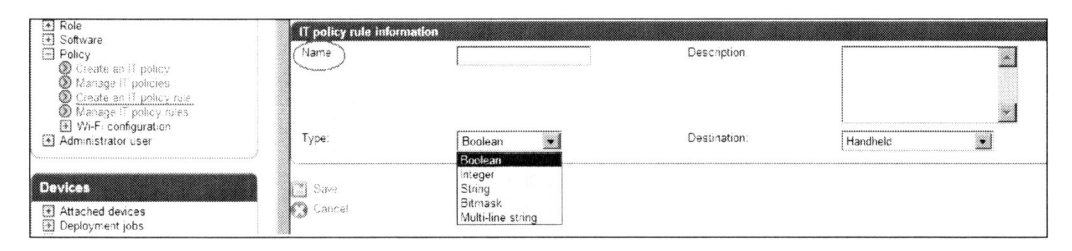

IT Policies

3. In the **Type** drop-down, select the value that the rule would use:
    - Boolean: True, False, or Default
    - Integer: Number, which can further be specified by a minimum and maximum value
    - String: A single line of characters, for example, a web link
    - Bitmask: It is specified in binary numbers to enable or disable features
    - Multi-line string: To define a list of options

4. In the **Destination** drop-down list, choose whether you want the BlackBerry Device, or BlackBerry Desktop Manager to be able to use the IT policy rule, or both.

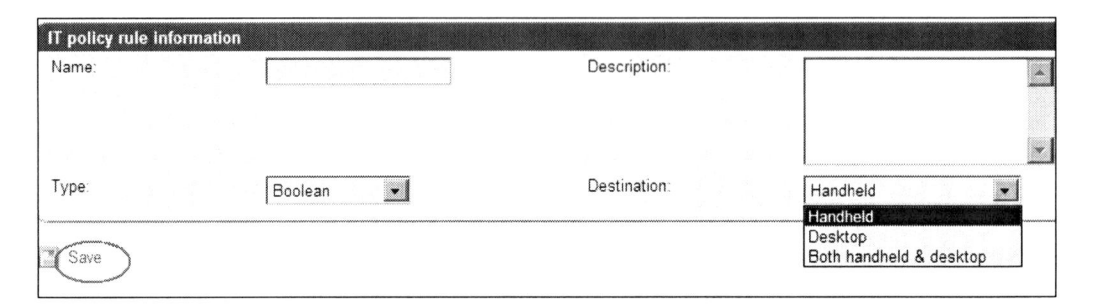

5. Click on **Save**.

Our IT policy rule for the third-party application will then appear on IT policies in our organization under the **User defined** tab. In Lab 4, we will be creating an IT policy rule for a sales application that our organization runs, to ensure we can disable the application on non-sales employees.

Before we move on to Lab 4, we need to take a look at how the IT policy is sent out to the device. We have mentioned previously that the IT policy is sent to a device within 15 minutes of the IT policy being created or changed. When we assign an IT policy to a user or a group of users, the BlackBerry Administration Service creates a deployment job, which has a default setting of creating job schedules every 15 minutes. In *Chapter 5, Software Configuration and Java Applications*, we will have a look at changing these default settings for job scheduling as a whole. Next, we are going to have a look at the options available to us regarding how IT policies are sent to BlackBerry devices.

[114]

Change how an IT policy is sent to a BlackBerry device

1. Expand **Deployment jobs**.
2. Click on **Specify IT policy distribution settings**.
3. Click on **Edit distribution settings**.

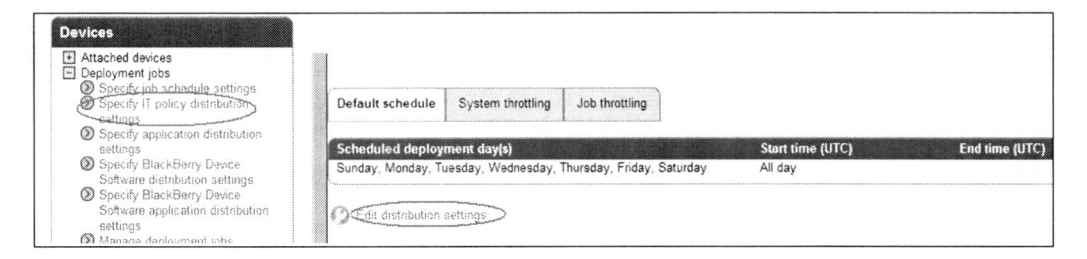

4. Under the **Default schedule** tab, we can change the default recurring day for sending out IT policy updates. By default the setting is to send out **Every day**, and the start time is **All day**.

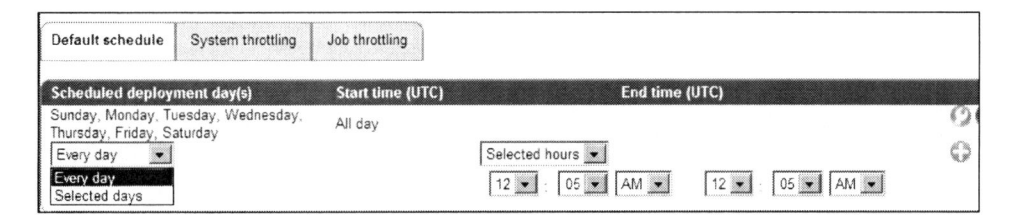

5. Under the **System throttling** tab, we can specify the maximum number of simultaneous tasks the BlackBerry Administration Service instance can carry out. The default setting is **1000** tasks at the same time (all types of job tasks not just related to IT policies).

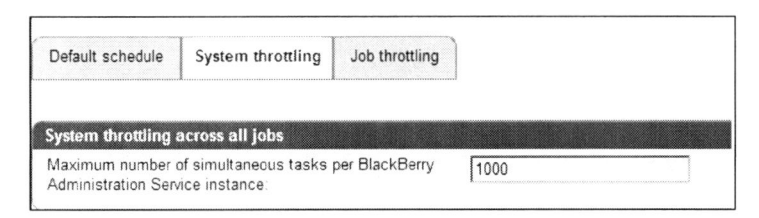

6. Under the **Job throttling** tab, we can set more load balance options regarding IT policies. Change the radio tab to **Enabled to reduce load on system**.

IT Policies

7. We can then set the maximum number of simultaneous IT policy tasks that the BlackBerry Administration Service instance can carry out in a day. (The time window by default is a day, which is set to **25** tasks by default.)
8. We can also specify the total number of IT policy tasks the BlackBerry Administration Service instance can carry out in a day; default is set to **150**.

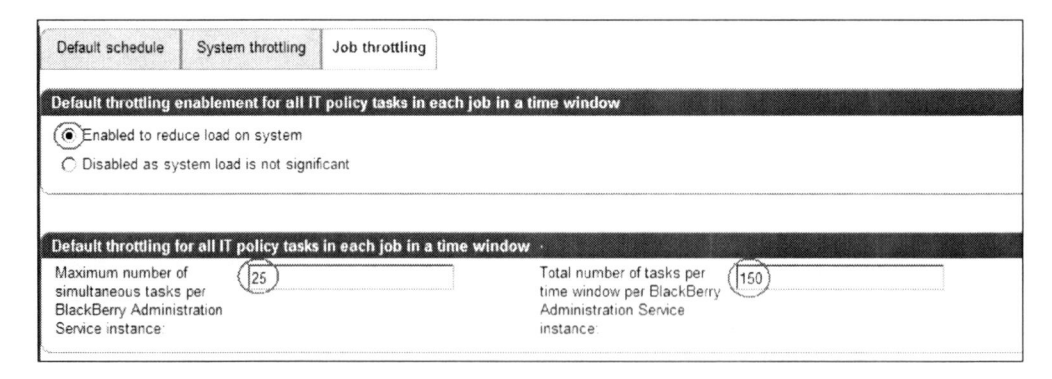

So the above settings allow us to control and change the way an IT policy is pushed out to user devices. These changes would be made depending on the number of users in the organization and the load balance requirements of your organization. The default values are generally accepted for a typical 500 user installation.

Lab 4

To illustrate the importance of IT policies and also to get you familiar with using them in your organization, we are going to create a mock lab that will set the following IT policy rules and IT policy for all user accounts that belong to sales employees.

So far our lab has a sales group which has around six users, who have been activated with the default IT policy. It is good practice not to edit the default IT policy and to create a new one. We need to ensure that the following requirements are met for the BlackBerry devices, for all sales employees:

- The user has to enter a new password every 45 days
- The minimum password length should be eight characters

Chapter 4

- Company security policy states that a duress e-mail must be set up—so if the sales user is forced to unlock the device, the head admin at the organization is notified
- Users cannot be allowed to use the BCC (Blind Carbon Copy) when sending messages from their devices
- Must allow access to the third-party application SalesStock

Creating the Sales Team IT policy

1. Log on to the BlackBerry Administration Service.
2. Create an IT policy called Sales IT policy (see *Creating a new IT policy* section of this chapter for additional help).
3. Click on **Manage IT policies** and select the **Sales policy**.
4. Click on **Edit policy** and select the **Device only** tab.

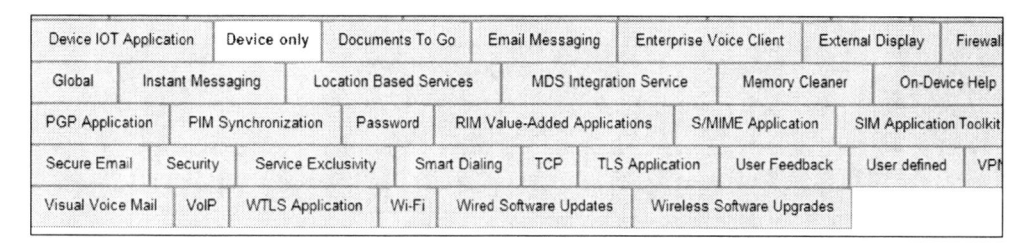

Device IOT Application	Device only	Documents To Go	Email Messaging	Enterprise Voice Client	External Display	Firewall
Global	Instant Messaging	Location Based Services	MDS Integration Service	Memory Cleaner	On-Device Help
PGP Application	PIM Synchronization	Password	RIM Value-Added Applications	S/MIME Application	SIM Application Toolkit
Secure Email	Security	Service Exclusivity	Smart Dialing	TCP	TLS Application	User Feedback	User defined	VPN
Visual Voice Mail	VoIP	WTLS Application	Wi-Fi	Wired Software Updates	Wireless Software Upgrades

5. For the rule **Password Required**, we must select **Yes** from the drop-down menu, as the default setting is **No** for this rule.
6. For the rule **Maximum Password Age** enter 45.
7. For the rule **Minimum Password Length** enter 8.
8. For the rule **User Can Disable Password** select **No**; by default this is set to **Yes**.

IT Policies

9. Scroll further down and change the drop-down menu for **Allow BCC Recipients** to **NO**.

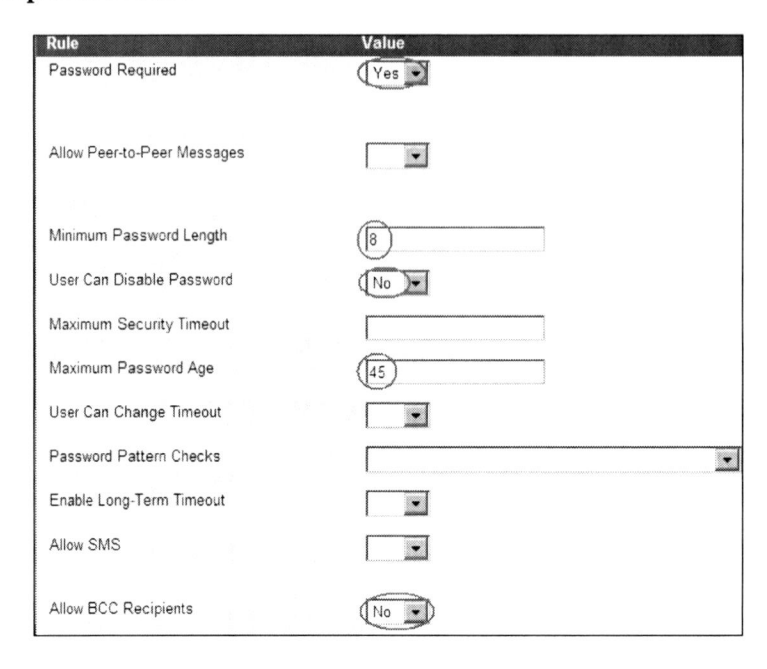

10. Select **Save all**.
11. Click on the **Password** tab and for the rule **Duress Notification Address** enter an e-mail address for the head admin so he is notified when the user is unlocking the device under duress.

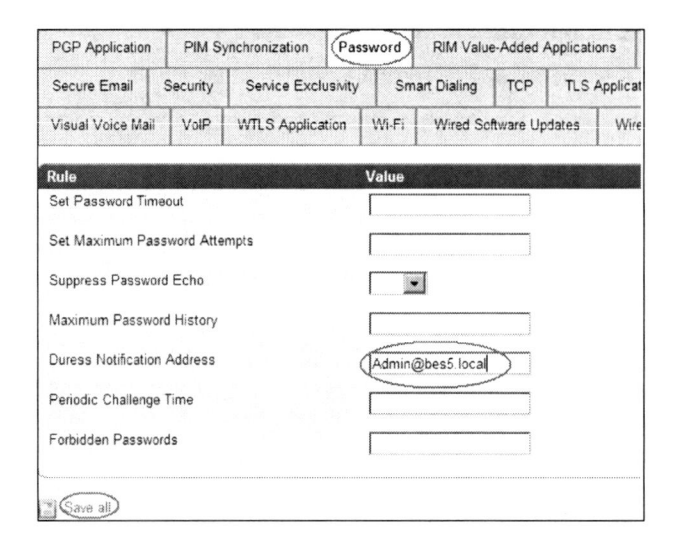

[118]

12. Please note when we enable this rule by default the number of password attempts are halved. By default the number of password attempts are 10, so once we enable this rule they will become 5.
13. For the user to enable the duress call of unlocking the BlackBerry, they would need to move the first character of the password to the end. For example, if the user's password was *blackberry*, then if they were unlocking the device under duress they would enter *lackberryb*. This would then send an e-mail message to the address above letting them know the device was unlocked under duress.
14. Save this IT policy.
15. For our final rule, we need to create a third-party application rule that has Boolean value, see *Creating a new IT policy* section of this chapter, give the policy name as SalesStock, choose a **Boolean** value, and for the **Destination** choose **Handheld**, as shown in the following screenshot:

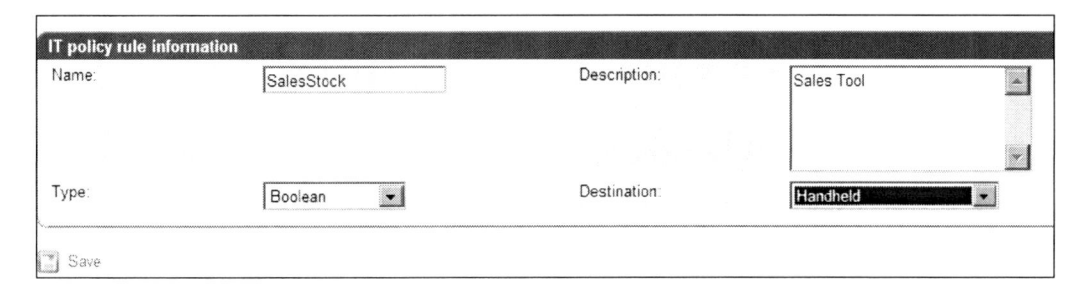

16. Go back to the Sales IT policy and click on the **User defined** tab and select **Yes** for **SalesStock** and click on **Save all**, as shown in the following screenshot:

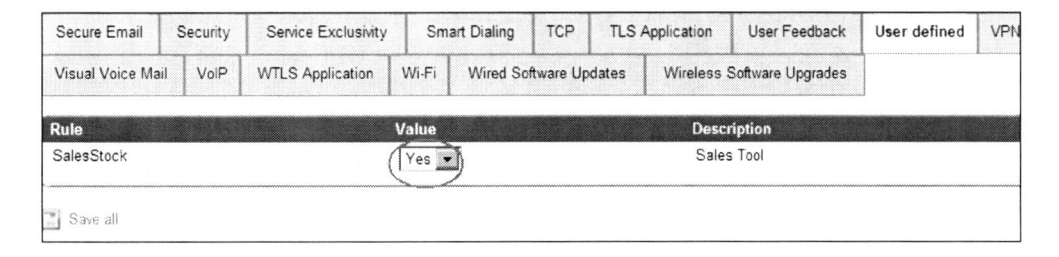

[119]

IT Policies

Applying the IT policy to the sales group

1. Click on **Manage groups**, select the **Sales Team** group.

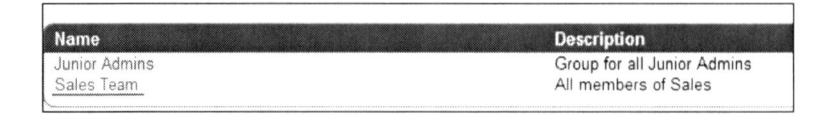

Name	Description
Junior Admins	Group for all Junior Admins
Sales Team	All members of Sales

2. Click on the **Policies** tab, and select **Edit group**.

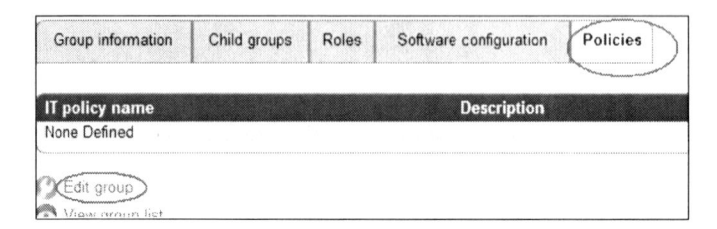

3. From the drop-down select the **Sales IT Policy** and click on **Save all**.

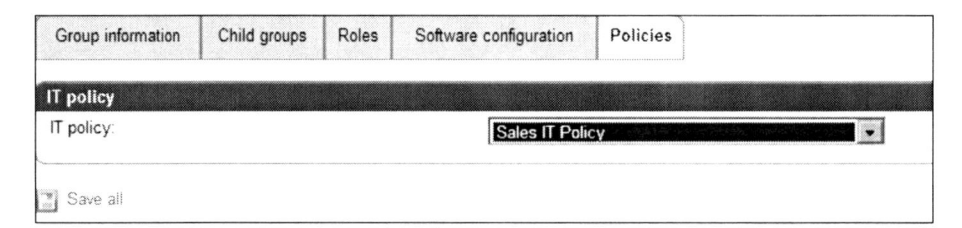

So we have successfully created the Sales IT Policy and applied it to our Sales Team group. From now on, any user created in that group will have the Sales IT Policy applied to them. We need to ensure that no member of our Sales Team has an IT policy directly applied to their user account, as doing so will mean that the directly applied policy will take priority.

We also need to make sure that if users belonging to the Sales Team are in different groups, we either set the IT policy priorities correctly, or we assign the user account a policy directly, so it is always used.

IT policy settings

As mentioned previously, we can resend an IT policy manually to a user account. This is shown next:

1. Click on **Manage users**.
2. Select or search for the user account which needs the policy sent to.
3. Select the **Policies** tab, and click on **View resolved IT policy data**.

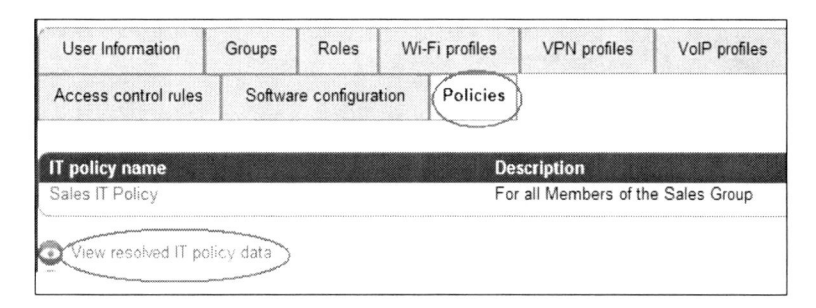

4. Select **Resend IT policy to a device**.

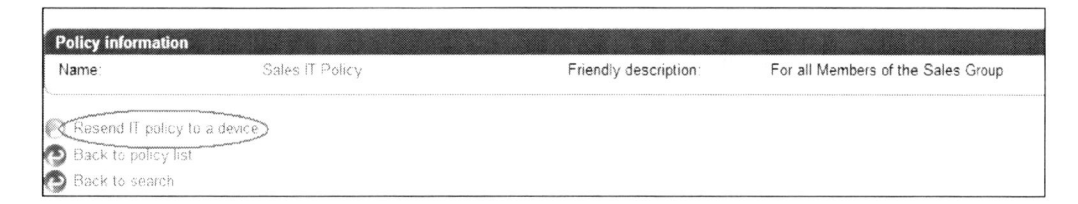

Now this IT policy will be sent to the device within 15 minutes. We can also, as mentioned, program the BlackBerry Enterprise Server to resend IT policies out to devices every X hours even if there is no update or change in the IT policies.

IT Policies

Resending the IT policy automatically to devices

1. Expand **BlackBerry Solution topology**, expand **BlackBerry Domain** and expand **Component view**.
2. Expand **Policy** and select the instance and click on **Edit instance**.

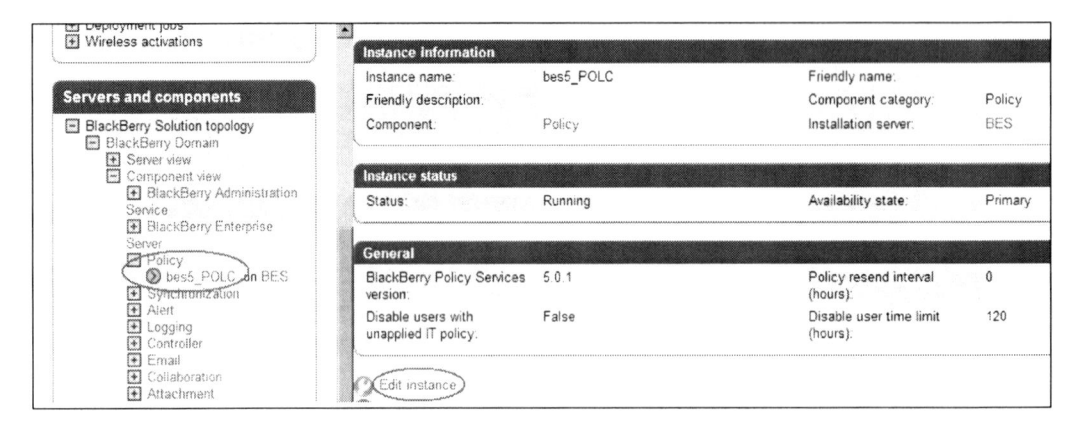

3. In the **General** section for the field **Policy resend interval (hours)** specify 3 to resend the IT policies every three hours automatically.

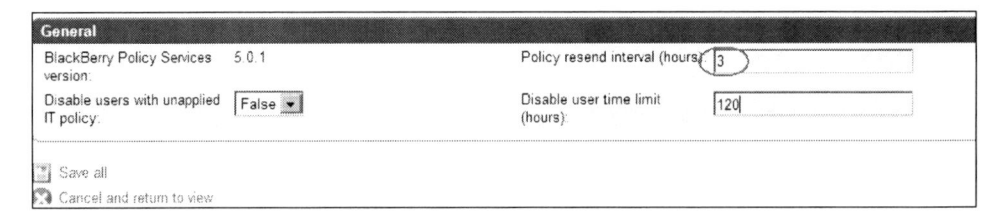

4. Select **Save all**.

Deactivating devices that do not have an IT policy

We can deactivate devices in our BlackBerry Enterprise Solution that do not have a valid IT policy assigned to them.

In the **General** section, change the drop-down for **Disable users with unapplied IT policy** to **True**, as shown in the following screenshot:

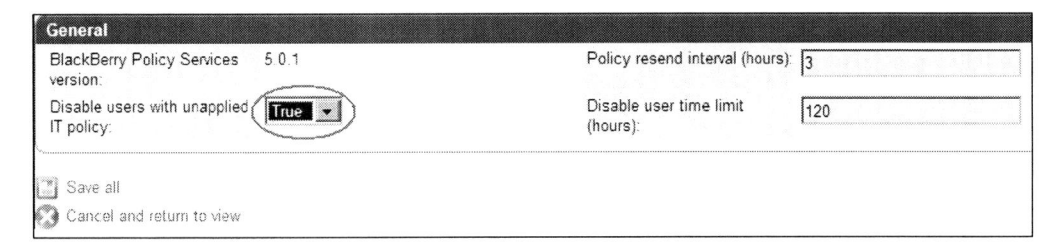

Troubleshooting IT policies

Ensure that you have viewed IT policy settings for users that belong to different groups, to ensure that they have the right IT policy applied. If they don't, check the priority settings for the IT policies within the organization.

If the IT policy seems to be stuck on waiting to apply to the device, this usually indicates that the device already has an IT policy assigned to it. Best practice is to wipe the device, by following the procedure in *Chapter 3, Activating Devices and Users*; this will clear the IT policy on the Smartphone. If the policy is still enforced after the wipe then you will need to refer to RIM documentation on how to use the policy bin tool to remove the IT policy.

Summary

In this chapter, we have examined the controls available to administrators to enforce specific policies on to a BlackBerry device. These capabilities facilitate administration and ensure that the BlackBerry device is used in accordance with organizational policies. With the aid of the lab, we should now be able to successfully create IT policies and assign them to our users and devices. In the next chapter, we will look at applications and software configurations.

Software Configuration and Java Applications

In this chapter, we will be looking at how we can send device software updates and Java-based applications to BlackBerry devices. We have the option of sending device software and Java-based applications over the air or via a wired approach. Please note that sending runtime MDS applications is covered in the next chapter.

Overview of the process

Before we are able to push device software and Java-based applications to our devices, we need to set up our software environment. This consists of the following (each area will be discussed in detail further on in this chapter):

- Creation of a shared folder on our network: This shared folder will be used by the BlackBerry Administration Service when installing Java-based applications on to devices. You do not place any application files into this folder or modify any files that are placed automatically by the BlackBerry Administration Service in to this folder.

- Addition of applications to the application repository: This feature is pre-installed on the BlackBerry Enterprise Environment, and can be accessed via the BlackBerry Administration Service. It will store and manage all versions of device software that you require for your organization alongside storage and management of Java-based applications for your organization.

- Creation of a software configuration: This specifies what versions of the BlackBerry device software and which Java-based applications we can install, update, or remove from BlackBerry devices. We can also use software configurations to specify what applications are required, are optional, or are not permitted on Blackberry devices. These configurations are then applied to individual user accounts or groups.

- Creation of an application control policy: This will specify what resources the application can access on the BlackBerry device. There is a default application control policy that can be used. Alternatively, we can create our own.
- Configure settings for deployment jobs: Once the software configuration is assigned to an individual user or group, the BlackBerry Administration Service creates a deployment job to install the device software or Java-based application on the BlackBerry devices, and deploys a job to apply the correct application control policies to the devices.

Now that we have a brief understanding of what is required to setup our software environment, let's have a look at each of these sections in more detail.

Developing Java applications for BlackBerries

When these applications are developed for a BlackBerry device, they will contain a .cod file that contains the complied application code for the application, which is then in turn executed on the BlackBerry devices to enable them to be installed on the device. During the same process, we can generate a .jad or more commonly an .alx file. These files are descriptor files that provide information about the Java BlackBerry application. So in essence, a BlackBerry Java application will have two main files associated with it—the .cod (executable) file and the .alx (descriptor) file. It is these two files in a ZIP format that we require to initiate a software deployment on BlackBerry devices.

Creating a shared folder on the network

When we create this shared folder, we need to bear in mind two vital points. Firstly, this shared folder is not the same one that is being used for the BlackBerry device software distribution and is completely independent of that folder (which we will be creating in the next section when we look at deploying BlackBerry device software). Secondly, this shared folder cannot be located in the following drive location X:\Program Files\Common Files\Research In Motion. This shared folder is used by the BlackBerry Administration Service to install Java-based applications on to the BlackBerry devices. Do not place any installation files, .cod or .alx into this shared folder. Also, do not make any changes to the files that the BlackBerry Administration Service stores in this folder during the software configuration process. We must create this shared folder before we add application files to the repository. The folder will require the following permissions:

- Administration accounts that you use for the BlackBerry Administration Service must have write permissions to the shared folder.
- The administration accounts that run the BlackBerry Administration Service Application Server service must have write permissions for the shared folder.

Let's have a look at setting up the shared folder required:

1. On the BlackBerry Enterprise Server, browse to the C:\ drive or a location of your choice that is not the same as the one mentioned previously or is not the same as where the BlackBerry device software is stored.
2. Create a new folder and name it BSC.

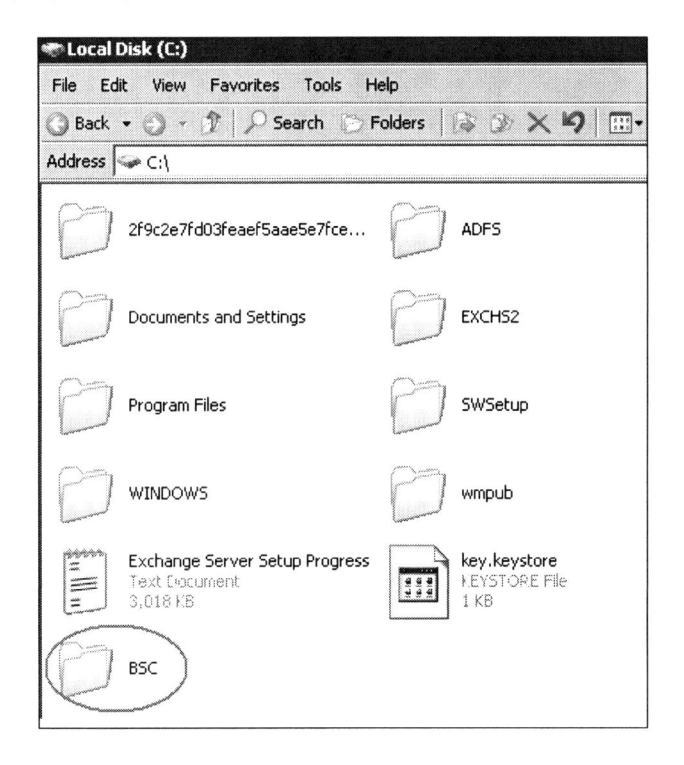

Software Configuration and Java Applications

3. Click on the properties of the folder, select the **Sharing** tab, place the radio button on to **Share this folder**, give the **Share name** as BSC, click on **Permissions** tab. Remove the everyone group and add the following users giving them full control:

    ○ The administration account that you use to log in to the BlackBerry Administration Service

    ○ The administration account that runs the BlackBerry Administration Service Application Server service

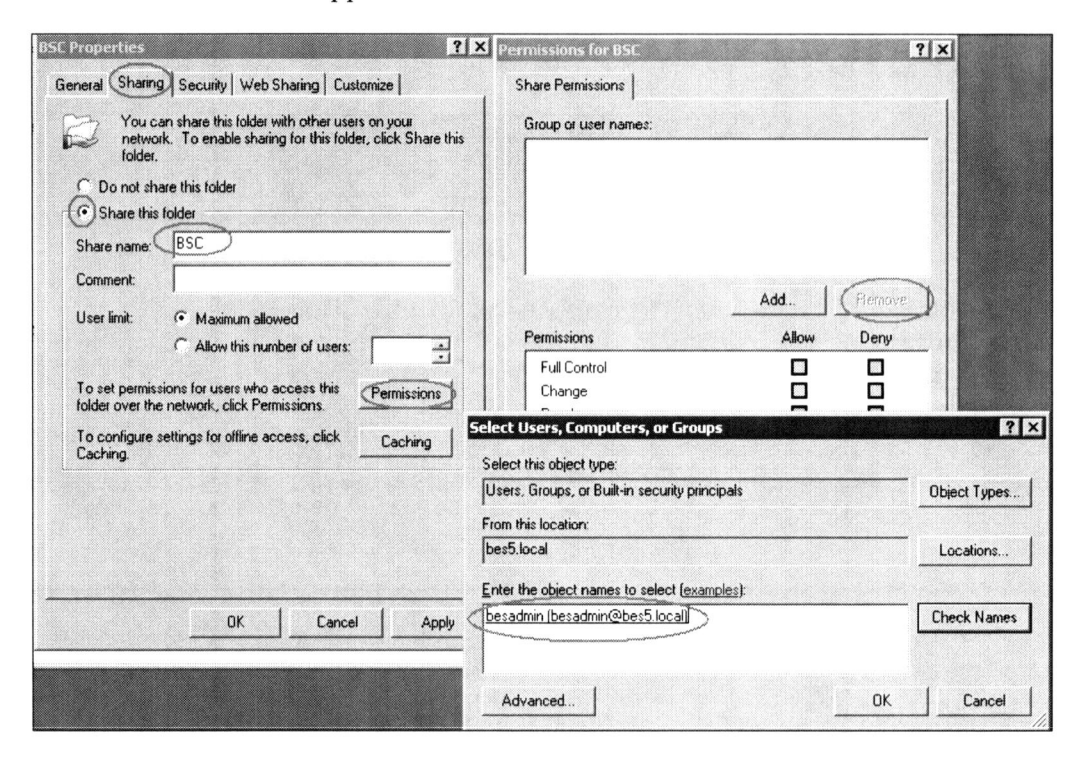

4. To double-check which account this is, we can go on the server that the BES is installed on and click **Start** and in the **Run** box type services.msc. In the window that opens, scroll to the BlackBerry Administration Service Application Server service, right-click and select **Properties**. Click on the **Log On** tab and the account will be displayed.

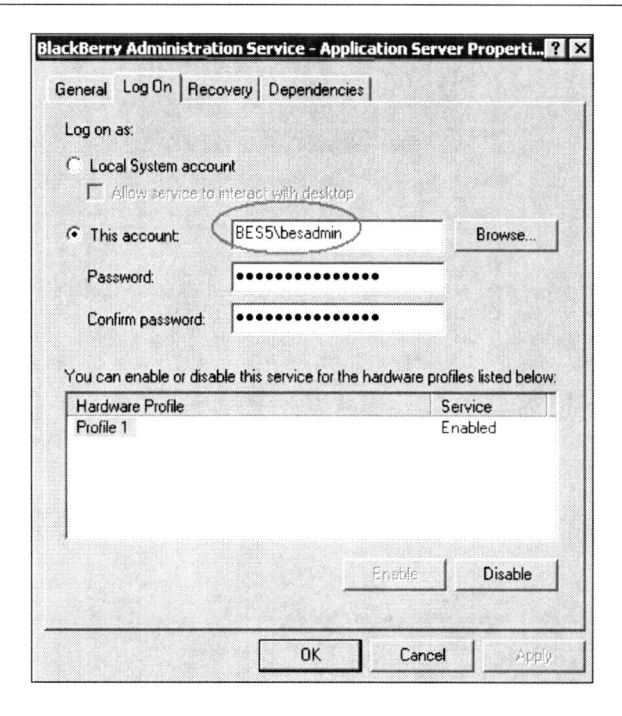

5. Give the account full control to the folder and click on **Apply**.

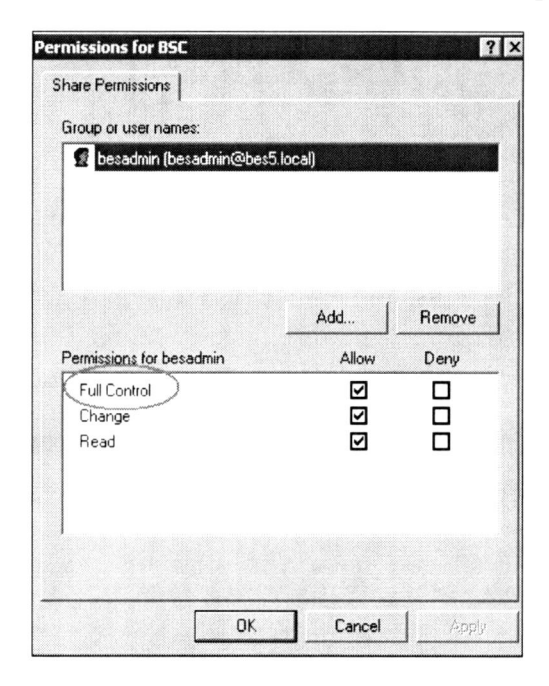

Software Configuration and Java Applications

6. Click on the **Security** tab and add the same accounts giving them write permissions, click **Apply** and **OK**.

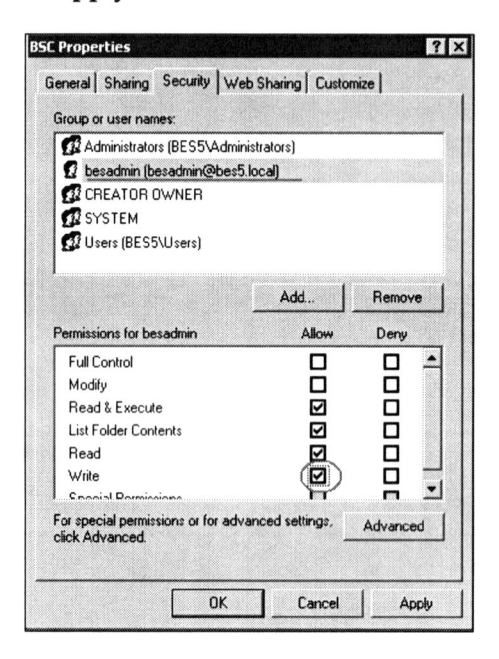

7. Next, we have to specify within the BlackBerry Administration Service, the location of our shared folder. When we specify the folder we must use a **UNC** (**Universal Naming Convention**) format for example, `\\servername\share_name`.

8. Log in to the BlackBerry Administration Service.

9. Expand **BlackBerry Solution topology**, expand **BlackBerry Domain** and expand **Component view**.

10. Click on **BlackBerry Administration Service** and select **Edit component**.

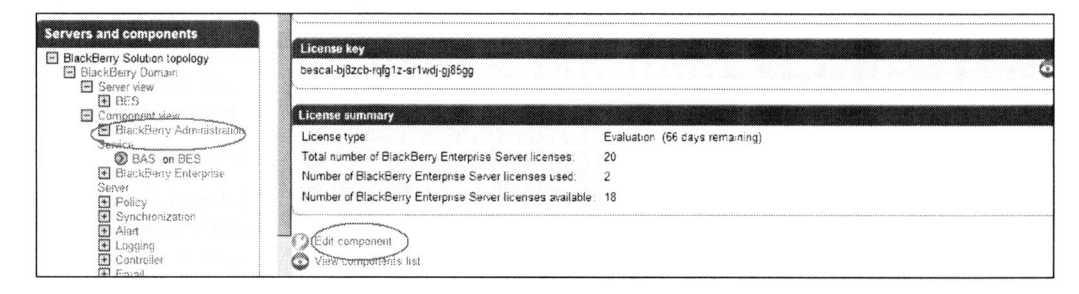

[130]

11. In the **Software management** section, type the UNC path to the shared folder.

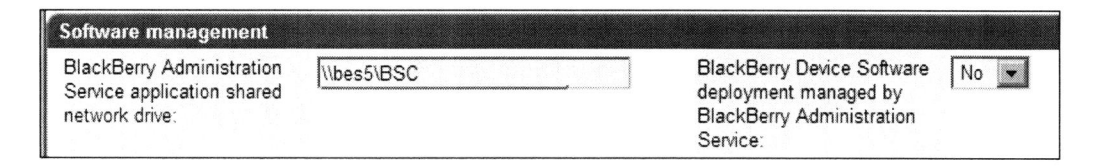

12. Click on **Save all**.

Application repository

Now we need to look at configuring the application repository. We need to add our application bundle (the application bundle includes the ZIP files we discussed previously, the .cdo, .alx, and/or .jad files) to the application repository. The following procedure demonstrates how to add the bundle to the repository. For users of older versions of BlackBerry Enterprise Servers—versions 5 and below—it should be noted that you can no longer copy the .cdo or .alx files to a shared location and index them. In BES version 5, the applications are published via the BlackBerry Administration Service and indexing is done automatically. For the following example, we can download the *smartview* application form.

1. Log in to the BlackBerry Administration Service.
2. Under **BlackBerry Solution Management**, expand **Software** then **Applications** and click on **Add or update applications**.
3. Browse to the ZIP files for the applications, and once selected click **Next**.

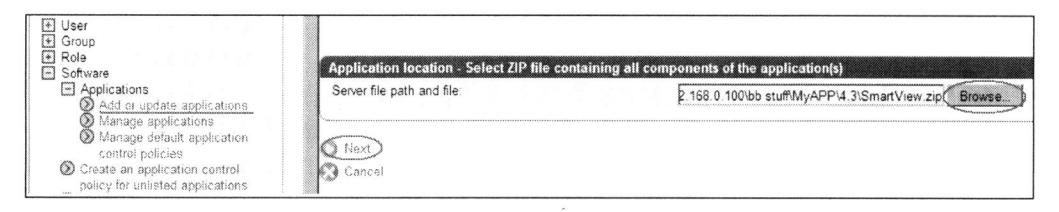

4. Click on **Add application**. If the application like the one in our example is a collaboration application, we need to click on the **Publish application**.

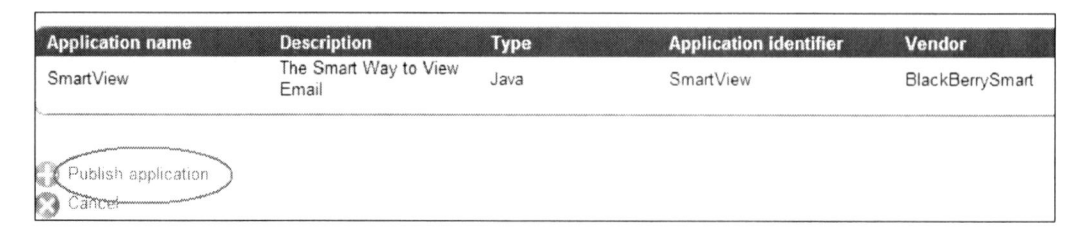

Application name	Description	Type	Application identifier	Vendor
SmartView	The Smart Way to View Email	Java	SmartView	BlackBerrySmart

Publish application
Cancel

Once you have published the application, you can see that the shared folder we created earlier will be populated with the application files along with a `PkgDBCache.xml` and `specification.pkg` file. Next, we are going to look at application control policies before we examine software configurations in more detail.

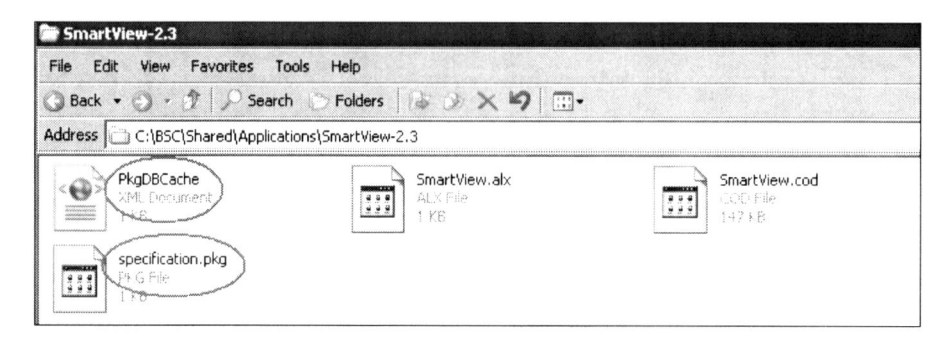

Application control policies

Similar to the IT policies we saw in the previous chapter, we can configure application control policies, which help us to control the data and APIs that the Java application can use and access on the device. It also allows us to control the external data sources and network connections that the application can access and utilize. The BlackBerry Enterprise Server has built-in application control policies or we can create our own. Let's examine the default built-in policies first.

Standard required

This policy will allow the Java application to be installed and permitted to run on the BlackBerry devices; furthermore, if this policy is applied then the application is installed automatically without any user intervention. The policy then has configurable access settings that can be edited, such as: "Is phone access allowed for the application", "Are external network connections allowed" and so on. More configurable settings will be seen later on.

Standard optional

This policy will make the Java application optional on the BlackBerry device; it won't be installed automatically and users can choose to install the application. It also has the same configurable access settings as the standard required policy that can be edited.

Standard disallowed

This policy will prevent users from installing and running the application on their device. For the first two policies, we can edit the access controls based on our organizational needs. This procedure is shown in Lab 5 under the *Changing a standard application policy* section of this chapter.

We can also create a custom application policy, and assign the policy to a Java application. This procedure is shown in Lab 5 under the *Creating a custom application control policy* section of this chapter.

We have already mentioned and seen the similarities between IT policies and application control policy; both can be applied to an individual user account or to a group. There is a policy precedence that takes place on the BlackBerry device, to avoid conflicts. An IT policy will always take precedence over an application policy. For example, let's say you have assigned for the same device an IT policy set that has a rule which states NO to Allow Internal Connections, and an application control policy that has an access rule stating Internal Connections are Allowed. The application will NOT be able to make internal connections, as the IT policy takes precedence.

The final set of application policies that we need to cover are for those applications that we have not listed in our software configuration. We will be looking at software configurations in more detail next, but just to recap, the software configuration specifies which device software and which Java-based applications can be installed or updated on devices. If our software configuration allows users to install applications that are not listed in the software configuration then we need to create an application control policy for these unlisted applications to specify what resources the applications can access on the device.

The BlackBerry Administration Service has two standard built-in application control policies for unlisted applications:

- One for unlisted applications that are optional
- One for unlisted applications that are not permitted

We can change the default access settings for the standard optional application control policy or we can create a custom application control policy for unlisted applications that are optional.

Software Configuration and Java Applications

To change the standard application control policy for unlisted applications that are optional, follow the procedure:

1. Log on to the BlackBerry Administration Service.
2. Under the **BlackBerry Solution Management**, expand **Software**.
3. Click on **Manage application control policies for unlisted applications**.

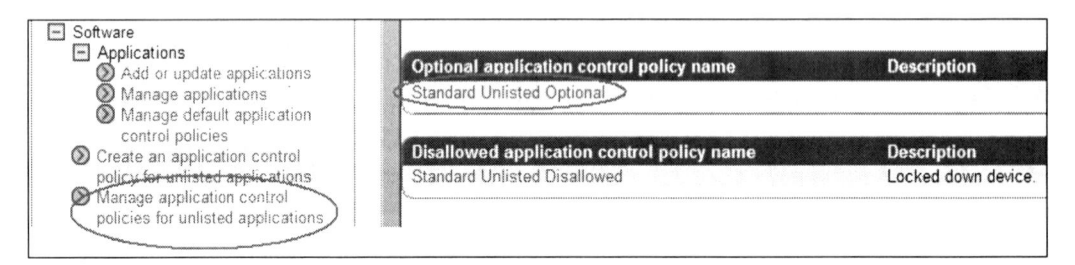

4. Click on **Standard Unlisted Optional**.
5. Select **Edit application control policy**.

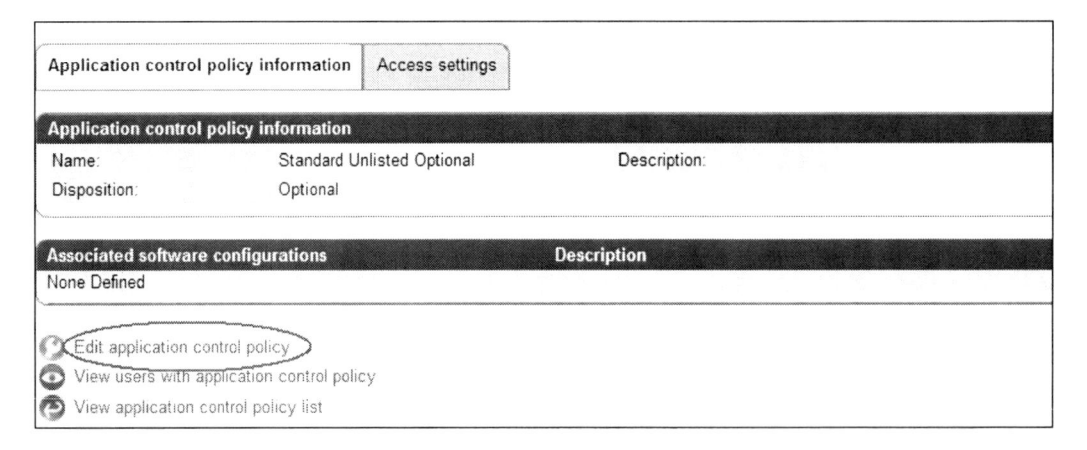

6. Select the **Access settings** tab, configure the settings for the policy and click on **Save all**.

[134]

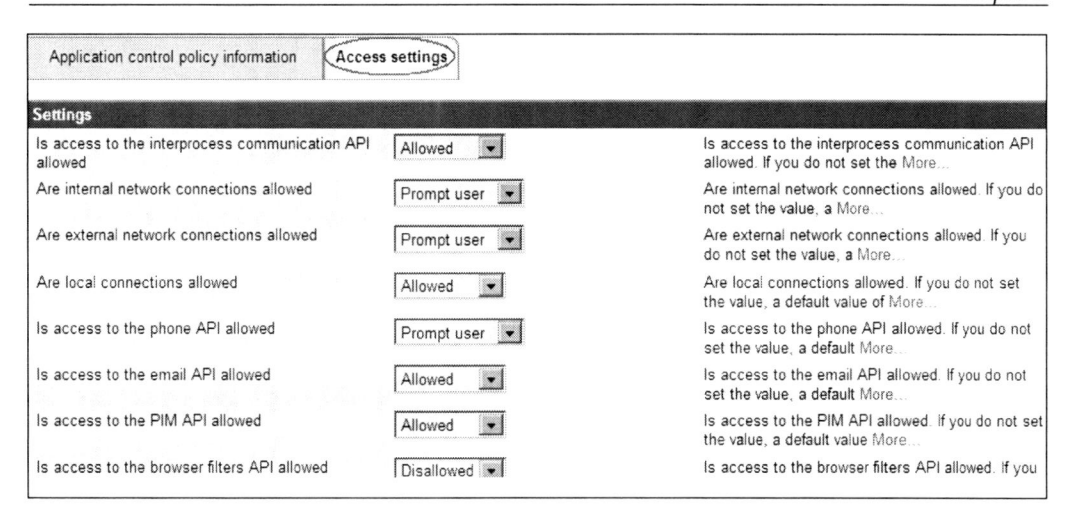

Setting	Value	Description
Is access to the interprocess communication API allowed	Allowed	Is access to the interprocess communication API allowed. If you do not set the More...
Are internal network connections allowed	Prompt user	Are internal network connections allowed. If you do not set the value, a More...
Are external network connections allowed	Prompt user	Are external network connections allowed. If you do not set the value, a More...
Are local connections allowed	Allowed	Are local connections allowed. If you do not set the value, a default value of More...
Is access to the phone API allowed	Prompt user	Is access to the phone API allowed. If you do not set the value, a default More...
Is access to the email API allowed	Allowed	Is access to the email API allowed. If you do not set the value, a default More...
Is access to the PIM API allowed	Allowed	Is access to the PIM API allowed. If you do not set the value, a default value More...
Is access to the browser filters API allowed	Disallowed	Is access to the browser filters API allowed. If you

As mentioned, we can also create a custom policy, this is demonstrated in Lab 5.

Software configurations

Within the BlackBerry Administration Service, we can create software configurations. These help us to specify the following:

- Specify the BlackBerry device software versions
- Specify BlackBerry Java applications that we want to install, update, or remove from the device
- Specify which applications are required, those that are optional or those that are not permitted on the device
- We can also specify what action to take if applications are not listed in the software configuration that we create

The following procedure will walk through the areas revolving around a software configuration from creating it, adding a Java-based application to it, and assigning it to users and groups.

Creating a software configuration

1. Log on to the BlackBerry Administration Service.
2. Expand **Software**, select **Create a software configuration**.
3. Type a name for the software configuration.

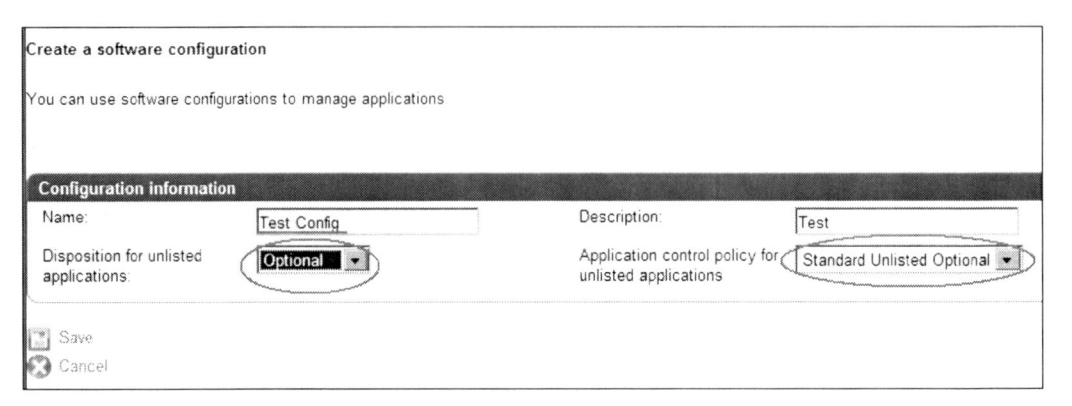

4. In the **Disposition for unlisted applications** drop-down, choose one of the following actions to perform:
    - **Optional**: To allow users to install applications that are not included in the software configuration, so users will be able to install applications outside of what is listed in our software configuration
    - **Disallowed**: To prevent users from installing unlisted applications, so no user will be able to install an application that is not defined in the software configuration
5. We are going to choose optional, therefore, we will also have to assign an application control policy for unlisted applications. We will choose one of the prepared application policies for unlisted applications — standard unlisted optional.
6. Save the changes made.

Next, we have to add an application to the software configuration that we have just created; this is shown in the following procedure. We are going to add the Smart View application, which we packaged earlier on in this chapter.

Adding a BlackBerry Java application to the software configuration

1. Log on to the BlackBerry Administration Service.
2. Expand **Software**, select **Manage software configurations**.
3. Select the **Smart View** software configuration we just created.

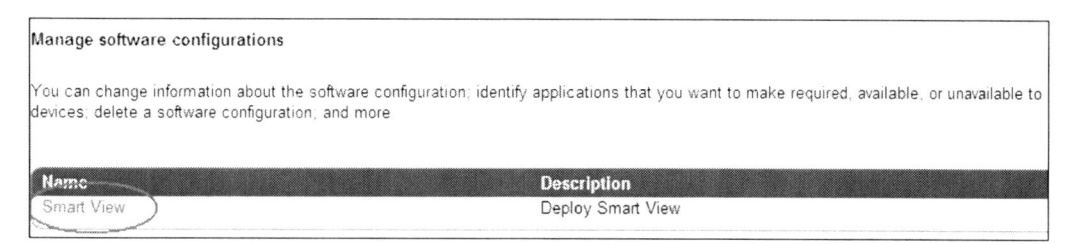

4. Click on **Edit software configuration**.

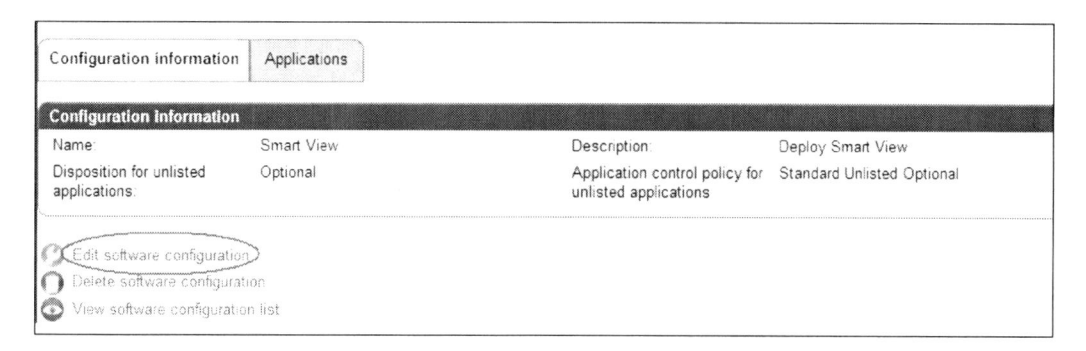

5. Select the **Applications** tab and click on **Add applications to software configuration**.

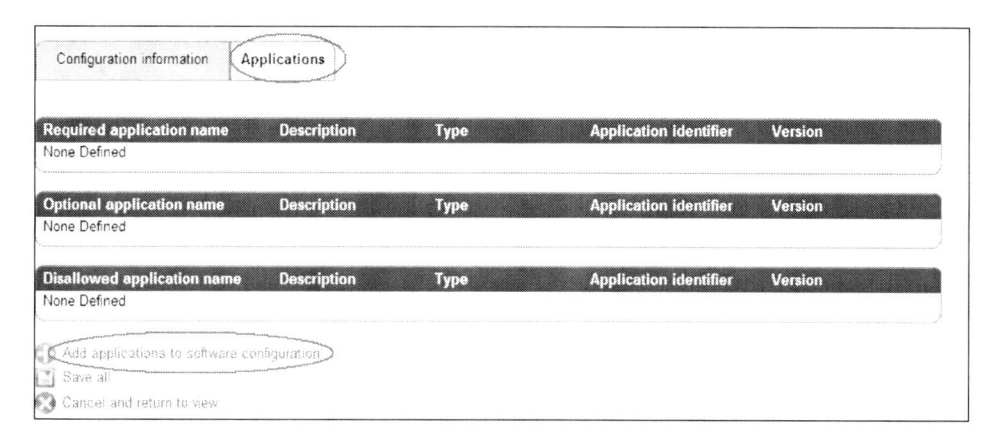

Software Configuration and Java Applications

6. Select the application we created earlier—**Smart View**.
7. In the Disposition drop-down box select one of the following options:
    - **Required**: This means that the application Smart View will be installed on the device automatically and the user cannot uninstall the application
    - **Optional**: This will allow users to install or remove the Smart View application
    - **Disallowed**: This will prevent the users from installing the Smart View application on their device
8. We are going to select **Required**.
9. Under the application information section, we need to assign an application control policy to the Java application. We will use the default standard required application control policy.
10. We then have to choose the method we are going to use to deploy the application: wireless to deploy the application to devices over the air, or wired to deploy the application to devices that will be connected via USB to a PC and access BlackBerry Web Desktop Manager. We are going to select the **Wireless** option.

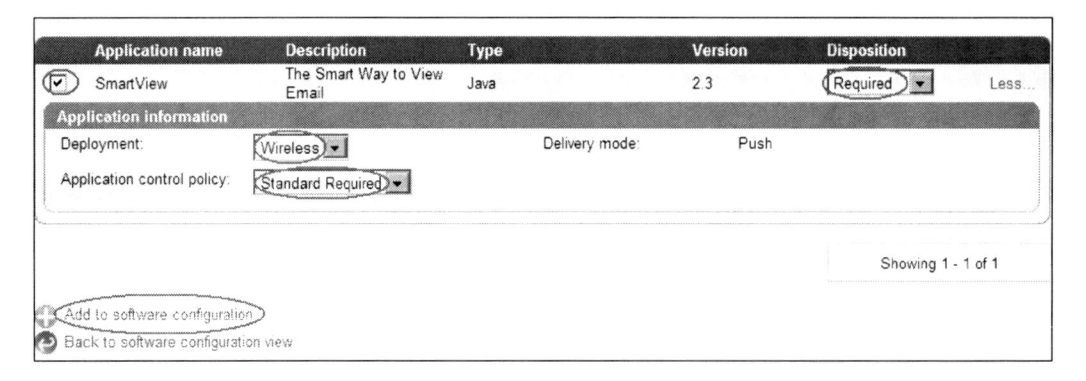

Application name	Description	Type	Version	Disposition
☑ SmartView	The Smart Way to View Email	Java	2.3	Required ▾ Less...

Application information

Deployment:	Wireless ▾	Delivery mode:	Push
Application control policy:	Standard Required ▾		

Showing 1 - 1 of 1

● Add to software configuration
● Back to software configuration view

11. We can add multiple Java applications to a single software configuration. In order to do so we would need to repeat steps 5 to 10.
12. Once we have added all the Java applications to this software configuration, select **Add to software configuration**.

Now that we have a software configuration, we need to apply it to a group of users or to an individual user. In the following procedure, we will see how to assign the software configuration to an individual user account, and then in Lab 5, we will take a look at assigning the software configuration to groups.

Assigning the software configuration to a user

1. Expand **Users**.
2. Click on **Manage users**.
3. Select the user account we want to apply the software configuration to.
4. Click on **Edit user**.
5. Select the **Software configuration** tab, select the software configuration we just created, and click on **Add** (if you want to assign multiple software configurations to a user, repeat the preceding three steps).

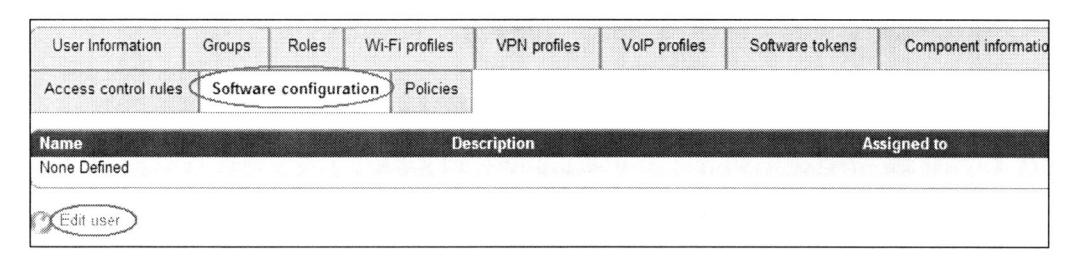

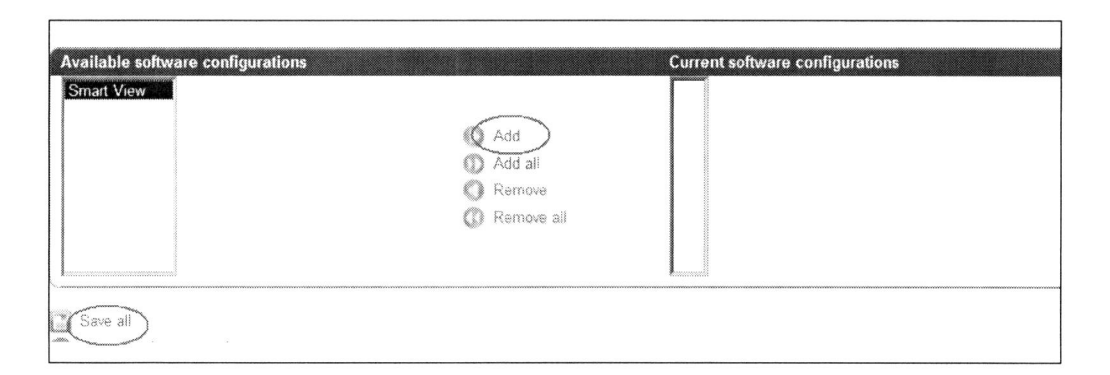

6. Click on **Save all**.

Job deployment

After you assign a software configuration to either a user or a group of users, the BlackBerry Administration Service creates a job to deliver the settings to the BlackBerry device. We can change the default settings of a job schedule and we can further customize the settings for software configuration deployment too. We should also bear in mind that IT policies also use the default settings of the job schedule, and IT policies are also sent out to devices via a job created in the job deployment section. Therefore, when we make changes to the job schedule default settings, we could experience a higher impact on our BlackBerry Enterprise Solution, as it's not just software configuration jobs that the job deployment carries out. Also, it's worth noting that these jobs are created for both IT policies and software configurations automatically by the BlackBerry Administration Service when a new addition or change is made to either an IT policy or a software configuration.

Default settings of a job schedule

1. On the **Devices** menu expand **Deployment jobs**.
2. Select **Specify job schedule settings**.
3. Click on **Edit job schedule settings**.

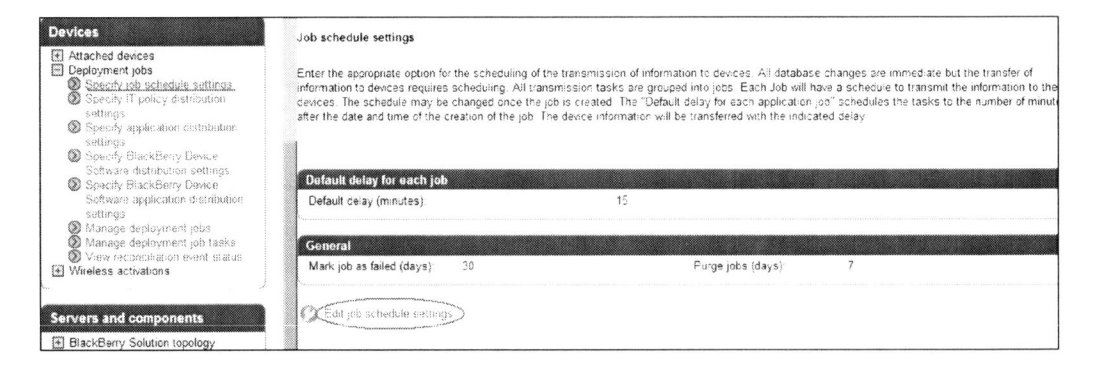

  - **Default delay**: specified in minutes, this is the time that the BlackBerry Administration Service waits before it creates and processes a job; default is 15 minutes.
  - **Mark job as failed**: specified in days, this is when the BlackBerry Administration Service marks the job as failed; default is 30 days.
  - **Purge jobs**: specified in days, this is how long the BlackBerry Administration Service waits before it deletes a job that is marked completed or failed; default value is 7 days.

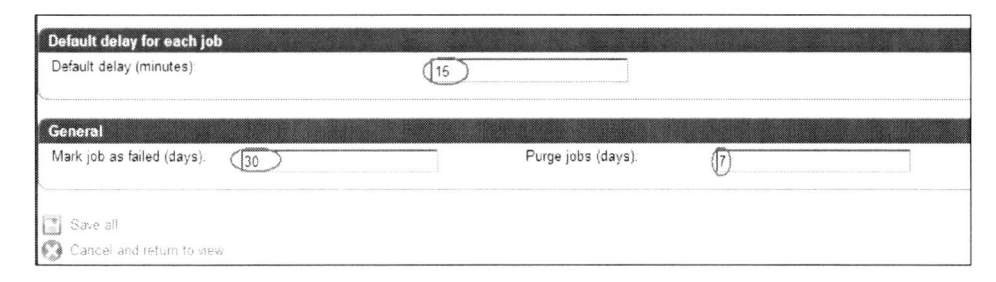

These can be edited to suit your organization's needs. For the purpose of this book, we are going to leave the default values.

Changing job settings of how applications are sent to devices

We can also change the way that applications are sent to a device, editing the *Specify IT policy distribution settings*. The options are the same as those discussed in *Chapter 4, IT Policies*, except they refer to how applications are sent to the device.

So once we have applied our software configuration to a user, we can check the status of the job by carrying out the following procedure:

1. Expand **Deployment jobs**.
2. Click on **Manage deployment jobs**.
3. Select the job we have just deployed for the software configuration for the user.

As mentioned, we can also push the software configuration over a wired platform. This can be achieved by using the BlackBerry Desktop Manager or the BlackBerry Web Desktop Manager. Next, we look at how this can be achieved.

Installing Java applications on BlackBerry devices using the wired approach

Once we have applied the software configuration to the user or group of users, connect the user's device to a PC that can access the BlackBerry Administration Service. Under the Devices menu, expand **Attached devices**, select **Device software**, and click on **Automatic installations of applications on the BlackBerry device** and follow the onscreen instructions.

In Lab 5, we will be looking at how to push device software to a BlackBerry. We have mentioned on several occasions that we can assign multiple software configurations to a user or to a group. Like with IT policies, this can lead to a conflict in the settings. The BlackBerry Administration Service uses specific rules to resolve conflicting settings when multiple software configurations are applied to users or groups. For example, a user called *Alex* could be assigned a software configuration that allows him to install Smart View, a BlackBerry Java application. Alex is a member of the Research Team group, this group having a software configuration assigned to it that states Smart View is not permitted and cannot be installed on user's devices that belong to this group. So we have a potential conflict that needs to be reconciled. Conflicts can happen at all levels of the software configuration. For example, there can be conflicts in the application control policies for the application, in the application control policy for unlisted applications.

The BES uses predefined reconciliation rules (as with IT policies) to resolve conflict settings when multiple software configurations are assigned to users or groups. The rules will determine if the application can be installed and what API the application can access on the device. This process occurs in the background and automatically. We can go and view the outcome of the reconciliation process and the final settings applied to the device for that user, as shown further.

Reconciliation rules for BlackBerry Java applications

To demonstrate this, we will assume we have the following set up on our BES4 **software configurations** (**SC**), which have the settings as shown:

- SC1 has 1 application—SMV version 1.0
- SC2 has 2 applications—BGV version 2.0 and NH version 1.9
- SC3 has 1 application—SMV version 2.0
- SC4 has 2 applications—JU version 3.0 and MND version 7.1

We have a user called *Alex* who is a member of the Research Team group. Let's take a look at scenario one:

Scenario one

If we assign software configuration SC2 and SC4 to Alex's user account and SC1 to the Research Team group, then each application in SC2, SC4, and SC1 will be installed onto the BlackBerry device, as long as the device software supports the application. So the device, if it has the right device software, will have the following applications installed on it: BGV, NH, JU, MND, and SMV.

Scenario two

If we assign software configuration SC3 to Alex's user account and SC1 to the Research Team group, then we have two software configurations that have the same application but different version numbers of the application. The latest version of the application is installed. So the device will have the following applications installed: SMV Version 2.0.

Scenario three

If we assign software configuration SC1 to Alex's user account and SC3 to the Research Team group (the opposite of the previous scenario), then we have two software configurations that have the same application but different version numbers of the application. This time round SMV version 1.0 will be installed on the device. This is because a software configuration applied to a user account takes precedence over a software configuration applied to a group if there is an application conflict such as the one above. So the device will have the following applications installed: SMV Version 1.0.

Scenario four

We will now take a look at reconciliation rules for more specific settings. For this assume the following setup on the BES:

- SC1 has an application called HR, which has the disposition set to **Require** and is set for wireless deployment
- SC2 has an application called HR, which has the disposition set to **Disallowed** and is set for wired deployment

We still have a user called Alex who is a member of the Research Team group.

So we have two software configurations both with the same application, but different disposition settings:

- **Required**: It installs automatically on the device
- **Optional**: It allows the user to choose to install the application
- **Disallowed**: It prevents the application being installed.

They also have different deployment settings:

- **Wireless**: It pushes the application over the air
- **Wired**: It installs the application via BlackBerry Desktop Manager or BlackBerry Web Desktop Manager

SC1 is applied to Alex and SC2 is applied to the Research Team group. The disposition setting for a software configuration assigned to a user will take precedence over the one assigned to a group. So Alex's device will have the application installed on the device automatically as the disposition setting for SC1 is required.

Scenario five

Using the same software configurations as those in scenario four, if SC1 and SC2 was assigned to the Research Team (so both software configurations are assigned to the same level groups) then the required disposition has precedence over the optional, which has precedence over the disallowed. So Alex's device would have the application installed automatically. Once the disposition is reconciled, then the BES will look at reconciling the deployment method.

Scenario six

SC1 is applied to Alex and SC2 is applied to the Research Team group. The deployment method for a software configuration assigned to a user will take precedence over one assigned to a group. So Alex's device will have the application installed wirelessly on the device.

Scenario seven

SC1 and SC2 are assigned to the Research Team, the wireless settings will take precedence over the wired settings when the applications are both the same. So Alex's device will have the application installed wirelessly over the air.

Scenario eight

Finally, there are reconciliation rules for when multiple software configurations are created, and the device is running out or is low on memory. The reconciliation takes place as follows:

- Required applications for wireless deployment are installed first
- Then required applications for wired deployment are installed next
- Then optional applications for wireless deployment are installed
- Finally, optional applications for wired deployment are installed

In Lab 5, we will be looking at reconciliation rules for BlackBerry device software and the options available for application control policies when deploying device software.

Lab 5

In this lab, we are going to look at deploying device software to BlackBerry handhelds. Throughout this chapter, so far we have had a look at the settings and options revolving around software deployment. To finish off this section, we are going to revisit some of the settings mentioned in the chapter so far before looking at device software deployment.

Changing a standard application policy

As mentioned earlier, we are going to have a look at how we can change a standard application policy. If we recall from an earlier section, when we add a Java application to a software configuration, we have to apply an application control policy. We have the standard default ones provided by the BES or we can edit them to suit our needs. Our organizational policy states that when using the standard required application control policy, we need to make sure that the applications can resolve our internal domains, this can be achieved by the following:

1. Expand **Software applications**.
2. Select **Manage default application policies**.
3. Select the policy we want to edit. For this example we will edit the **Standard Required policy** by selecting it.
4. Click on **Edit application control policy**.
5. Select the **Access settings** tab.
6. Under the section **List of internal domains**, populate the internal domain names.

Creating a custom application control policy

We also have the option of creating a custom application control policy for a Java application that we want to deploy.

> We need to make sure that we create this custom application control policy before we add the application to a software configuration.

Software Configuration and Java Applications

As mentioned before, if we choose to create multiple custom application control policies, we must apply priorities to the policies, so if there is a conflict it can be resolved. To create a custom application control policy, follow these steps:

1. Expand **Software applications**.
2. Select **Manage applications**.
3. Search for the Java application that we want to create a custom application control policy for—for our example we can select the **Smart View** application.
4. Select the application version for which we want this policy for.
5. Click on **Edit application**.
6. Select the **Applications control policies** tab.
7. Radio box to **Use custom application control policies**.
8. We can then create a custom application control policy for the three options:
    - Required
    - Optional
    - Disallowed
9. Choose the policy type and enter a name and select the custom settings—as shown next, we have created a custom required policy.

Assigning the software configuration to a group

As mentioned earlier in the *Assigning the software configuration to a user* section, we can also assign the software configuration to a group. We will be assigning the software configuration that we created earlier to the Sales Team group as shown next:

1. Expand **Groups**.
2. Select **Manage groups** and click on the **Sales Team** group.
3. Select **Edit group**.
4. Select the **Software configurations** tab.
5. Select the **Smart View** software configuration and click on **Add**.
6. Select **Save all**.

We can now move on to deploying device software to our BlackBerry handhelds.

Deploying device software to BlackBerry devices

In this section, we are going to look at the methods available to deploy device software to BlackBerry handhelds. This can be achieved by any of the following methods, each having pros and cons.

Using Desktop Manager

Using the application loader tool within Desktop Manager, users can update their device software. The device software needs to be downloaded from the provider's website and extracted into a network share folder that is available to the users. If you use this method, you need to bear in mind the following points:

- Users must have the BlackBerry Desktop Manager software installed on their PC
- We cannot use software configurations to manage deployment, so we cannot make device software update mandatory
- Also, network traffic will be increased

Using Web Desktop Manager

As before, we would need to download the software and extract it to a network share. This time round, we need to create a software configuration so that we can distribute the device software to BlackBerry device software users. When using this method, you need to bear in mind the following:

- We can use software configurations and application policies to control the update of device software
- Users do not require the BlackBerry Desktop Manager software installed
- Can increase network traffic to the share

Updating the BlackBerry device software over the wireless network

We would need to create a software configuration and send a required BlackBerry device software update to a user. Once the user receives the update, he or she has the option of carrying out the update immediately or can defer the process for up to 72 hours.

Software Configuration and Java Applications

> When using this method the BlackBerry device must have 16 MB of RAM and at least 64 MB of flash memory available to start the upgrade process. The device will try to free up memory if the above values are not met by deleting cached data, applications, and old message lists. Also the battery level of the device must be 50 percent or greater for the device to retrieve the software update package.

Deploying device software using Web Desktop Manager—an example

For the purpose of this lab, we will be looking at deploying the device software using the Web Desktop method. In our organization, we have BlackBerry Curve 8900 devices. We have a strict security policy in place, which states the devices software must be current and up-to-date at all times. Our policy states that device software updates will be carried out using Web Desktop Manager. Also, when the device software upgrade is carried out, we must ensure that the setting for hide sent e-mail messages is still enforced. To accomplish this, we need to carry out the following steps and stages.

For each different BlackBerry that connects to your BES, you will need to download the corresponding BlackBerry software and create a software configuration for each BlackBerry Smartphone.

> In our example, we only have BlackBerry 8900 Curve, so we will be creating just the single software configuration.

Installing the BlackBerry device software

Firstly, we need to download and install the latest device software versions for all the BlackBerry devices in our BES environment. These can be downloaded from your providers' website. Once we have obtained the device software, we need to install it on a server that all the users can reach. For the purpose of this lab, we will install the device software on our BES server.

1. Copy the BlackBerry device software on to the server.
2. Double-click the `.exe` setup file.

Chapter 5

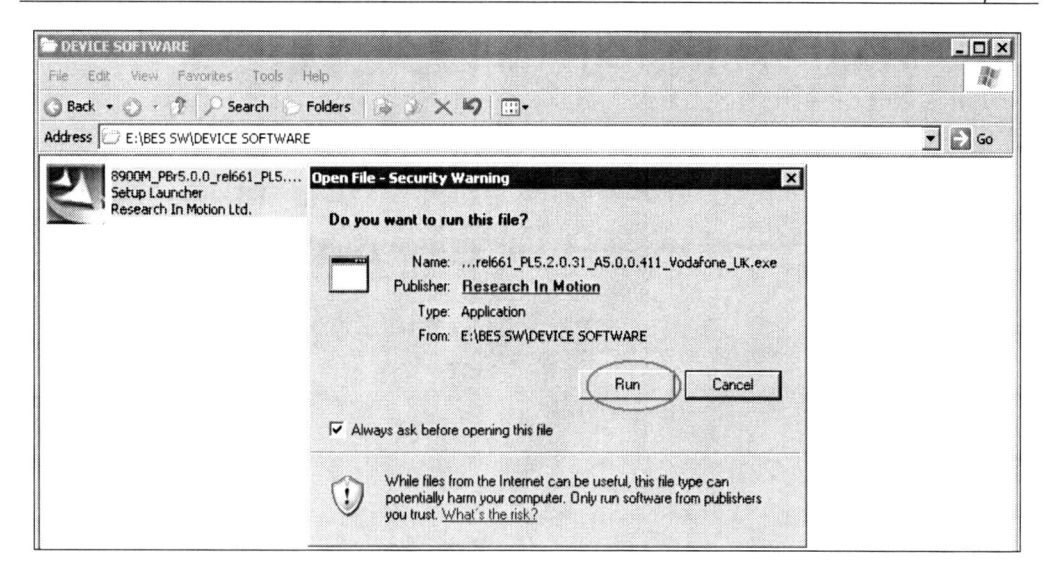

3. Select the appropriate language.

4. Select the appropriate region, click **Next**, accept the license agreement and click **Next**.
5. When prompted, do not place a tick in the start the application loader tool.

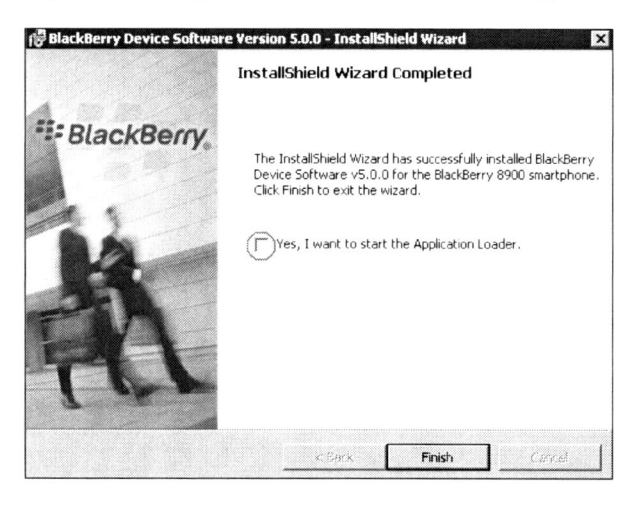

[149]

Creating the shared folder

Next, we need to create the shared folder (as we did previously) as follows:

1. Browse to the following folder on the server where we have installed the device software: `C:\Program Files\Common Files\Research In Motion`.

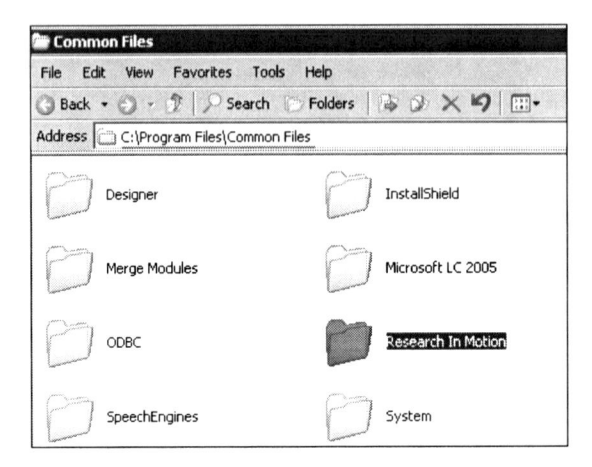

2. Right-click the folder and select the **Sharing** tab, share the folder and accept the default share name. Select the **Security** tab and add the account that is running the BlackBerry Administration Service — Application Server service — and assign the **Full Control** to that account.

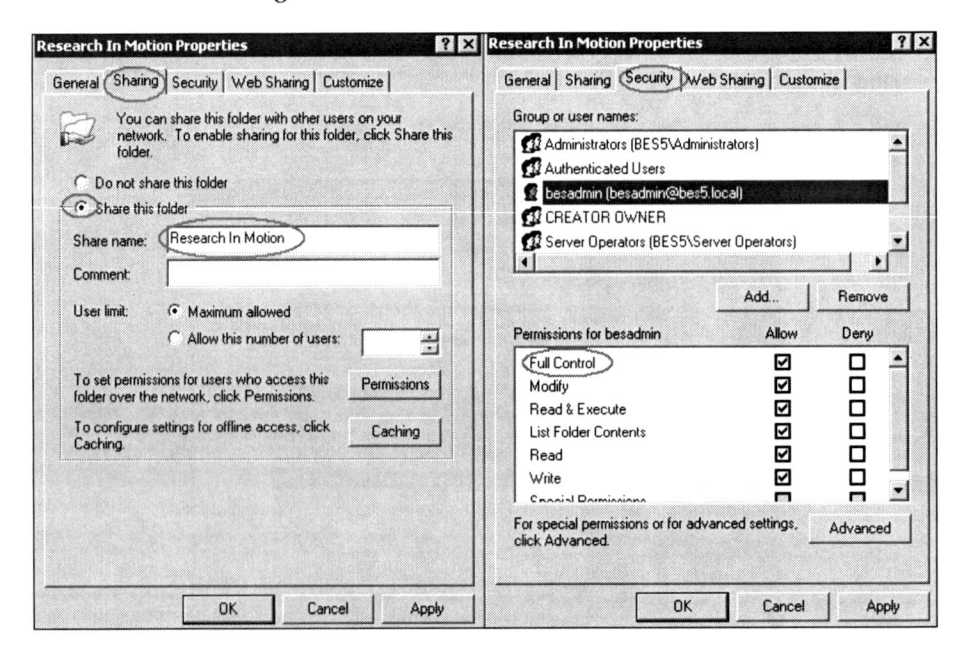

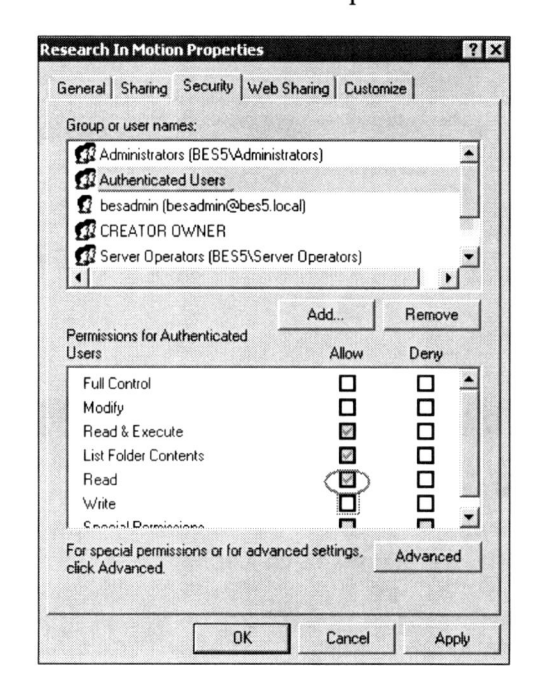

3. Ensure that all network users have **Read** permission to this folder.

Allowing the BlackBerry Administration Service to display the device software configuration settings

Next, we need our BlackBerry Administration Service to allow us to create a BlackBerry device software configuration. By default this is not enabled on the BlackBerry Administration Service. It should be noted that once we enable this option the following changes are made to the IT policy rules:

- The Allow Non Enterprise Upgrade IT Policy rule changes to NO
- The Disallow Device User Requested Upgrade IT Policy rule changes to YES
- The Disallow Device User Requested Rollback IT Policy rule changes to YES

To display the BlackBerry device software pages, carry out the following:

1. Under **Servers and components** menu expand **BlackBerry Solution topology**. Select **BlackBerry Domain**, **Component view** and select **BlackBerry Administration Service**.
2. Click on **Edit component**.

Software Configuration and Java Applications

3. In the **Software management** section, where it states **Blackberry Device Software deployment managed by BlackBerry Administration Service** drop-down, select **Yes**.

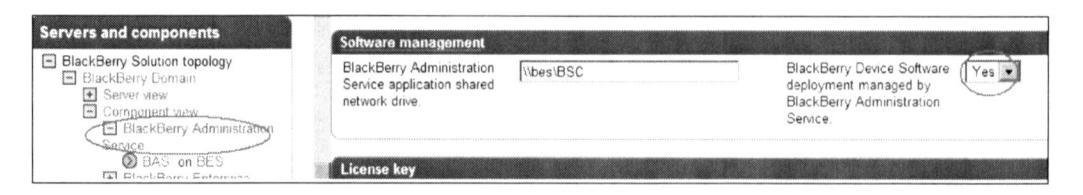

4. Select **Save all**.

Adding the shared folder to the BlackBerry Administration Service

We now have to add our shared folder to the BlackBerry Administration Service, so it can find the device software that we have just installed. To do this carry out the following steps:

1. Expand **Software**.
2. Select **BlackBerry Device Software**.
3. Click on **Add shared network drive**.
4. Populate the fields as shown in the following screenshot, remembering that the network path must be referenced as a UNC.

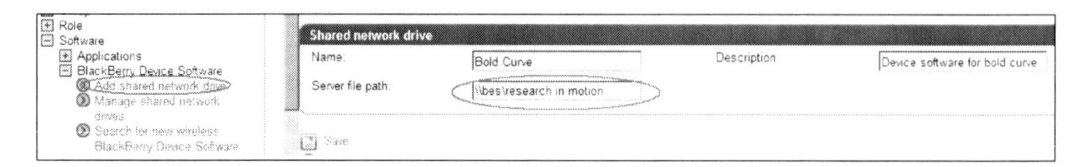

We now need the BlackBerry Administration Service to find the device software. This is achieved by carrying out the following steps:

1. Expand **Software**, then **BlackBerry Device Software**, and click on **Manage shared network drives**.
2. Click on the shared folder that we just created.

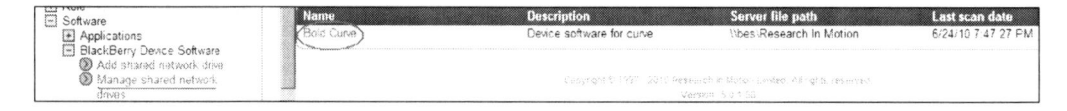

[152]

3. Select **Execute shared network drive scan**.

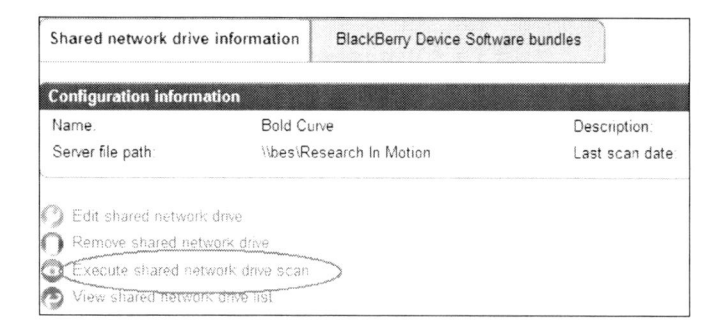

The preceding procedure will make the BlackBerry Administration Service aware of all the BlackBerry device software bundles that we have created. In this lab example, we have only downloaded one device software. If your organization runs different devices, then you must download the device software for all devices and prepare the software bundles for each version, as we have done before. To verify that the BlackBerry Administration Service has found all of the software bundles that we have installed, we can click on the BlackBerry Device Software bundles tab and see a list of the device software bundles. Once the scan is finished, a message will be displayed, as shown in the following screenshot:

Creating the BlackBerry device software configuration

We are now ready to create a BlackBerry device software configuration; this will include the device software and will allow us to distribute it to users.

1. Expand **Software** and then **BlackBerry Device Software**.

2. Click on **Create BlackBerry Device Software configuration** and enter a name for the software configuration and click on **Save**.

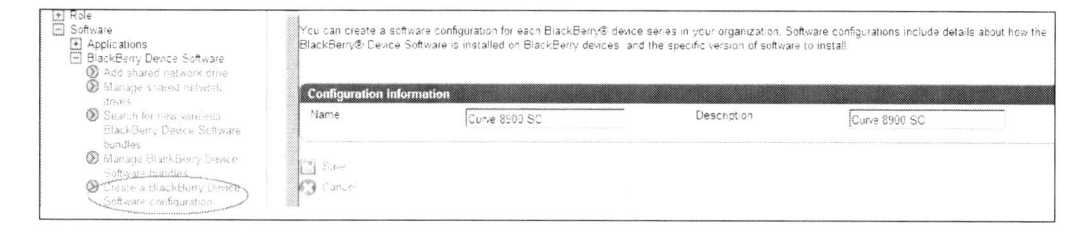

Software Configuration and Java Applications

3. Within the configuration data section, click on the software configuration that we just created.

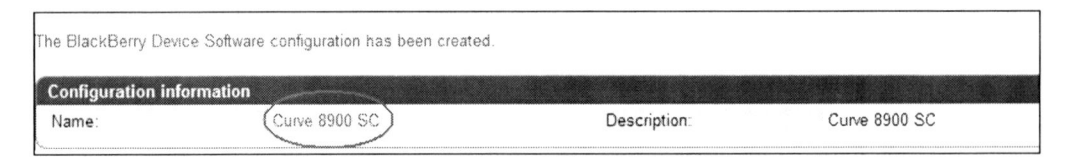

4. Click on **Edit BlackBerry Device Software configuration**.

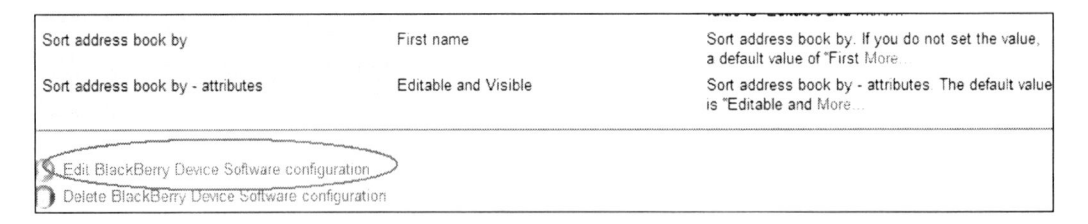

5. Within the **Native application settings**, we can make sure that the rule in our policy — **Hide sent email messages** — is enforced. We can also make any other changes to suite our organization needs.

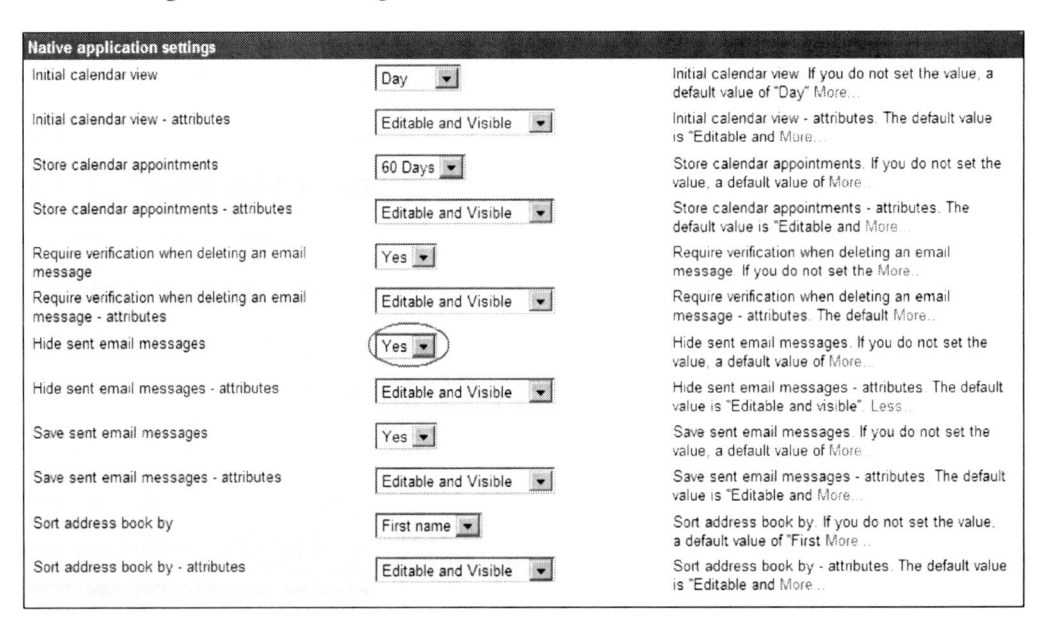

[154]

6. Once we have made the change, click on the **BlackBerry Device Software bundles** tab, and select **Add BlackBerry Device Software bundles to BlackBerry Device Software configuration**.

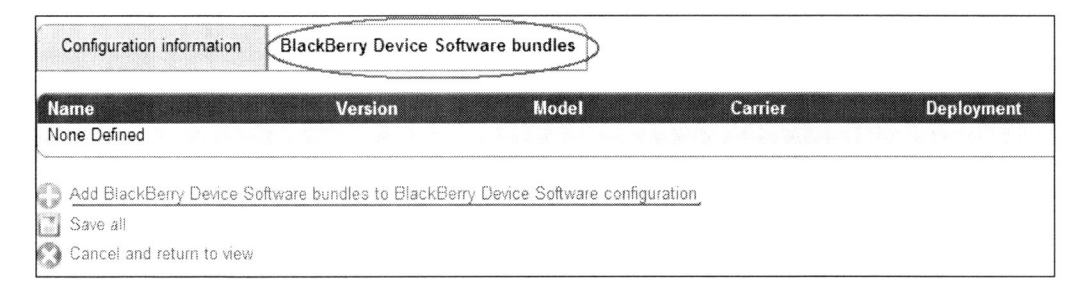

7. Search for the software configuration that we have just created. Select the configuration, click on **Add to BlackBerry Device Software configuration**, and then click on **Save all**.

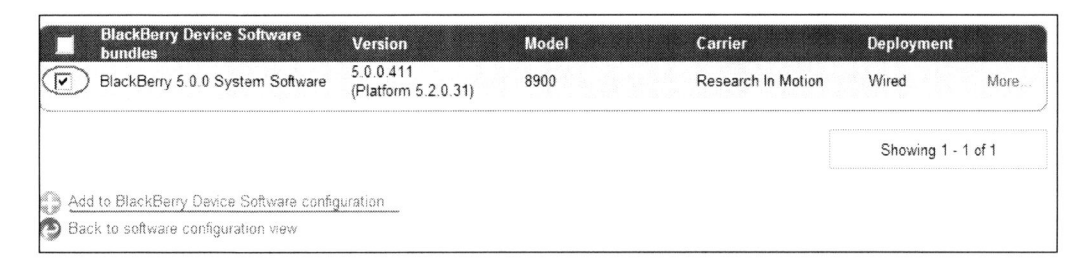

Now we need to create a software configuration that will house the software configuration for the BlackBerry device software that we have just created. This will let us distribute the software to all users in our organization.

Creating a software configuration for the BlackBerry device software

1. Expand **Software**.
2. Click on **Create a software configuration**.

Software Configuration and Java Applications

3. Type a name for the software configuration, for **Disposition for unlisted applications.** We are going to choose **Disallowed** as we only want users to install the device software and nothing else. We will also use the default application control policy — **Standard Unlisted Disallowed**.

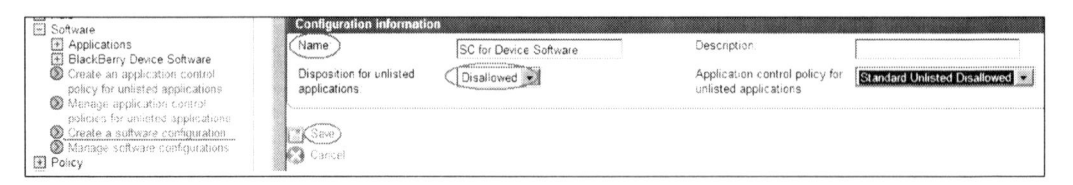

4. Click on **Save**.
5. Under the **Configuration information**, click on the software configuration that we have just created.

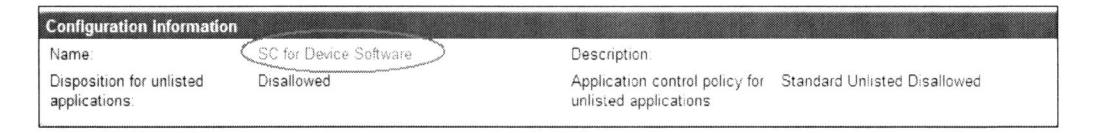

6. Click on **Edit software configuration**.
7. In the **BlackBerry Device Software configuration** section, click on the drop-down and select the BlackBerry device software configuration that we have created earlier — **Curve 8900 SC**.

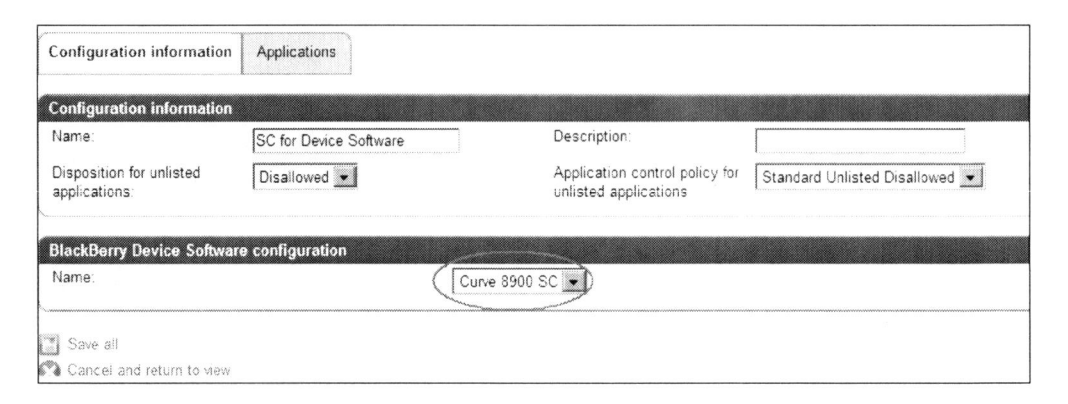

8. Click on **Save all**.

We now have a software configuration that houses the BlackBerry device software configuration that is ready to be assigned to users or groups.

Assigning the software configuration to a user

1. Click on **Manage users**.
2. Select the user we want to apply the software configuration to. For our example we will choose **Mark Ross**.
3. Select **Edit user**.
4. On the **Software configuration** tab, in the available software configurations list, click on the **SC for Device Software** and select **Add**.

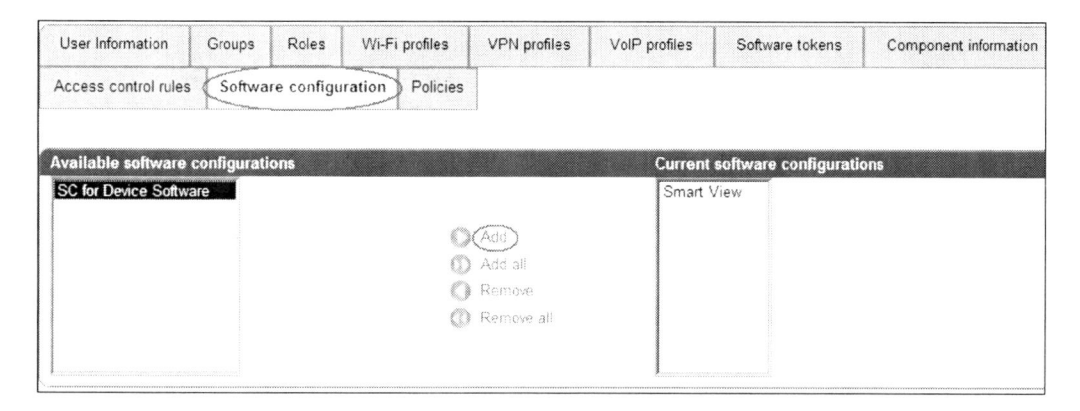

5. Click on **Save all**.

Assigning the software configuration to a group

1. Click on **Manage groups**.
2. Select the **Sales group**.
3. Click on **Edit group**.
4. On the **Software configuration** tab, in the available software configurations list, click on the **Curve 8900 SC** and select **Add**.
5. Click on **Save all**.

So, now that we have assigned the software configuration to a user or group, when they connect their BlackBerry devices to the Web Desktop Manager they will be prompted to upgrade the device software.

Summary

In this chapter, we have looked at creating software configurations, so we can roll out Java-based applications to the BlackBerry devices in our environment and still maintain tight control over the applications by using and deploying application control policies. We also had a look at creating software configurations that enabled us to deploy device software updates to our BlackBerry devices. In the next chapter, we are going to have a look at MDS runtime applications and how these are published and distributed to BlackBerry devices within our BES environment.

MDS Applications

In this chapter, we are going to have a look at **MDS** (**Mobile Data Service**) runtime applications. These are custom applications that are developed for your organizational needs. MDS runtime applications are created using BlackBerry MDS Studio or Microsoft Visual Studio—a BlackBerry plugin. In general, these applications are form-based applications that users can use on their device to access databases or web services based inside your organization's firewall—the corporate LAN.

For the purpose of this chapter you can download a sample MDS application from the BlackBerry website under the development section, current link is: `http://us.blackberry.com/developers/javaappdev/devtools.jsp`. This application is an Expenses Tracker, which an employee can populate in real time from his device as business expenses occur during a trip. Once the trip is complete, the application e-mails your finance department and attaches an Excel spreadsheet outlining the employee's business trip expenses. This chapter will show you how to distribute an MDS application to a BlackBerry device.

> This chapter will act as a lab in itself, so there will be no lab at the end of this chapter.

Understanding and setting up our MDS environment

The MDS has two component services:

- **MDS Connection Service**: This service provides access to content on the Internet, intranet, and access to the organization's application servers
- **MDS Integration Service**: This service facilitates installation and management of applications and allows access to the server system in your corporate LAN via database connections or web services

MDS Applications

Firstly, we need to set up our MDS environment. This includes the following:

- Ensure that the BlackBerry MDS integration Service is installed and running on our BlackBerry Enterprise Server.
- This service should have been selected during the initial installation of the BES; if it was not selected we can run the setup and install the MDS services. If the MDS service is already installed, you will see the services running in the Windows server.
- Send the BlackBerry MDS Runtime platform to devices in our BlackBerry domain.
- This can be achieved by using Software Configuration policies, as shown next:
    - Publish the BlackBerry MDS application
    - This will be done using the MDS console that is installed during the installation of MDS services
    - Configure our IT policy and any application control policies for the MDS application
    - Using IT policies and application policies we can lock down our MDS application
    - Install the MDS application on the devices
    - Using the MDS console and the application repository for MDS applications, we can deploy and install the MDS applications on the devices

Each of the preceding sections will now be looked at in greater detail.

Running MDS services

During the installation of our BlackBerry Enterprise Server in *Chapter 1, Introduction to BES 5*, we chose to install the MDS components. We need to ensure that the MDS service is running in our environment. This can be checked by going to services on the server that hosts the BlackBerry Enterprise Server and ensuring that the **BlackBerry MDS Connection Service** and **BlackBerry MDS Integration Service** are started, as shown in the following screenshot:

| BlackBerry MDS Connection Service | Provides s... | Started | Automatic | BES5\bes... |
| BlackBerry MDS Integration Service | Provides m... | Started | Automatic | BES5\bes... |

[160]

Installing MDS runtime platform

For MDS runtime applications to work, we need to ensure that the MDS runtime platform is installed on to devices in our corporate network. The version of MDS runtime platform that you need to install on to the devices will depend on the following:

- Model of the device
- BlackBerry software version on the device

So, depending on the different devices and the different BlackBerry device software running on the devices, you might need to create several MDS runtime software configuration packages to cover the different models and device software within your corporate environment.

As in the previous chapter, we can use a software configuration to deploy the MDS runtime platform that is needed on the devices. For the purpose of this lab, we are going to assume all our devices are the same make and have the same device software: BlackBerries 8900.

Creating a software configuration to deploy the MDS runtime platform to devices

1. Download the appropriate MDS runtime platform for your device from the BlackBerry website-the current link is: https://www.blackberry.com/Downloads/entry.do?code=F9BE311E65D81A9AD8150A60844BB94C. For our example, we are going to download the MDS runtime package for a BlackBerry 8900 device, which is entitled BlackBerry MDS runtime v4.6.1.21.

2. Extract the contents to a shared folder on the BES server.

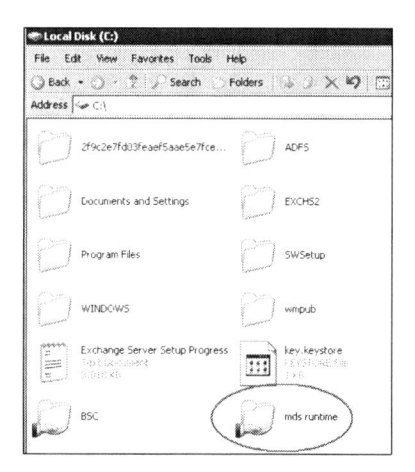

MDS Applications

3. Log in to the BlackBerry Administration Service.
4. Under **BlackBerry solution management** expand **Software** then **Applications** and click on **Add or update applications**.

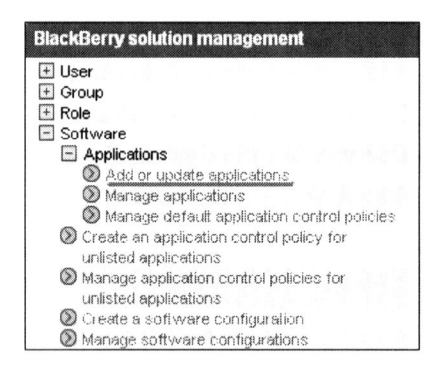

5. Browse to the ZIP files for the MDS runtime application, and once selected click **Next**.

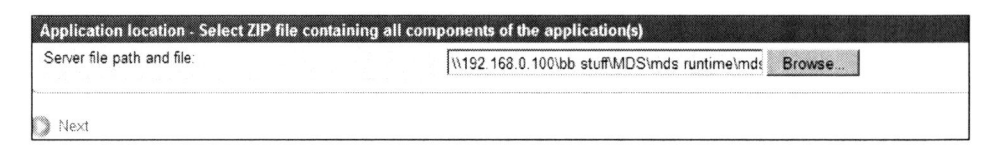

6. Select to publish the application.
7. To ensure the correct packages were created browse to the BSC share created in *Chapter 5*, *Software Configuration and Java Applications* and ensure the following files are present:

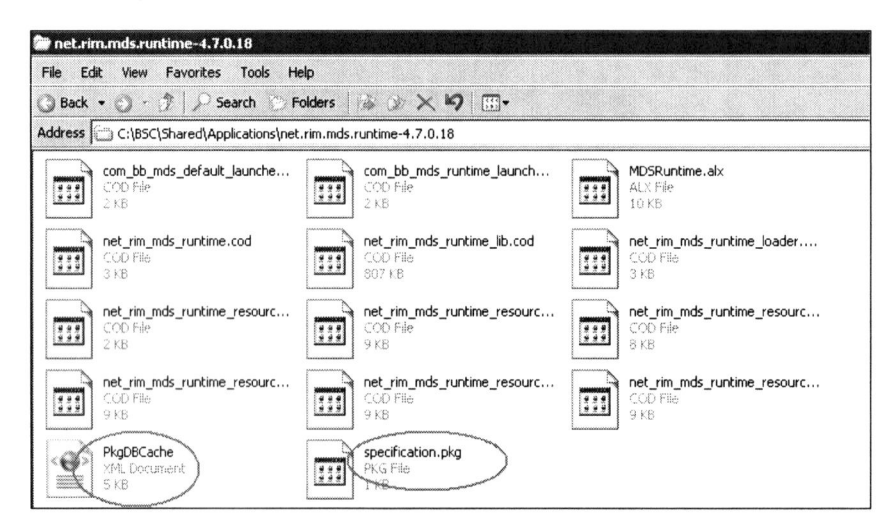

8. We now need to create our software configuration (if you recall from *Chapter 5, Software Configuration and Java Applications*, the preceding steps have just added the MDS runtime application to the application repository only). Select **Create a software configuration**.

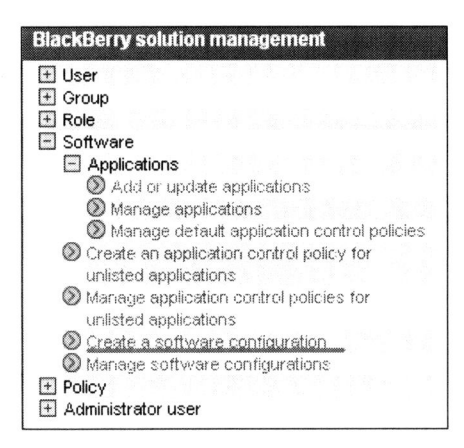

9. Enter the name Runtime, and leave the other settings as default.

10. Click on **Manage software configurations** and select **Runtime**.

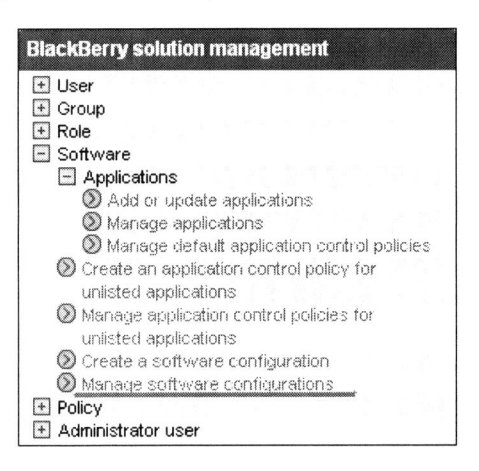

MDS Applications

11. Select the **Applications** tab and click on **Edit software configuration**, as shown in the following screenshot:

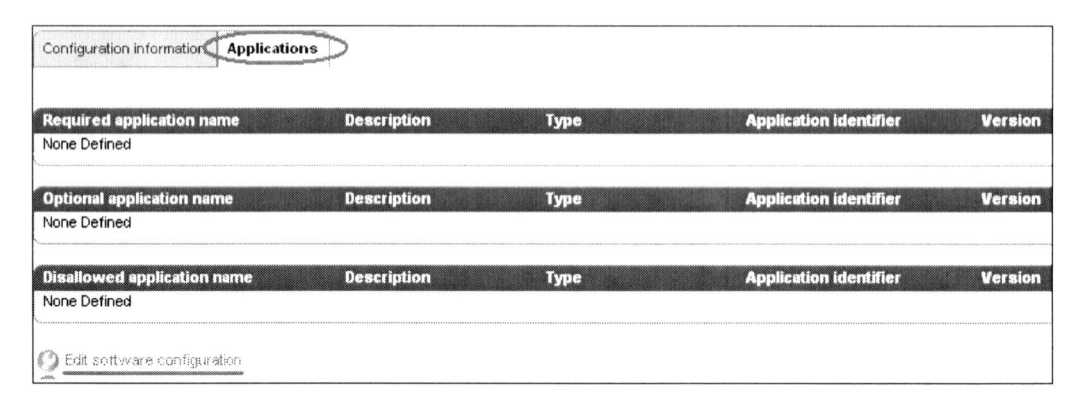

12. Click on **Add applications to software configuration**.

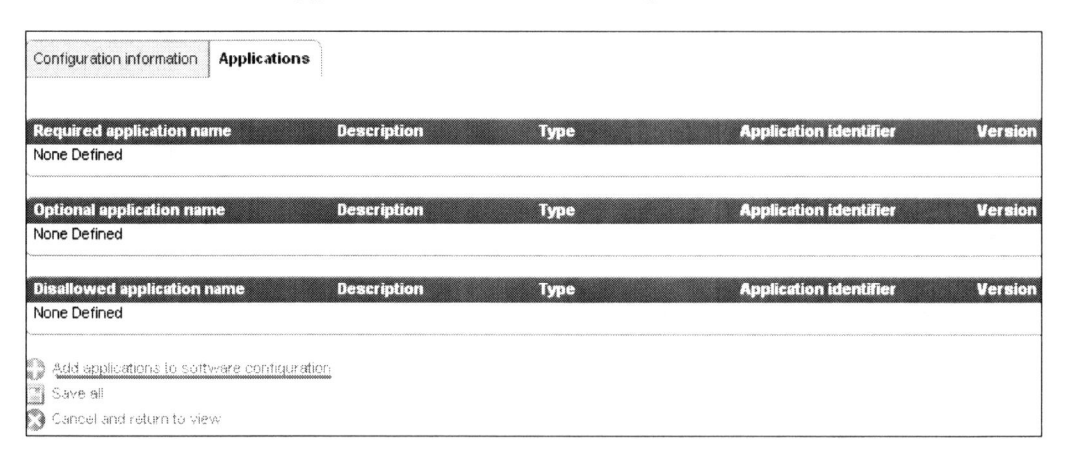

13. Click on **Search** or fill in the search criteria to display the Runtime packages. Select the Runtime applications (in some cases two applications may have been created; select both, one is the default launcher and one is the runtime platform, this is dependant on the device). In our example, we need both the **MDS Runtime** and the **MDS Default Launcher**, so we need to place a tick in both to show additional configuration steps, as shown in the following screenshot:

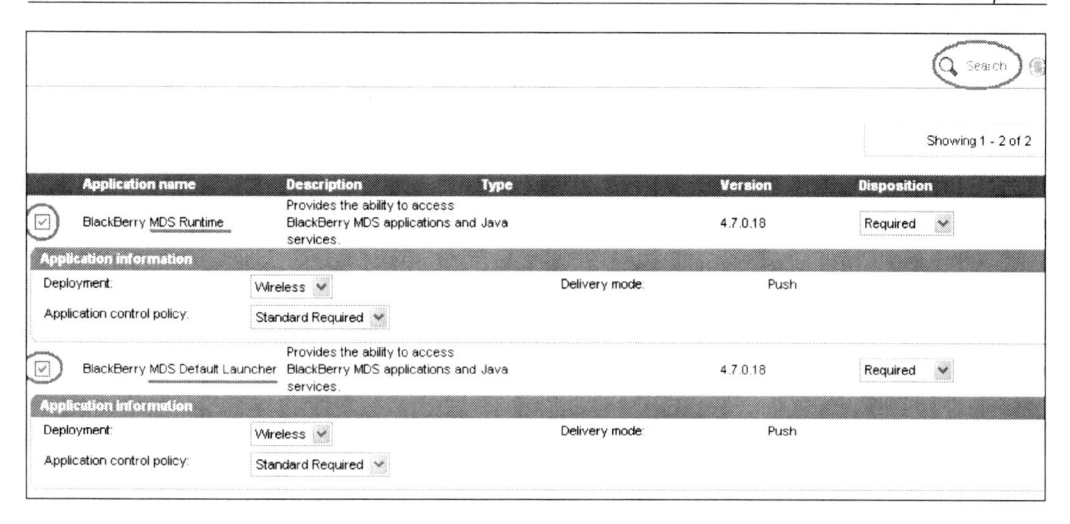

14. Select **Wireless** as the **Deployment** method and the **Standard Required** for the **Application control policy**, and **Required** for the **Disposition** setting.

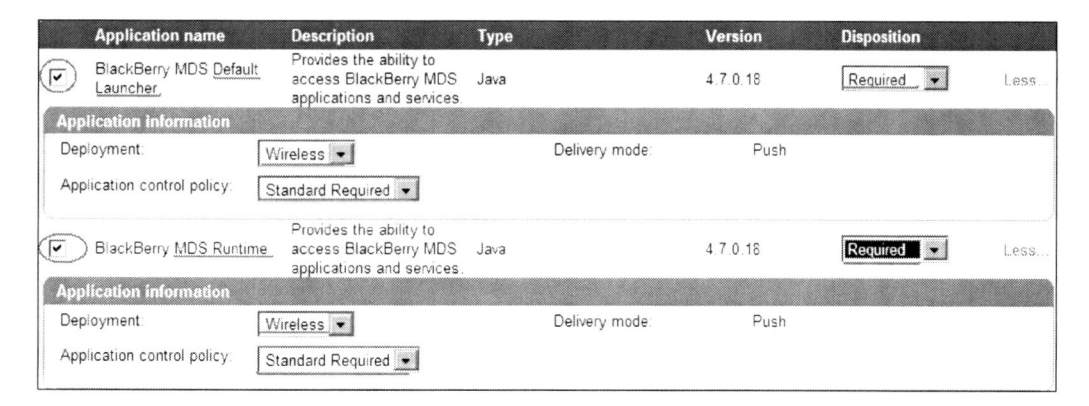

15. Once added, click on **Save all**.
16. We now need to assign this software configuration to the devices in our BES environment. For the purpose of this lab, we are going to assign it to the Sales Group.

> Please bear in mind that—as mentioned before—if you have different devices or same devices but with different device software operating on them then you will need to download the right MDS runtime platform for each scenario and configure the appropriate number of software configurations.

17. Click on **Manage groups**.

MDS Applications

18. Select the **Sales Team**.

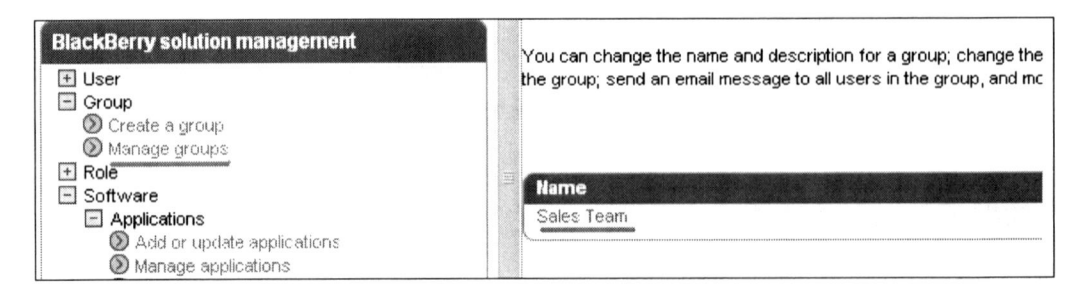

19. Click on **Edit group**.

20. Select the **Software configuration** tab. In the **Available software configurations** list, click on **Runtime** and select **Add**, as shown in the following screenshot:

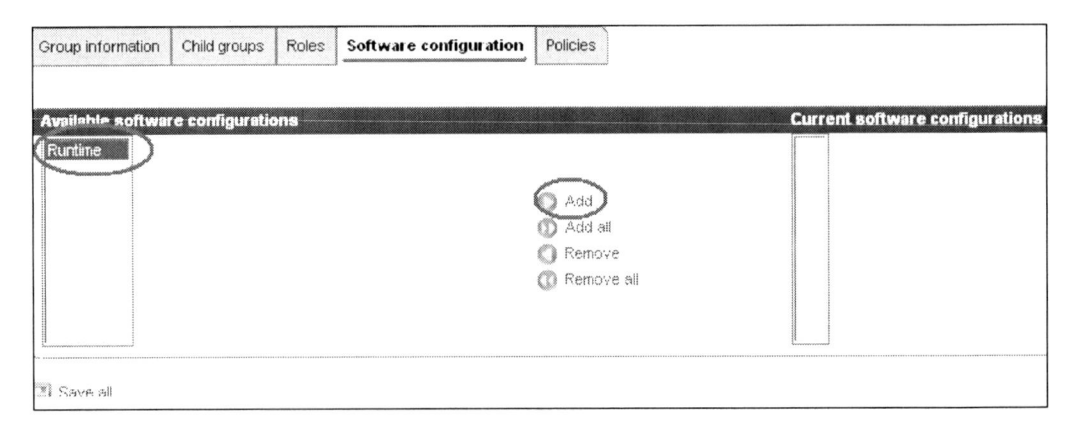

21. Click on **Save all**.

Now that our devices are ready to run MDS applications we need to add our MDS application to the MDS application repository. The MDS application repository is installed by default during the initial installation of the BES as long as we choose to install all default components of MDS. The MDS application console is a web-based administration tool, like the BlackBerry Administration Service, which is used to control, install, manage, and update MDS applications.

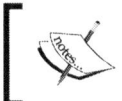

> Please note that you use the BlackBerry Administration Service to control Java-based applications and you use the MDS console to administer MDS applications.

Logging in to the MDS console

The console was created during the installation of the MDS Integration Service. We can log in to it using the details we specified during installation in *Chapter 1, Introduction to BES 5*.

1. Open up an Internet Browser.
2. Type the FQDN of the server that hosts the BlackBerry Administration Service followed by the subdirectories listed next. For example, `https://bes.bes5.local/mdsisconsole/app`.
3. In the **MDS-IS Host** drop-down list, select our MDS-IS instance, and type in the user name and password created during the installation process.

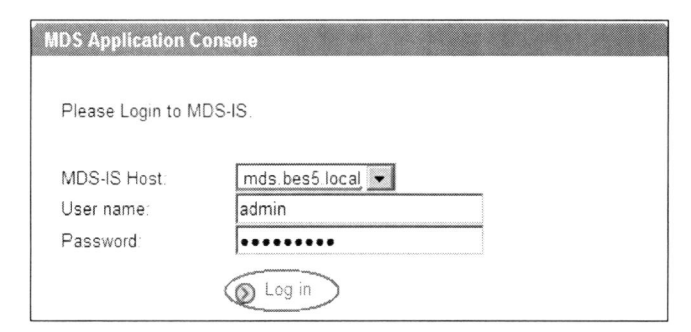

Now that we have logged into our MDS console, we can add the MDS application to the MDS application repository.

MDS Applications

> If you get an error while logging in stating "*unable to connect to MDS services*", ensure that your internal DNS has an A host record pointing to the MDS-IS service. In our example, we would need an A record created in internal DNS that points *mds* to the *ip* address of our BES server. Then restart the MDS-IS service.

Adding an MDS application (Expense Tracker) to the MDS repository

1. Within the MDS console under the **MDS Application management** menu, click on **Publish Application**.

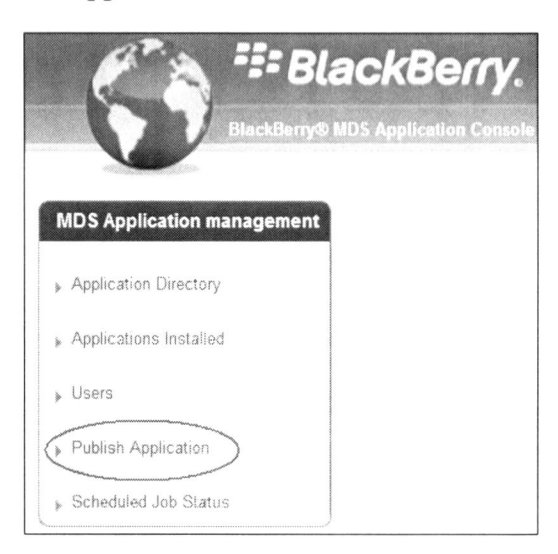

2. In the **Upload application bundle** section, browse to the Expense Tracker ZIP file (the one downloaded from the link in the introduction of this chapter).

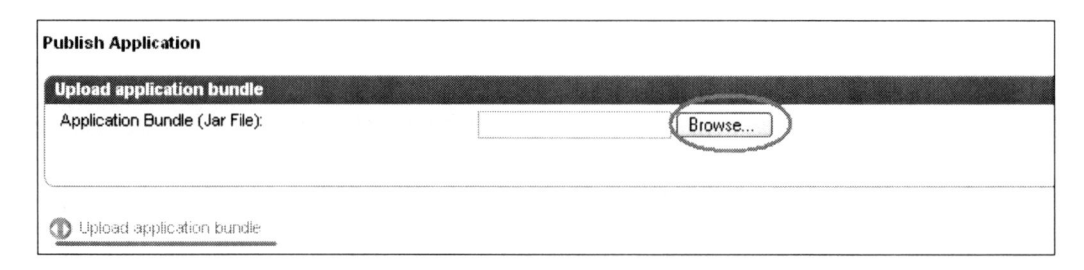

3. Click on **Upload application bundle** and then click on the **Update application bundle** link again.

We have now added the Expense Tracker to the MDS application repository using the MDS console. Please note that the MDS sample application that we downloaded was already primed for publication. If you are developing your own MDS application, please make sure that you have taken the appropriate steps to make the application publishable.

We now need to look at sending this MDS application to our users' devices.

Sending the Expense Tracker MDS application to BlackBerry devices

We can send the MDS application to BlackBerry devices over the air. Users will then use the BlackBerry MDS control centre on their BlackBerry device to search the MDS application repository and find the Expense Tracker application. This will enable them to then go ahead and install the application. The MDS control centre is available on the BlackBerry device once the MDS runtime platform has been installed and activated on the device.

1. Log into the MDS console.
2. On the **MDS Application management** menu, click **Application Directory**.
3. Browse for the Expense Tracker application.
4. Click on the install icon. We now have the following options:
    - We can install the application based on groups, and using the drop-down we can select an existing group that we want to install the MDS application to.
    - We can install the application based on BlackBerry PIN numbers. Select the PINs option and we can import a list of PINs from the BlackBerry Administration Service or we can type the PINs in separating each PIN by a semi colon (;).
    - We can install the application on BlackBerry devices based on usernames. Select the users option, and as mentioned earlier we can either export the users or type them individually.
5. We are going to use the group option and select the **Sales Group**.
6. We can then choose some scheduling options:
    - We can specify the date and time we want the application to be installed.

- We can specify how many devices at one time the application install request will be sent to the default setting; the default setting is 10 at a time and is configured under the group setting.
- The push interval allows us to set the interval at which the MDS Integration Service tries to send the application to devices; the default value is 5 minutes.

7. Click **Install** to proceed.

We can check to see if the process was completed successfully by viewing the scheduled job status in the MDS console under the MDS Application management.

So using the MDS console, we have successfully deployed the MDS Expense Tracker application to all the devices within the Sales Group.

You should now be able to go to a device that belongs to the Sales Group and see the MDS Expense Tracker application functioning on their device.

Configuring IT policies with respect to MDS applications

We have settings available in our IT policy with regards to MDS applications; these can be configured to provide tighter control of the applications.

As with Java-based software, we can apply application control policies to our MDS applications. This feature is outside the scope of this book but further information can be found at http://www.blackberry.com/developers/.

Summary

In this chapter, we had a look at the MDS applications that can be deployed to the BlackBerry Smartphone. MDS enables the BlackBerry to truly become a Smartphone by allowing administrators to deploy critical applications to the Smartphone. As we saw in this chapter, we can custom develop applications to run on the BlackBerries or use third-party applications to push on to the devices. We can then further secure the application usage on the device by using IT policies.

We were able to carry out the above tasks by using the MDS console, and downloading the appropriate MDS runtime packages for our devices.

In the next chapter, we will be looking at providing High Availability to our BES system to ensure we have continual service in case of a disaster.

7
High Availability

BES version 5 offers **high availability (HA)** straight out of the box. Unlike all previous versions where disaster recovery was offered as an active-passive model with a manual intervention, BES 5 offers this feature as a standard. In the previous versions, this meant that we would have to configure a standby server, which would usually mean an additional BlackBerry Server license, and at the time of failure, users would need to be issued with new service books if the SRP ID changed. In this chapter, we are going to have a look at the vast improvements made in this area with BES version 5, starting with how high availability is offered straight out of the box without any additional licensing issues. You would still need an additional server to run the standby BlackBerry Server.

Understanding high availability

The first improvement is that the manual intervention when a failure occurs has been removed.

With BES version 5 there is an automatic failover between BES instances (actually BES Servers) and BES components (individual services running, as seen in *Chapter 1, Introduction to BES 5*). Instead of the old model of active-passive, the new one is a primary standby, where the instances exchange health scores to ensure components are running at an optimal level. There is still the option to force a manual failover for maintenance tasks. No longer do we need to worry that the SRP ID will be locked out (this occurs if two instances of a BES join the RIM network with the same SRP ID), this is avoided when running the BES in high availability mode. We can also use the primary-standby architecture to aid in limited downtime for upgrades, such as applying MR releases. The key about this architecture is that no additional BlackBerry Server license is needed for the standby server.

Understanding how it works

The primary BES would have all live connections and communications with the organization's mail servers, the RIM network and the local BES configuration database. The standby server would have a live connection to the BES configuration database, and a warm connection to the mail server, and no connectivity to the RIM network.

The primary BES running all the services with live connections fails the dispatcher component in the standby BES, identifies the failure, and automatically begins the failover process. The standby BES will then try to establish a connection to the `SRP.xx.blackberry.net` (where xx is the country location). The standby server now becomes the primary server and verifies it as the only BES with the SRP connection and creates an active connection. Once online, the original primary BES server becomes the standby server and attempts to make a live connection to the database server and a warm connection to the mail servers.

The primary standby model works on health scores; these are calculated for each BES component and shared as a heartbeat between the two instances.

The threshold values for scores of each component are configured once on the primary server (these are known as failover thresholds) and on the standby server (these are known as promotion thresholds). Scores above these threshold values would trigger a failover or promotion.

A default threshold score is configured for each component. There is room for an administrator to change the default health scores, which trigger a failover or promotion; this is shown later on in the chapter.

> It should also be noted that the BlackBerry configuration database is a vital component to high availability of your BES server; therefore, if it is housed on an SQL server, I would strongly recommend setting up mirroring of the database, which is now a certified option with RIM.

Configuring high availability

1. On a new server extract the BlackBerry Enterprise media.
2. Select **Install standby server**.
3. If mirroring has been set up, point the database location to the mirror database location, so if a failover of the primary database occurs, the mirror takes over.

As mentioned in the introduction of high availability, the architecture revolves around health scores being exchanged between the primary and standby server. If the value of a component's health score goes above or below the failover threshold or promotion threshold then an automatic failover is triggered.

The components send their health scores to the BlackBerry dispatcher, which in turn writes them to the configuration database. There are 17 health components or parameters that are measured; each can be set with a threshold health score from 0 to 63.

For example, let's say the default promotion threshold value for the wireless network access is 57. If the primary BES reports a health score of 20 and the standby server reports a health score of 58, then an automatic failover will occur and the standby server will initiate the process to become the primary BES. It's important to understand the following when we are setting thresholds:

- **Promotion thresholds**: These are examined when the standby instance needs to determine whether it can promote itself to the primary instance
- **Failover thresholds**: These are examined when the primary BES needs to determine whether it should demote itself or not

Let's have a look at these settings.

Examining the default threshold values and setting failovers

The following are the steps you can take to have a look at the settings mentioned previously. Again, the following steps show how you can change the default values to meet your network needs:

1. Expand **Servers and components**, then expand **High Availability**, and select **Highly available BlackBerry Enterprise Servers**.
2. Select the BlackBerry Enterprise pair.
3. Click on **Automatic Failover Settings**.
4. We can now change the order and threshold values of the 17 parameters.

In the same section, we can choose whether we want the failover to happen automatically. This can be done by selecting **Turn on automatic BlackBerry Enterprise Server failover**.

Forcing a manual failover

We also have the option to perform a manual failover—ideal for applying maintenance packs on the primary server. To force a manual failover we need to:

1. Expand **Servers and components**, then expand **High Availability**, and select **Highly available BlackBerry Enterprise Servers**.
2. Select the BlackBerry Enterprise pair.
3. Click on **Manual failover**.
4. In the list, choose the BlackBerry Enterprise instance that we want to failover to.
5. Click on **Yes**—failover to standby instance.

Introducing HA for databases

If your environment is using MS SQL Server 2005 with SP2 or later, we can introduce high availability for the database that the BES server uses by utilizing database mirroring. In principle, database mirror is run in a RAID 1 configuration and produces a copy of the databases on to a separate physical hard disk drive. If the primary hard disk drive was to fail, active connections would be made to the mirrored database automatically. In this type of RAID 1, disk mirroring provides fault tolerance to the BES infrastructure. If the database connection fails on our primary BES, it will try and open a connection to the mirrored databases. If this fails then the primary BES will lower its health score in anticipation that the standby server will now assume the role and try to open an active connection to its BES database.

Most of the components within the BES environment have some sort of feature to help with high availability by either using load balancing, DNS round-robin, (demonstrated during the installation for the BlackBerry Administration Service site) and failover with active connection to one instance and standby connections to another warm instance. There is no high availability for one of the BES components and that is the monitoring website that was created during the installation. We will be having a look at this site next.

Using the BlackBerry monitoring website

The BlackBerry monitoring service is used to monitor and troubleshoot issues with the BES and the devices that are attached to the BES. This feature works by using **SNMP (Simple Network Management Packets)** traps. Each component that is associated with the BES has SNMP enabled. The SNMP string will poll each component to retrieve monitoring data, which it will then process and record in to the BES database. This data is then projected to administrators on the Blackberry monitoring website that was created during the installation. We need to set up SNMP traps within our environment for the website to collect the data. Let's launch this site to see what type of information is produced on this site and how to configure our SNMP traps.

1. Open up a Browser.
2. Navigate to `https://fqdn:8443/webconsole/app`. Ensure you use the `8443` port.
3. Log in to the site, using the same credentials used for the BlackBerry Administration Site.
4. As you can see from the following screenshot, there are three main sections relating to configuration. Before we can make use of the monitoring website, we need to set up SNMP on our network.

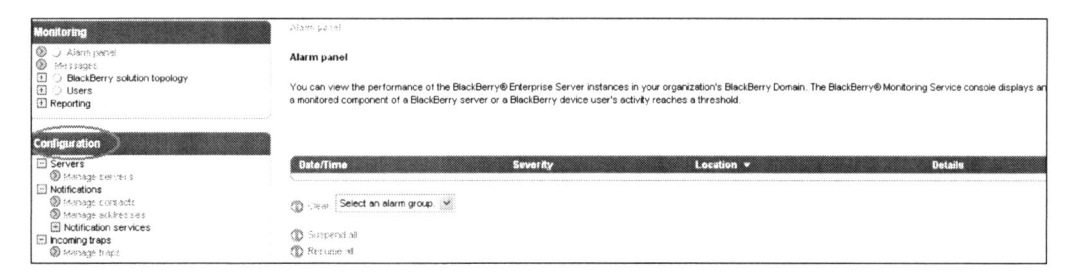

High Availability

Setting up SNMP on the BES Server

If you have a distributed component installed, then you will need to set this up on each server that has a component that you want to be monitored.

1. On the BES server, right-click on **My Computer** and select **Manage**.

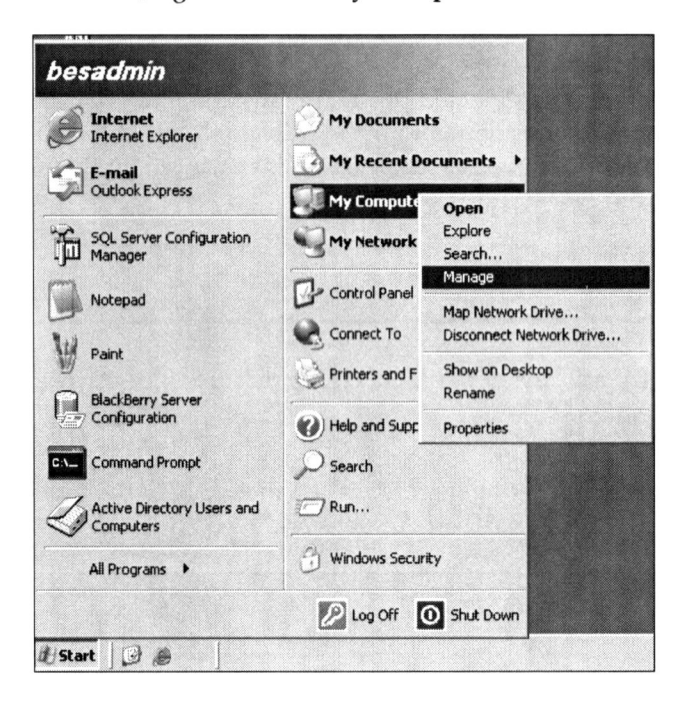

2. Expand **Services and Applications**.

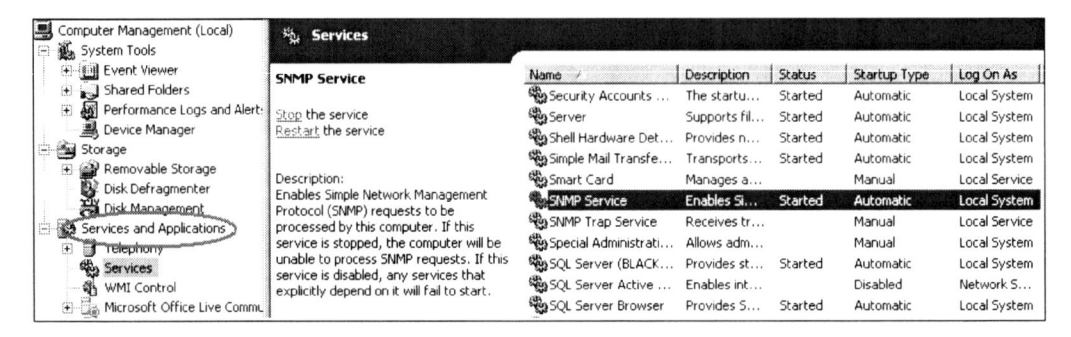

3. Click on **Services** and on the right-hand pane double-click **SNMP Service** (if the service is not present, it needs to be installed on that server via **Add Remove Windows components** under **Management and Monitoring tools**).

4. Select the **Agents** tab and ensure **Physical** is ticked.

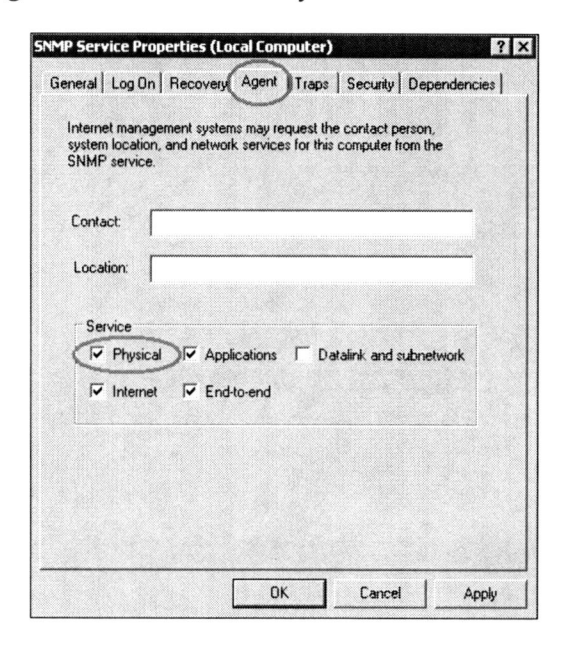

5. Select the **Traps** tab.
6. In the community name box, type `public` — this is case sensitive.

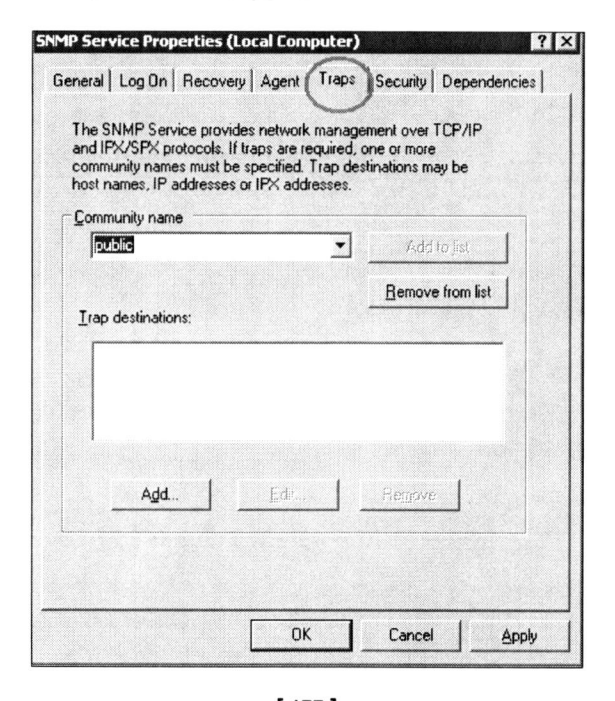

High Availability

7. Select the **Security** tab.
8. Click the **Add** button in the accepted community names.

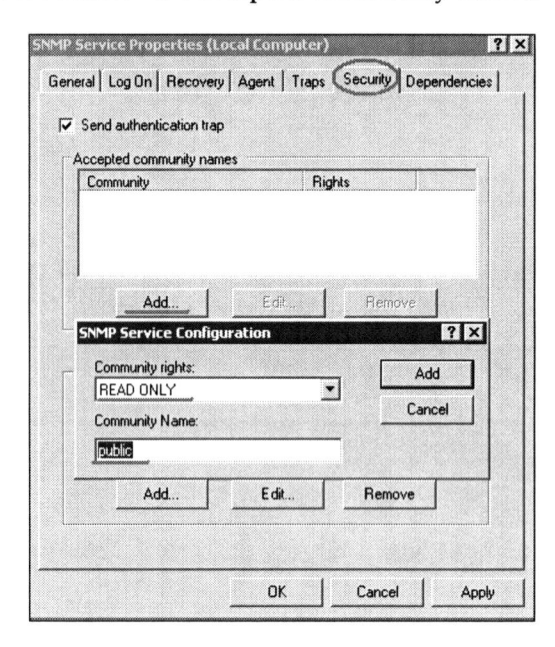

9. Select **READ ONLY**.
10. Enter `public` in the community name field. Ensure it is case sensitive as entered in step 6.
11. Click the **Add** button.
12. Ensure that default ports on the firewall are open; 161 for SNMP general messages on UDP and 162 for SNMP trap messages on UDP.

Now that we have our SNMP trap in place, we can go back to the monitoring website and populate the remaining details and activate some monitoring of BES core components.

1. Log back on to the monitoring site.
2. On the **Configuration** menu expand **Servers** and select **Manage Servers**.
3. Click on the spanner like icon next to BES server for which we want to turn SNMP monitoring on.
4. Leave the SNMP port as 161 (unless you changed it in the previous paragraph).

5. SNMP Community name is `public`.
6. Place the tick in the box to **Turn monitoring on**.
7. We can click on **Test Connection** to ensure all the services are running and that the information we entered is correct.
8. Click on **Save**.

You will now be able to use the monitoring site to run reports on the network activity of your BES infrastructure.

Summary

In this chapter, we have discussed the new features of high availability that is ready to use straight out of the BlackBerry Enterprise Server 5.0 installation. There is no additional licensing that is needed to run the high availability setup, and it can provide a useful feature when it comes to carrying out maintenance tasks on our BES servers. We also have had a look at the monitoring console that is built into the BES, which enables us to keep a close eye on the performance of our BES.

In the next chapter, we will be looking at upgrading our BES and the methods available to upgrade from previous versions of BES, including using the BES Transporter tool.

8
Upgrades

Now that you have played around with the new BES and have got accustomed to it, if you have any previous versions of BES you are properly itching to upgrade them to BES version 5. You would have noticed that there are new features and components to BES version 5. In this chapter, we are going to have a look at the process of upgrading previous versions of BES.

Upgrading from supported versions

You can upgrade to BES 5 from the following versions:

- BES 4.1 with SP3 or later.
- BES 4.0 with SP7 or later. If you have more than one BES instance in the BlackBerry domain then you will need to upgrade to BES 4.1 with SP3.

All other BlackBerry Enterprise Servers need to be upgraded to either of the preceding two versions.

Upgrading considerations

With BES version 5, high availability is available straight out of the box, so we need to consider the previous disaster recovery plans that you may already be running. Best practice is to upgrade any other BES server to support standby high-availability configuration.

With regards to the BlackBerry configuration database, most administrators would have been replicating the database to provide redundancy. With BES 5, the option of mirroring the Microsoft SQL database is supported straight out of the box, and this can replace replication of the database. If your organization needs to keep the replication going, it needs to be turned off during the upgrade process and then manually reconfigured.

Replacing the BlackBerry manager

During the upgrade process the BlackBerry Manager will be replaced with the BlackBerry Administration Service, as we discussed in *Chapter 1, Introduction to BES 5*. This will mean that we will need to configure the appropriate accounts so administrators can gain access to the new BlackBerry administration tool through the BlackBerry administration site. We can recall that the access to the BlackBerry administration site is controlled by adding administrators within the BlackBerry administration site.

Upgrading the database

When we upgrade the BES to version 5, we need to upgrade the BlackBerry configuration database as well. This would be a good time to move the database to an SQL server, if it is currently running on the lightweight MSDE SQL.

> This is just best practice suggestion; BES 5 still supports SQL Express — the lightweight database.

The database is upgraded automatically during the upgrade process. There is an option to upgrade the database manually by running the scripts, but please bear in mind that you cannot manage the BlackBerry Administration Service until the configuration database is the same version as the BlackBerry Administration Service. So again, for best practice, it is advisable to upgrade the configuration database during the upgrade process. Other components of the BES are upgraded during the upgrade process.

Upgrading options

We can upgrade our existing infrastructure to the new BES environment or we have the option of setting up a completely new BlackBerry domain and using the BlackBerry Enterprise Transporter tool to move user accounts from the old BlackBerry domain to the new one. The latter method does not require devices to be reactivated, and the process is demonstrated in the lab at the end of this chapter. We are going to focus on upgrading a single BES server in a BlackBerry domain.

Upgrading procedure

We are going to assume that we have already carried out the prep work needed prior to an upgrade, as shown in *Chapter 1, Introduction to BES 5*. This prep work includes:

- Configuring the messaging environment
- Configuring the permissions for the windows accounts
- Configuring access and permissions for the BES configuration database

Firstly, we are going to backup the existing BlackBerry configuration database.

> This is best practice and will also ensure that if there is any issue during the upgrade, we can revert back.

The following examines two procedures of backing up the database, each one depending if you are using an SQL server to house the database or if you are using MSDE.

Backing up the BlackBerry configuration database on an SQL server

1. Log into the SQL server with the appropriate account that allows you to administer the SQL databases. Then expand the **Databases** folder and select the **BESMgmt** database.

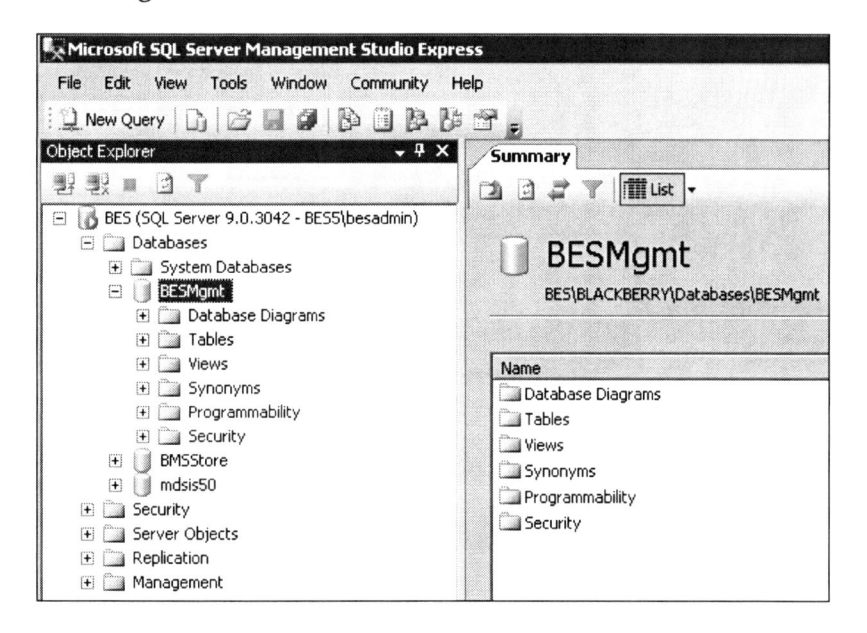

Upgrades

2. Right-click on the database and select **Tasks** and click on **Backup**.

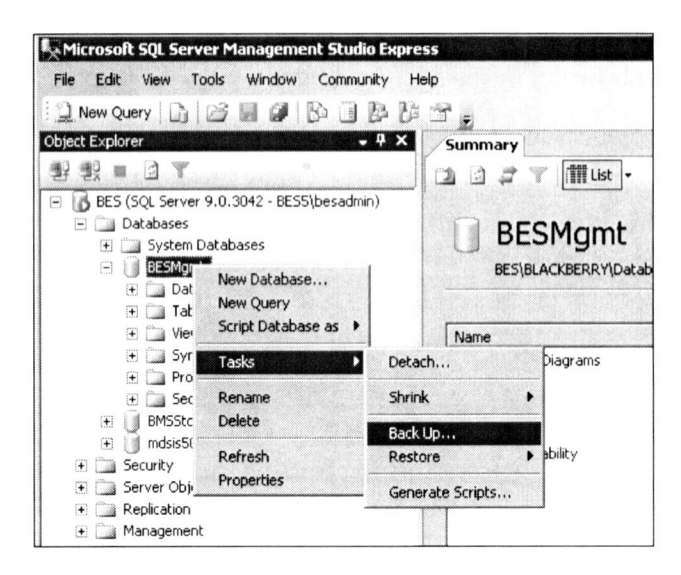

3. Ensure **Backup type** is **Full** and the **Backup Component** is set to **Database**.

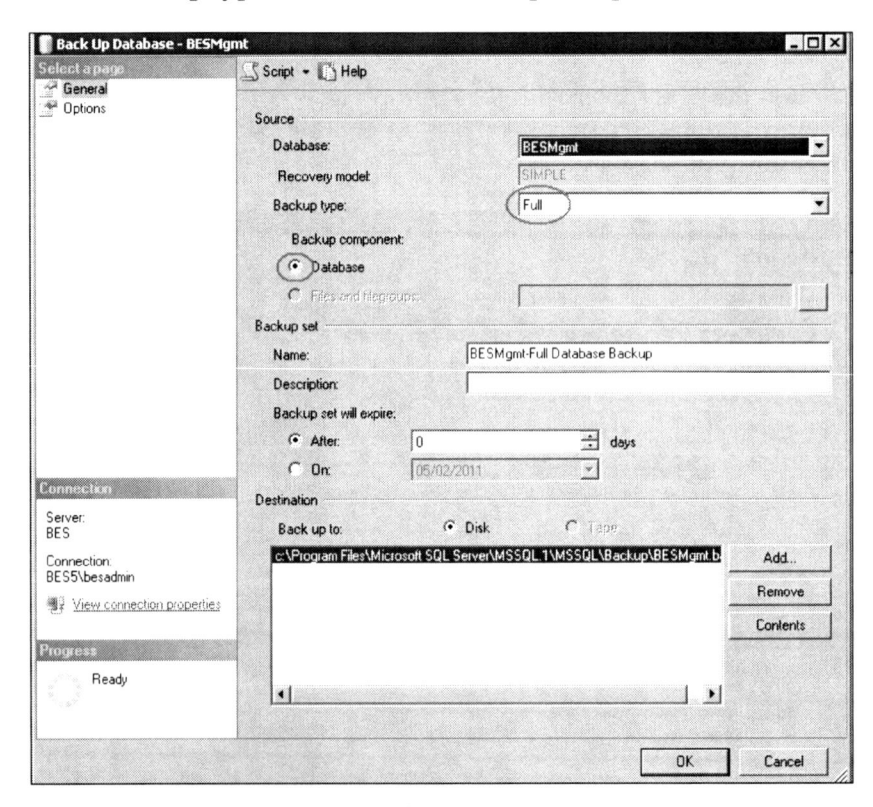

4. Select the destination and click on **OK**.

It is also advisable to copy the raw `.mdf` and `.ldf` files from the default Microsoft SQL storage folder. The path to these files can be found by selecting the properties of the BESMgmt database and then on the left-hand side select **Files** and scroll across until you see **Path**-this will be the location of the mdf and ldf files. Browse to this location and copy the files to a network store.

Backing up the BlackBerry configuration database on lightweight MSDE

We will assume that our BlackBerry configuration database is called BESMgmt and we want to back it up to a folder called BESDB on the `D:\` drive of the local server. The local account is the *sa* account with the password set as *apple*.

1. Extract the BlackBerry software on to the server that hosts the current BlackBerry configuration database.
2. Open a command prompt and browse to the `Tools` folder from the command prompt.
3. Enter the following:

   `BlackBerryDbBackup.exe -d BESMgMt - f D:\BESDB - U sa -P apple`

> The preceding command is case sensitive and we can use Windows Authentication to the database by using the E-Switch instead.

If you have an MDS database running, BES version 5 no longer uses the MDS integration service discovery database—`mdss-dis`. These house the publish MDS Runtime applications that you currently have available in the BlackBerry domain. During the upgrade process, the data will be merged and MDS Runtime Applications will need to be republished on the new BES 5 as shown in *Chapter 6, MDS Applications*.

There are different procedures we can use to upgrade our existing BES to BES version 5. Next, we will examine them as each organization will have different needs.

Using the 'in place' procedure

This upgrade procedure will allow you to upgrade your current BES to BES 5, by upgrading the BES software and the BlackBerry configuration database; this procedure should be used if you only have one instance of BES running in your organization. This procedure means that you don't require any extra hardware for the upgrade. BlackBerry devices are auto activated when using this procedure. New IT policies are sent and new service books are sent. The main issue with this process is that there will be downtime in your organization when you perform the upgrade as the BES services will be switched off.

1. Ensure that all the BlackBerry Manager consoles and connections have been disconnected.
2. Extract the new BES 5 software on to the server.
3. Click on `setup.exe`.
4. Select **Use existing database**.
5. Point to the database that is currently in use ensuring that the ports are correct, as BES 5 offers high availability straight out of the box. We have the option to put in details of an SQL mirror database (please note that this does not create the mirror, it just lets the server know the location of a mirror database).
6. Enter the details of the Exchange Server.
7. Install the BlackBerry Administration Service console by selecting it from the additional components (this will need to be installed in order to manage the BES).
8. Enter the DNS pools of the MDS and BAS service as demonstrated in *Chapter 1, Introduction to BES 5*.
9. Select the Besadmin account in the Active Directory Settings.
10. Start the BES services, and make a note of the new console addresses, this will replace the BlackBerry Manager Console as the tool to administer the BES environment.

Upgrading your BES environment using the End Transporter tool

In many organizations, the impact of taking the BES server offline is not a viable option, hence, there is an improvement in high availability straight out of the box, which allows us to schedule maintenance on our BES server by using the warm standby instance, as pointed out in the last chapter. If the strategy of upgrading is not viable for your infrastructure, we can upgrade to BES 5 by installing a fresh instance of the new BES server on a new server (you can still use the same BESAdmin account to carry out the installation) and then using the Transporter tool to migrate the users across. Using this tool means that we do not need to wipe handhelds down and reactivate them on the new server.

This tool helps us to migrate users to our new BlackBerry domain that we create on the new server. This scenario requires the following:

- A fresh server to install a new copy of BES 5
- Downloading the transporter tool

Migrating users to the new BES server

As mentioned earlier, we can install a fresh copy of BES 5 on a new server. This can be done using the guide from *Chapter 1, Introduction to BES 5*. Once the new server is installed with its new SRP ID and keys, use the following procedure to transport users to the new BlackBerry domain.

Recording the database paths

In preparation for the migration, we need to gather the following information to simplify terminology. In the following example, the source server is the old BES currently running on the network and the destination server is the new BES 5 that we have just installed on a fresh server install.

- Database location of the source server
- Database location of the destination server
- Login details of the BESAdmin account (bear in mind that you can use the same existing BESAdmin account when installing the new BES 5 version).
- Download and install the Transporter tool on each server — the tool is found in the Resource Kit.

Using the Transporter tool to move BES users

Once we have downloaded the Transporter tool, which is available from the BlackBerry Resource Kit, install it on the new BES server.

1. Double-click on the MSI to install the software.
2. Select the appropriate language, accept the license agreement and default installation location and click on **Finish** once installed.
3. Launch the Transporter tool.
4. Under **Step 1: User Manifest**, select **New**.

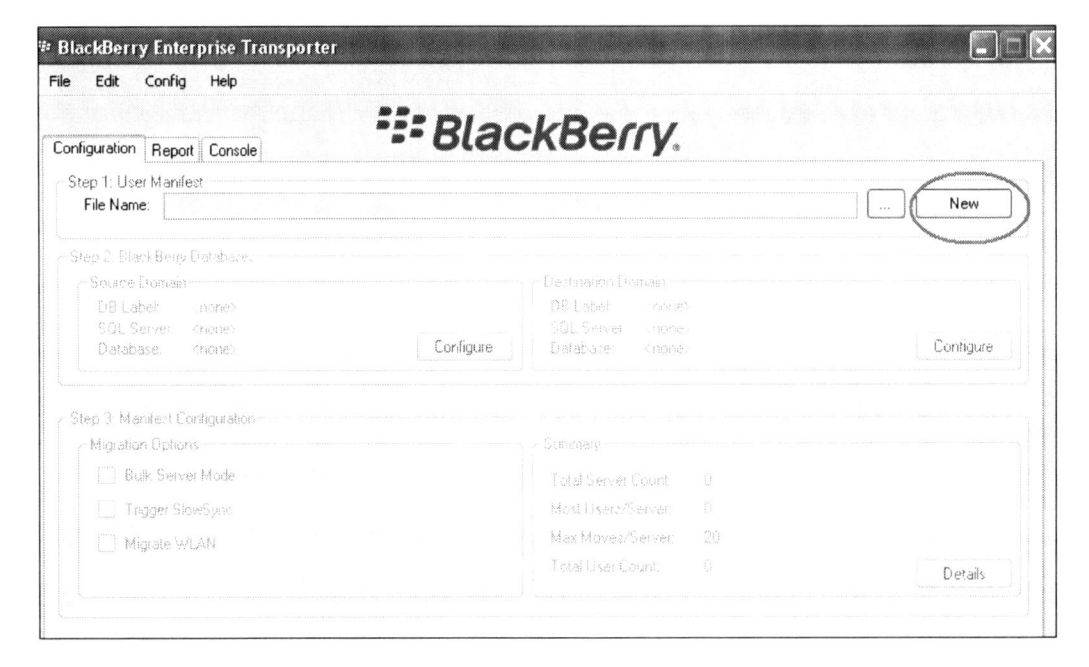

5. Enter a name for the XML file that we are going to create—`BES50 move` and select **Save**.

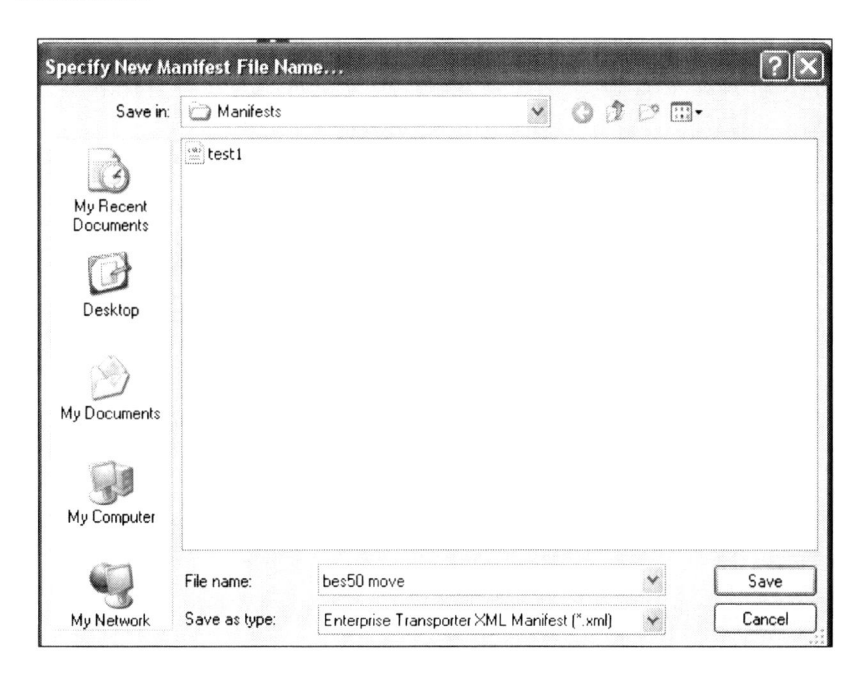

6. Under **Step 2: BlackBerry Databases**, click the **Configure** button for the source domain.

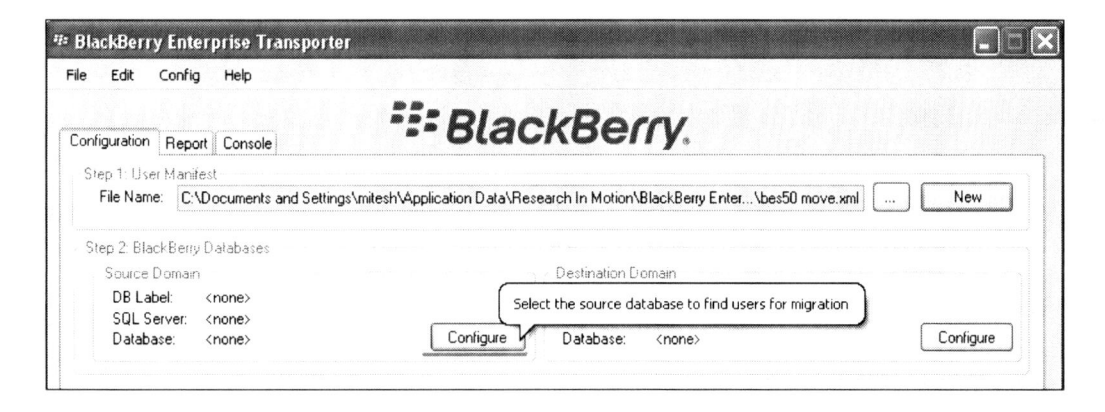

7. In the new box that opens up, use the drop-down to change the **Label** to **<new>** as shown in the following screenshot:

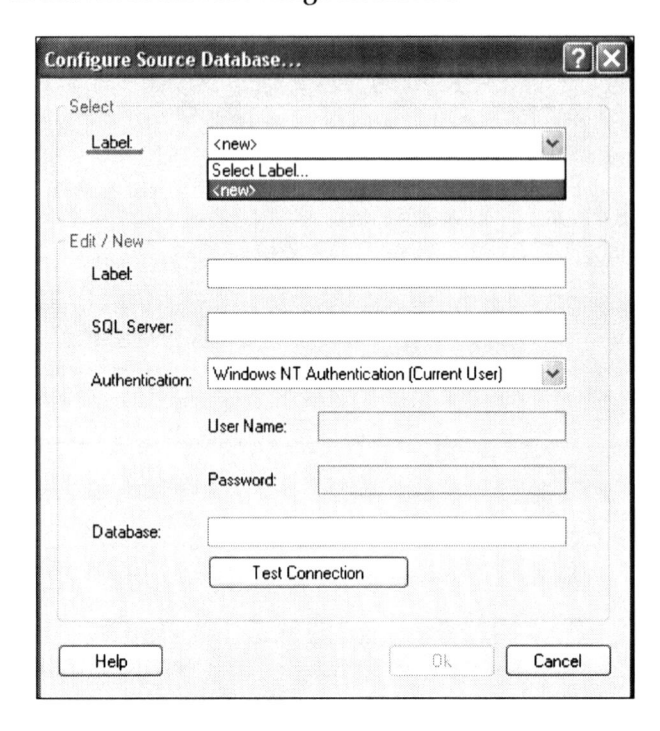

8. Enter name for the label — `Conn_Old_BES`.
9. Enter the name of the Microsoft SQL server that houses the old BES database. If you are using instances, make sure you give the full instance name by using `servername\instancename`.
10. Select the **Authentication** type that is set up on the old BES database.
11. Click on **Test Connection** and then click on **Ok**.
12. Click on **Configure Destination Database**.
13. Select new label and enter name as `conn_new_bes`.
14. Enter the name of the SQL server.
15. Select the **Authentication** type and click on **Test Connection** and select **Ok**, as shown in the following screenshot:

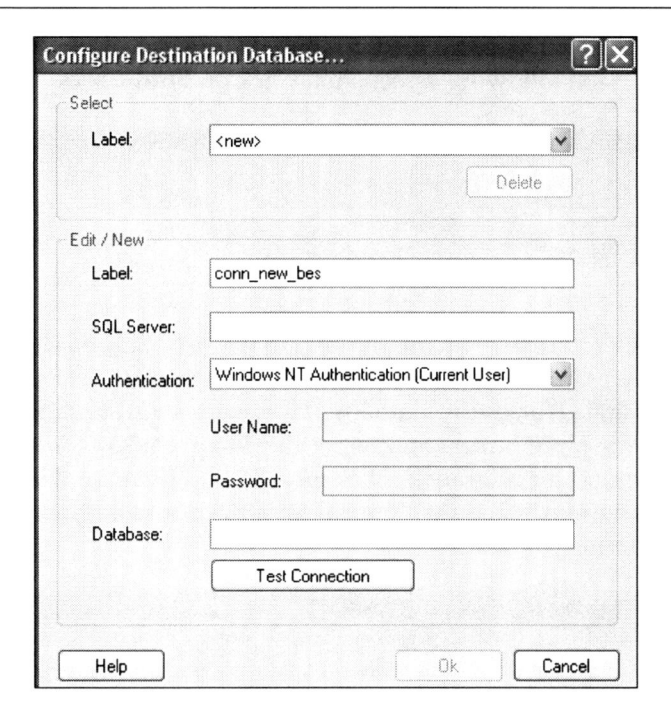

16. Under **Step 3: Manifest Configuration**, we have three options:
    - **Bulk Server Move**: This will allow us to move users in Bulk format from the source database to the destination database (advisable to use when moving a large amount of users—say, 500 plus)
    - **Trigger SlowSync**: This will initiate a slow synch of the user's device to the new BES, once they have been moved to the new BES server
    - **Migrate WLAN**: This option is selected if the setup is done using a WLAN

17. For the purpose of this label, we are going to leave all three unticked. Click on **Details**, as shown in the following screenshot:

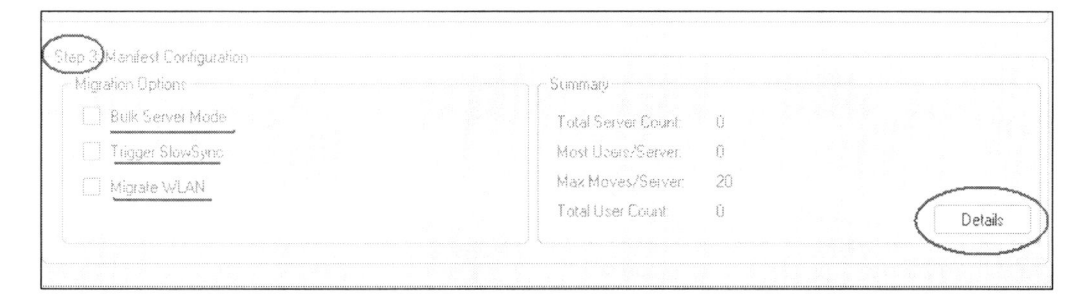

Upgrades

18. After clicking on **Details**, a **User Manifest Configuration** window opens up, as shown in the following screenshot. Click on **Find Users**.

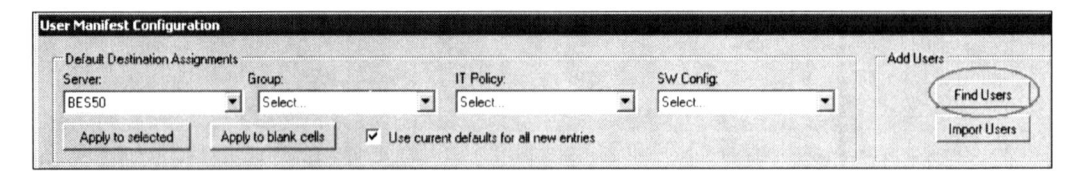

19. Select a user to move from the old BES to the new BES, as shown in the following screenshot. Ensure that the radio button is selected to show users from the whole Blackberry domain. If there are a vast number of users we can move the radio button to other options to granulize the search. Once the users are found for migration, click on **Add** and then the **Done** button. RIM recommendations based on a typical server is not to migrate more than 10 users at a time.

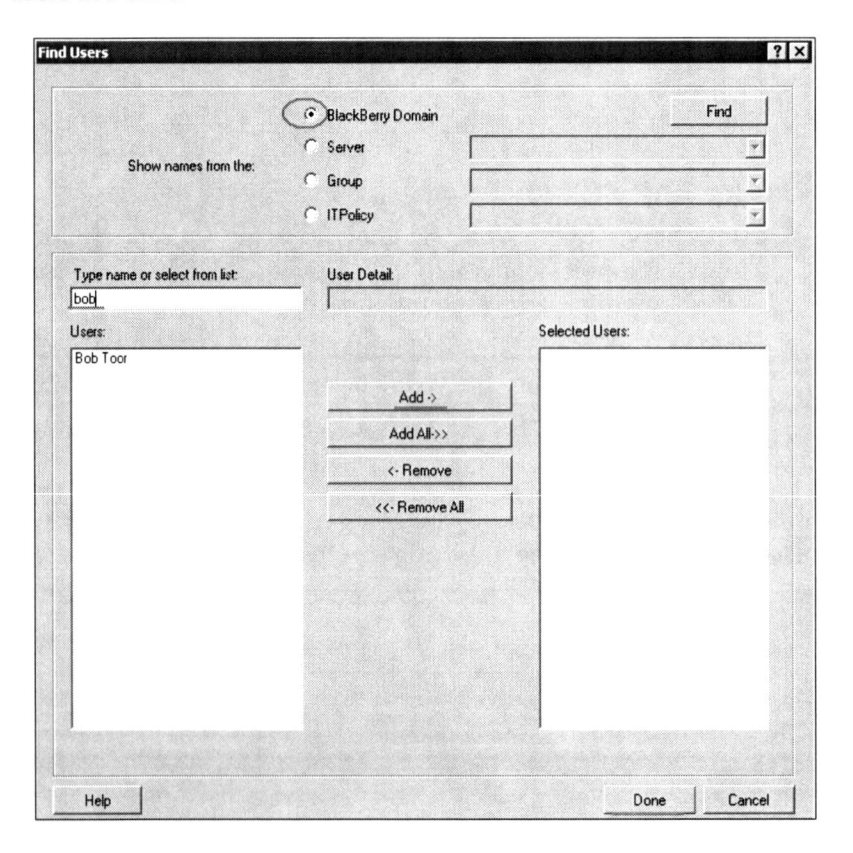

20. In **Step 4: Preview**, we are going to select **Preview**, so we can see any errors that might crop up during the move of the user.

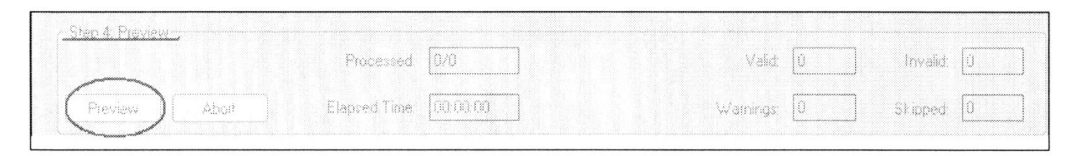

21. While the preview is taking place, select the **Console** tab so we can take a look at what the move is testing. As we can see from the following screenshot, it will make sure the user is available for the move and has the correct permissions. In our case, the validation has been successful, which means we can move on to Step 5. If any errors are indicated, we need to sort these out before moving on to Step 5, (see the *Transport Errors* section of this chapter). If there is any warning indicated, we can still move on to Step 5, but would have to tick the **Ignore Warnings** box; most warnings resolve around data not being moved, or a noncompliant IT policy.

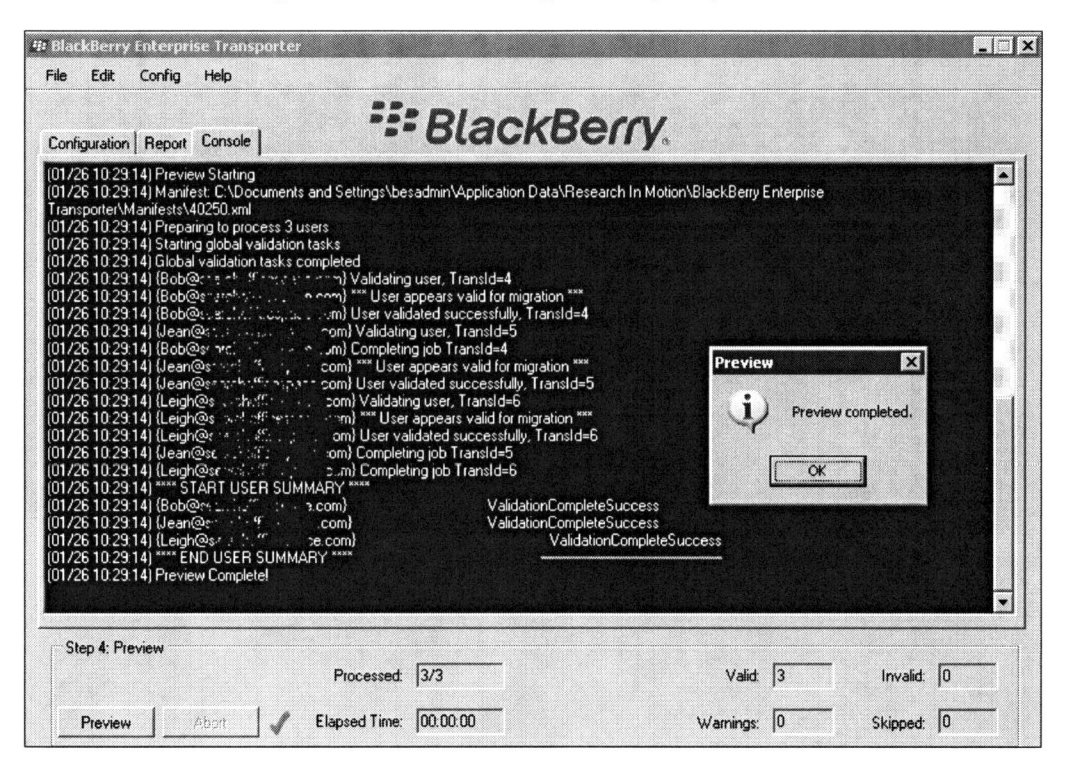

Upgrades

22. Once the preview is complete and we have sorted out any errors, we can begin **Step 5: Migration**, the **Migrate** option. Depending on the errors seen during the preview, we may want to continue migrating a user with the errors, which means that we would need to place a tick in the **Ignore Warnings** box.

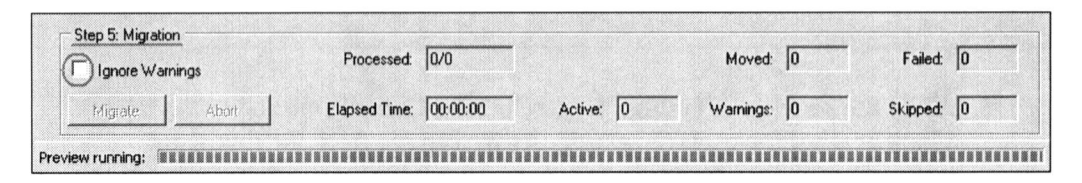

23. We can keep an eye on the migration by selecting the **Console** tab. A user usually takes 15 minutes to migrate, depending on network traffic and size of the user's database settings.

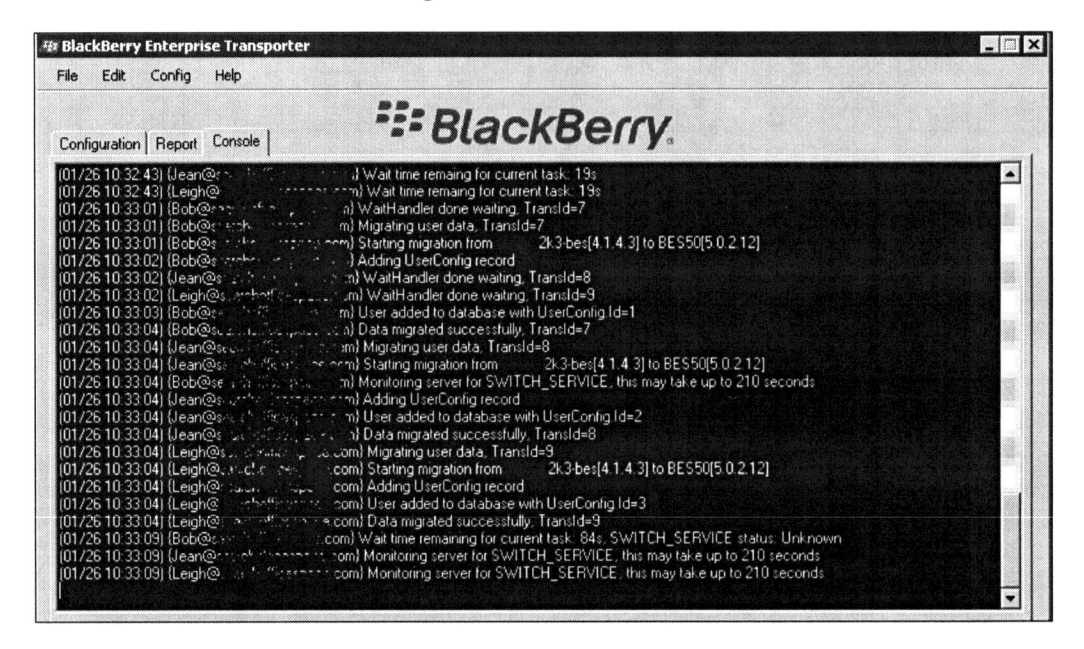

24. We can view the report once the migration has finished by selecting the **Report** tab and as we can see from the following screenshot the user has been transferred successfully along with the IT policy.

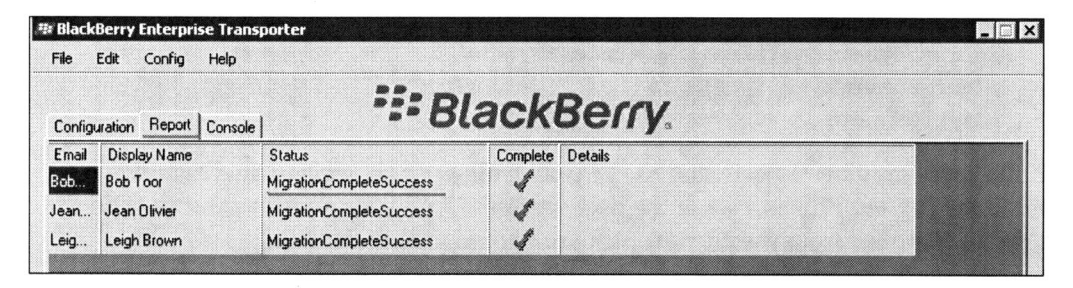

25. As a final check we can log on to the new BES and see if the user has appeared there and ensure that messages are being delivered to the device.
26. The user should also have been deleted from the old BES server.
27. The user should have the new IT policy successfully sent to the device along with the correct service books. All this can be checked using the following steps:
    - Check that user is on the new BES and messages have been delivered. Click on **Manage Users** and search for the user we have just migrated across
    - Click on the user and ensure under **Associated Device Properties** the times and dates are current
    - Click on the user's PIN number, click on the **Messaging** tab and ensure message history is current, and shows no errors.
    - Click on the **Service Books** tab and ensure that the user has the right service books and that they are pointing to the SRP of the new BES, not the old one.

Understanding transport errors

Common transport errors are related to BlackBerry Administration Login failed. We need to ensure that we have stated the correct details. A common cause is that a proxy setting is not letting the connection through. If this is the case, then you can follow the procedure so that the Transporter tool bypasses any proxy settings.

In the `EnterpriseTransporter.exe.config` file, add the following section inside the `<configuration>` tags:

```
<system.net>
<defaultProxy>
<proxy usesystemdefault = "false" />
</defaultProxy>
</system.net>
```

If the users preview reports that the IT policy may not be applied successfully, log on to the current BES and see if the user has any IT policies pending and re-send the user an IT policy from the current BES prior to migrating the user.

To ensure a smooth migration make sure that the user has 50 percent or more battery life on the Smartphone and is in good GRPS coverage.

Summary

In this chapter we have had a look at the options available to us to upgrade prior versions of BlackBerry Enterprise Servers. As mentioned in the chapter, there are strict upgrade paths that need to be followed to get to the 5.0 version. Alternatively, many upgrades—if new hardware is available—can be conducted by following the second method shown in this chapter, which utilizes the Transporter tool. This method would allow you to carry out the upgrade in a way that would provide the most up time, as both old and new BES can run together while you are moving the users from the old BlackBerry domain to the new BlackBerry domain. It is also a safer method of upgrading because if a user fails to upgrade to the new BES, we can reinitialize that user back on the old BES.

Index

A

activation passwords
  setting 102
administrative roles
  enterprise role 56
  junior helpdesk role 56
  security role 56
  senior helpdesk role 56
  server only role 56
  system administrator, monitoring 56
  users only role 56
  view administrator, monitoring 56
administrative user
  creating 67-69
Advanced Encryption Standard (AES) 51
application control policies
  standard disallowed 133, 134
  standard optional 133
  standard required 132
application repository 131, 132

B

BAS 8
BES
  about 7
  databases 13
  high availability 171
  MAPI and CDO files 14
  MDS integration database 13
  monitoring database 13
  network, requisites 14
BES 4.1 to BES 5, upgradation
  BlackBerry configuration database, backing up on lightweight MSDE 185
  BlackBerry configuration database, backing up on SQL server 183-185
  BlackBerry manager 182
  considerations 181
  database 182
  in place procedure 186, 187
  options 182
  procedure 183
BES 5.0
  architecture 10
  components, overview 11
  features 8
  installing 29-34
  users, creating 75-77
BESAdmin
  account 14, 15
  BlackBerry configuration database, creating 23, 25
  database server, enabling 23
  Microsoft Exchange permissions, assigning to Service account 18-20
  Microsoft Windows permissions, assigning to Service account 20-22
  Microsoft Windows permissions, configuring for Service account 22
  preinstallation checklist 29
  service account, creating 16, 17
  service account permissions, setting automatically 28
  service account permissions, setting manually 25-28
  user, mailbox assigning to 17
BES environment
  upgradation, End Transporter tool used 187

BES server
  BES users moving, transporter tool used 188-195
  database paths, recording 187
  SNMP (Simple Network Management Packets), setting up 176-179
  transport errors 195, 196
  users migrating, procedure 187
BlackBerries
  Java applications for 126
BlackBerry
  message, delivering 47
BlackBerry Administration Service
  about 11, 83
  logging into 57-60
  settings 62, 63
  shared folder, adding 152, 153
  used, for activating device 84
BlackBerry Administration Service, settings
  about 62, 63
  administrative roles, creating 63
  administrative user, creating 67-69
  administrators, creating 63
  group, creating 66, 67
  role, creating 64-66
BlackBerry Administration Service console. *See* BAS
BlackBerry Alerts 12
BlackBerry Attachment Service 12
BlackBerry Collaboration Service 12
BlackBerry configuration database
  about 12
  creating 23, 25
  service account permissions, setting automatically 28
  service account permissions, setting manually 25-28
BlackBerry Configuration Panel 12
BlackBerry Controller 12
BlackBerry device
  device software, deploying 147
  distributing 80-82
  expense tracker MDS application, sending 169, 170
  IT policy, sending 115, 116
  Java applications installing, wired approaches 141, 142
  message, sending from 49, 50
  message, sending to 48, 49
BlackBerry device software
  installing 148, 149
  software configuration, assigning to group 157, 158
  software configuration, assigning to user 157
  software configuration, creating 155, 156
  updating, over wireless network 147
BlackBerry device software configuration
  creating 153, 155
BlackBerry Dispatcher 12, 50
BlackBerry Enterprise Server. *See* BES
  users, importing to 97, 99
BlackBerry Java applications
  adding, to software configuration 137, 138
  reconciliation rules 142, 144
BlackBerry Mail Store Service 12
BlackBerry MDS Connection Services 12
BlackBerry MDS Integration Service 12
BlackBerry Message Agent 50
BlackBerry Messaging Agent 12, 48, 50
BlackBerry Monitoring Service 11
BlackBerry Policy Service 12
BlackBerry Router 12
BlackBerry Synchronization Service 12
BlackBerry Web Desktop Manager
  about 11, 83
  devices, activating 87

C

CDO files 14
console
  logging into 61
corporate peer-to-peer key, Enterprise policy
  setting 72, 73
custom application control policy
  creating, for Java application 145, 146

D

databases
  for high availability 174
Desktop Manager
  using 147

[198]

device
  activating, BlackBerry Administration Service used 84
  activating, BlackBerry Web Desktop Manager used 87
  activating, over corporate Wi-Fi 87, 88

device software
  BlackBerry Administration Service, allowing to display software configuration settings 151, 152
  deploying, to BlackBerry devices 147
  deploying, Web Desktop Manager used 148

disclaimer
  setting at server level, for all users 100

E

Elliptical Curve Cryptography (ECC) key 54
encryption
  about 51, 52
  Advanced Encryption Standard (AES) 51
  BES encryption method 53
  transport keys 51
  Triple Data Encryption Standard (3DES) 51

End Transporter tool
  used, for upgrading BES environment 187

enterprise activation 84

Enterprise policy
  activating 70, 71
  corporate peer-to-peer key, setting 72, 73
  transport keys, regenerating 74

enterprise role 56
ETP.dat message 84
Exchange System Management (ESM) 14
expense tracker MDS application
  adding, to BlackBerry devices 169, 170

F

Failover thresholds 173

G

GAL 14
get more option 49
Global Address List. *See* **GAL**
group
  creating 66, 67

H

HA. *See* **high availability**
high availability
  about 171
  configuring 172, 173
  default threshold values, examining 173
  for databases 174
  manual failover 174
  setting failovers, examining 173
  working 172

I

IT policy
  about 107, 108
  applying, to sales group 120
  assigning 109
  assigning, to group 110
  assigning, to user 110
  conflicting, rules 111
  creating 108, 109
  devices without IT policy, deactivating 122
  priorities, setting 112
  resending, manually 121
  resending automatically, to devices 122
  sales team IT policy, creating 117-119
  sending, to BlackBerry device 115, 116
  sending out every three hours, by configuring BES 121
  troubleshooting 123
  user IT policy, verifying 112-115

J

Java application
  custom application, creating 145, 146
  for BlackBerries 126
  installing on BlackBerry devices, wired approach 141, 142

job deployment
  job schedule, default settings 140, 141
  job settings, changing 141

job schedule
  default settings 140, 141

junior helpdesk role 56

L

LCS. *See* Microsoft Live Communication Server
Level One message filter
  applying, to user 103, 104
Lightweight Directory Access Protocol (LDAP) 45

M

maintenance pack
  applying 45, 46
manual failover 174
manufacturer 55
MAPI 14
MDS
  about 159
  application, adding to MDS repository 168, 169
  component services 159
  console 167
  environment, setting up 160
  expense tracker MDS application, sending to BlackBerry devices 169, 170
  IT policies 170
  runtime platform 161
  services 160
  software configuration, creating to deploy MDS runtime platform to devices 161, 162, 163, 164, 165, 166
MDS application
  adding, to MDS repository 168, 169
MDS Connection Service 159
MDS Integration Service 159
MDS repository
  MDS application, adding 168, 169
MDS runtime platform
  deploying to devices, by creating software configuration 161-166
message
  delivering 47
  sending, by BlackBerry device 49, 50
  sending, to BlackBerry device 48, 49
messaging environment
  about 89-91
  organizational data 92-96

Microsoft Exchange permissions
  assigning, to service accounts 18-20
  configuring, for service accounts 22
Microsoft Internet Information (IIS) 31
Microsoft Live Communication Server 9
Microsoft Windows permissions
  assigning, to service accounts 20-22
Mobile Data Service. *See* MDS
model 55
MR (Maintenance Releases) 46

N

network
  shared folder 126-130

O

over-the-air (OTA) 87
Over the LAN
  about 83
  devices, activating 86, 87
Over the Wireless Network (OTA) 83-86
Over your corporate organizations Wi-Fi network 83

P

PIM (Personal Information Management) 89
PIN (Personal Identification Number) 54, 55
PIN message
  sending 103
PIN Range 55
Promotion thresholds 173

R

Research In Motion. *See* RIM
RIM 7
RIM NOC (Research In Motion Network Operation Centre) 48
role
  creating 64-66

S

sales group
  IT policy, applying 120

sales team IT policy
  creating 117, 118, 119
security options
  BES encryption method, setting 53
  content protection 54
  encryption 51, 52
  PIN-to-PIN messages 54, 55
  security options setting 50
security role 56
senior hepldesk role 56
server only role 56
Server Routing Protocol. *See* SRP
service account, BESAdmin
  creating 16, 17
  Microsoft Exchange permissions, assigning 18-22
  Microsoft Windows permissions, assigning 20-22
  permissions, setting automatically 28
  permissions, setting manually 25-28
shared folder
  adding, to BlackBerry administration service 152, 153
  creating 150
  on network 126-130
Simple Network Management Protocol. *See* SNMP
SNMP 9
SNMP (Simple Network Management Packets)
  about 175
  setting up, on BES server 176-179
software configurations
  about 135
  assigning, to group 146, 157, 158
  assigning, to user 139, 157
  BlackBerry Java application, adding 137, 138
  creating 136
  creating, for BlackBerry device software 155, 156
  job deployment 140
SRP 8
standard application policy
  changing 145
symmetric key algorithms
  authenticity 51
  confidentiality 51
  integrity 51
system administrator
  monitoring 56

T

transport keys
  regenerating 74
  storage 52
Triple Data Encryption Standard (3DES) 51

U

UNC (Universal Naming Convention) 130
upgradation
  from BES 4.0 to BES 5 181
  from BES 4.1 to BES 5 181
user-based group
  creating 77-79
users
  activating 83
  adding, when missing in directory lookup 99, 100
  disclaimer, setting at server level 100, 101
  importing, to BlackBerry Enterprise Server 97, 99
  migrating to new BES server, procedure 187
  software configuration, assigning 139
users only role 56

V

view administrator
  monitoring 56

W

Web Desktop Manager
  used, for showing device software deployment 148
  using 147
wired approach
  to install Java application, on BlackBerry devices 141, 142

Thank you for buying BlackBerry Enterprise Server 5

About Packt Publishing

Packt, pronounced 'packed', published its first book "*Mastering phpMyAdmin for Effective MySQL Management*" in April 2004 and subsequently continued to specialize in publishing highly focused books on specific technologies and solutions.

Our books and publications share the experiences of your fellow IT professionals in adapting and customizing today's systems, applications, and frameworks. Our solution based books give you the knowledge and power to customize the software and technologies you're using to get the job done. Packt books are more specific and less general than the IT books you have seen in the past. Our unique business model allows us to bring you more focused information, giving you more of what you need to know, and less of what you don't.

Packt is a modern, yet unique publishing company, which focuses on producing quality, cutting-edge books for communities of developers, administrators, and newbies alike. For more information, please visit our website: `www.packtpub.com`.

Writing for Packt

We welcome all inquiries from people who are interested in authoring. Book proposals should be sent to `author@packtpub.com`. If your book idea is still at an early stage and you would like to discuss it first before writing a formal book proposal, contact us; one of our commissioning editors will get in touch with you.

We're not just looking for published authors; if you have strong technical skills but no writing experience, our experienced editors can help you develop a writing career, or simply get some additional reward for your expertise.

BlackBerry Java Application Development

ISBN: 978-1-849690-20-1   Paperback: 368 pages

Build and deploy powerful, useful, and professional Java mobile applications for BlackBerry smartphones, the fast and easy way.

1. Develop professional, rich, and smart Java applications using BlackBerry SDK
2. Discover the powerful components provided by the SDK to build a powerful user interface with a common look and feel
3. Explore the complex, but important, topic of network communications
4. Integrate with the standard applications on all BlackBerry Smartphone to make your application even more useful

Cocos2d for iPhone 0.99 Beginner's Guide

ISBN: 978-1-849513-16-6   Paperback: 368 pages

Make mind-blowing 2D games for iPhone with this fast, flexible, and easy-to-use framework!

1. A cool guide to learning cocos2d with iPhone to get you into the iPhone game industry quickly
2. Learn all the aspects of cocos2d while building three different games
3. Add a lot of trendy features such as particles and tilemaps to your games to captivate your players
4. Full of illustrations, diagrams, and tips for building iPhone games, with clear step-by-step instructions and practical examples

Please check **www.PacktPub.com** for information on our titles

Lightning Source UK Ltd.
Milton Keynes UK
UKOW021109310113

205651UK00003B/153/P